NATIONAL GEOGRAPHIC LEARNING | CENGAGE Learning

Life

5b

Combo Split

Student Book

Paul Dummett
John Hughes
Helen Stephenson

NATIONAL GEOGRAPHIC LEARNING | CENGAGE Learning

Life Level 5b Combo Split

Paul Dummett

John Hughes

Helen Stephenson

Publisher: Sherrise Roehr

Executive Editor: Sarah T. Kenney

Editorial Assistant: Patricia Giunta

Director of Global Marketing: Ian Martin

Senior Product Marketing Manager: Caitlin Thomas

Director of Content and Media Production: Michael Burggren

Production Manager: Daisy Sosa

Senior Print Buyer: Mary Beth Hennebury

Cover Designers: Scott Baker

Cover Image: © Steve Bloom Images / Alamy

Compositor: MPS Limited

Cover Image

A male panther chameleon stalking prey in beach-side vegetation, Bay of Antongil, Masoala Peninsula National Park, Madagascar.

Combo Split B + CD-ROM
ISBN-13: 978-1-305-26774-9

Combo Split B + Online Workbook
ISBN-13: 978-1-305-26780-0

National Geographic Learning/Cengage Learning
20 Channel Center Street
Boston, MA 02210
USA

Cengage Learning is a leading provider of customized learning solutions with office locations around the globe, including Singapore, the United Kingdom, Australia, Mexico, Brazil, and Japan. Locate our local office at **international.cengage.com/region**

Cengage Learning products are represented in Canada by Nelson Education, Ltd.

Visit National Geographic Learning online at **NGL.Cengage.com**
Visit our corporate website at **www.cengage.com**

Printed in the United States of America
Print Number: 02 Print Year: 2016

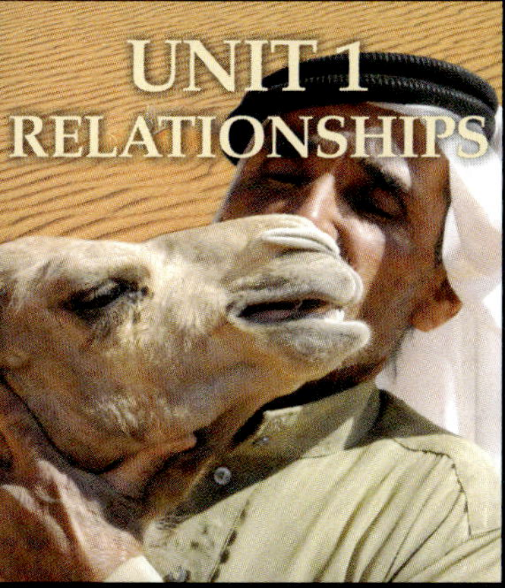
UNIT 1
RELATIONSHIPS

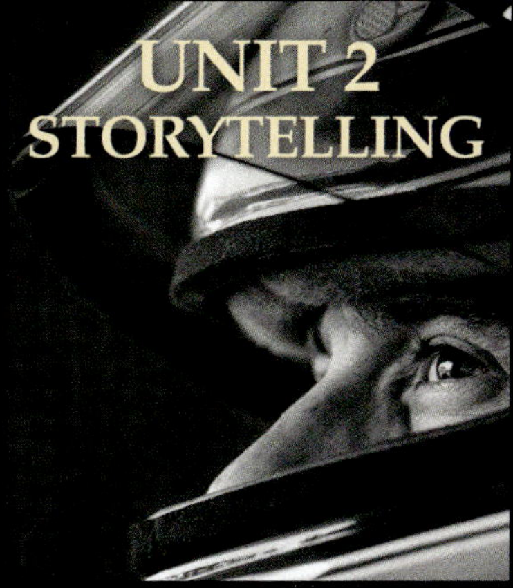
UNIT 2
STORYTELLING

UNIT 3
SCIENCE AND
TECHNOLOGY

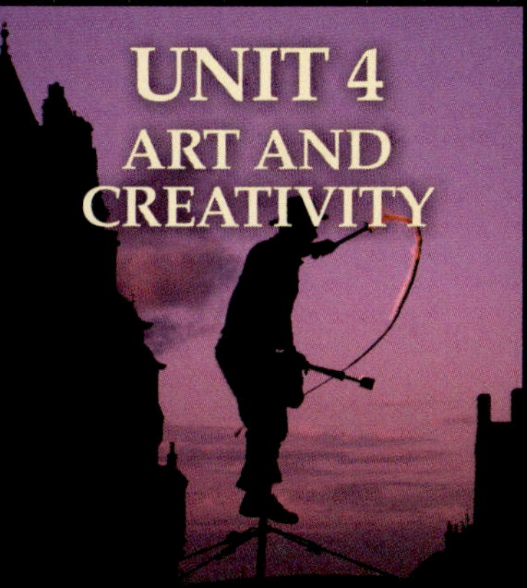
UNIT 4
ART AND
CREATIVITY

UNIT 5
DEVELOPMENT

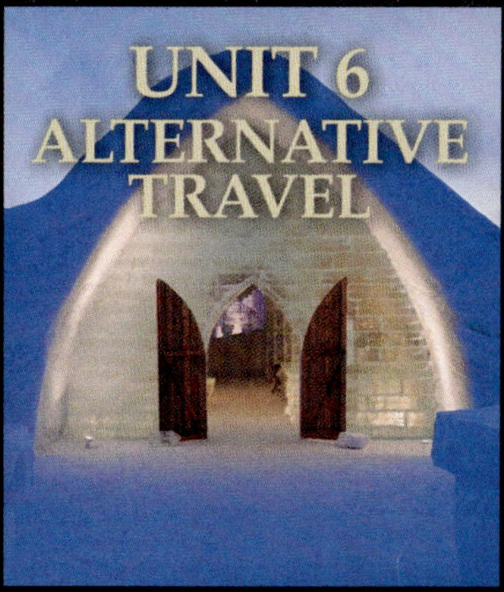
UNIT 6
ALTERNATIVE
TRAVEL

UNIT 7
NATURAL
RESOURCES

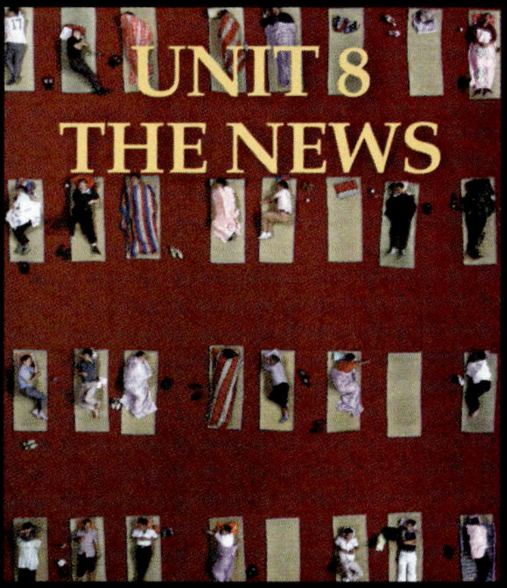
UNIT 8
THE NEWS

UNIT 9
TALENTED
PEOPLE

UNIT 10
CUSTOMS AND
BEHAVIOR

UNIT 11
KNOWLEDGE
AND LEARNING

UNIT 12
THE ECONOMY

LISTENING	READING	CRITICAL THINKING	SPEAKING	WRITING
four people talking about saving water	an article about Ecuador's plan to protect resources an article about Madagascar's unique ecology	emotive language	how we use water conservation wishes	text type: a letter to the editor writing skill: giving vivid examples
four feel-good news stories	an article about an iconic image an article about the power of the press	different perspectives	the ethics of taking photographs feel-good news stories reputations	text type: minutes from a meeting writing skill: impersonal language
an interview about Emerging Explorers	an article about an extraordinary career an article about a woman who was king	weighing the evidence	a career path personal qualities women at work	text type: an online profile writing skill: writing in note form
part of a radio show about a tribe with an unusual diet	an article about the "tiger mother" approach to parenting an article about body language	sources	typical behavior food and eating habits customs in your country wedding traditions	text type: an informal email (2) writing skill: elision in informal writing
a talk by a psychologist on memory	an article about an ethnobotanist an article about a parrot	reinforcing ideas	acquiring knowledge memory tests why you forgot types of learners	text type: an email about a misunderstanding writing skill: linking contrasting ideas
an interview with the author of *The Servant Economy*	an article about Norway's riches an article about an alternative economic model	signposts to key information	the economy in your country getting things done gift giving and exchange	text type: a report writing skill: subheadings and bullet points

Life around the world

Unit 10 Eating insects

Discover why eating insects could be good for you, and why one man is on a mission to change our tastes.

Unit 1 Immigration

The history of immigration in the United States.

Unit 2 History of film

A history of film, from its early beginnings in the 19th century to the Hollywood blockbusters of today.

Unit 4 Urban art

Discover the world of graffiti and innovative music.

Unit 5 Aquarium on Wheels

A special aquarium that gives its student teachers lessons in life.

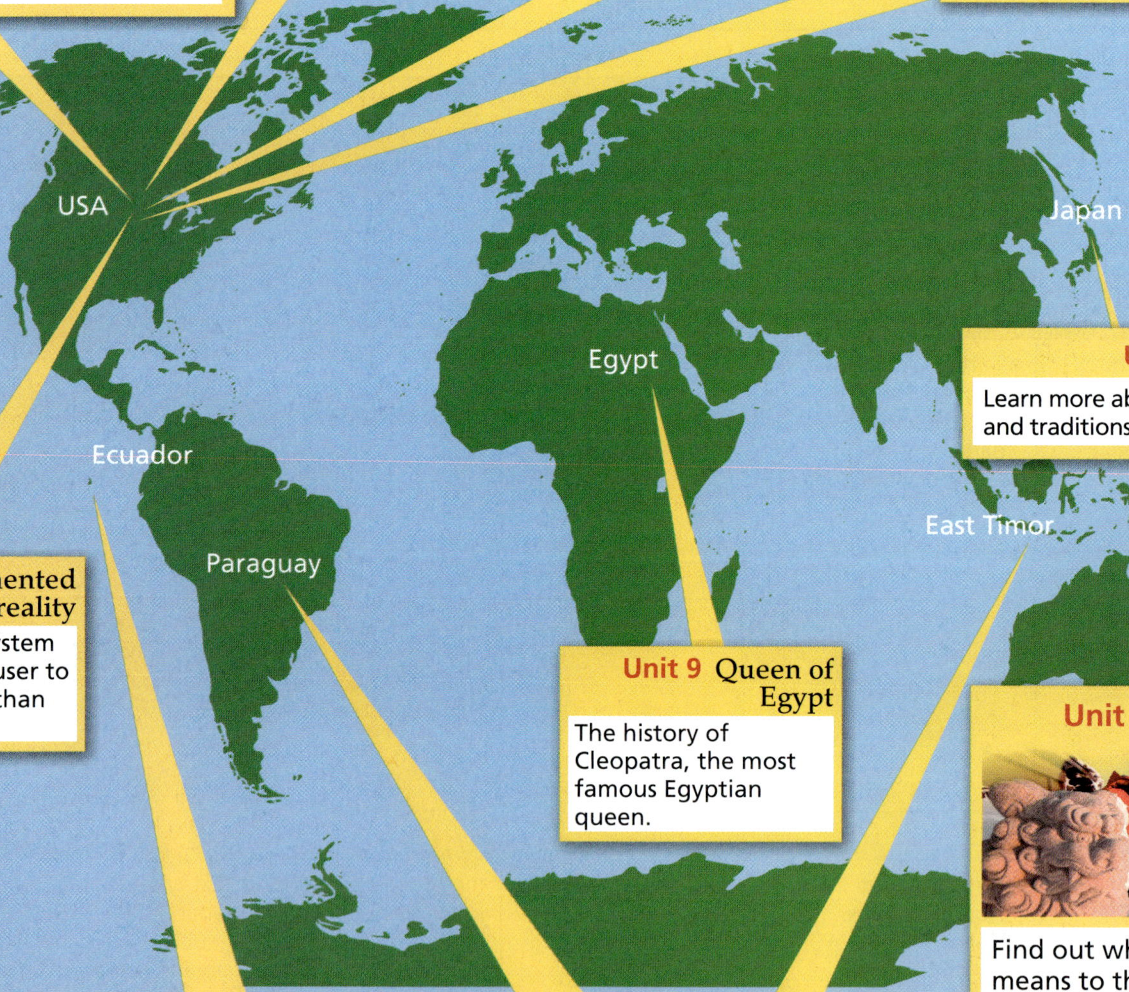

Unit 12 Japan

Learn more about the history and traditions of Japan.

Unit 3 Augmented reality

Learn about a system that allows the user to see much more than simple reality.

Unit 9 Queen of Egypt

The history of Cleopatra, the most famous Egyptian queen.

Unit 8 Mount Fuji

Find out what Mount Fuji means to the Japanese.

Unit 7 Galapagos energy

Find out about the impact of humans and tourism on the Galapagos Islands.

Unit 11 Paraguay shaman

Find out why it's essential to record plants from the rain forests of Paraguay before they disappear.

Unit 6 East Timor

The slow process of creating a new tourist destination.

Unit 7 Natural resources

This photo taken half above, half under water shows fishermen on an Indonesian coral island.
Photograph by David Doubilet

FEATURES

1 Work in pairs. Look at the photo. How many natural resources can you identify?

air	soil
animals	sunlight
fossil fuels (coal, oil, gas)	trees
minerals	water
plants and fruits	wind

2 Match the words (1–5) to their definitions (a–e). Then discuss which words apply to the natural resources in Exercise 1.

1	abundant	a	nature can replace what is used
2	exhaustible	b	in plentiful supply
3	inexhaustible	c	can be used up
4	renewable	d	difficult to find
5	scarce	e	will never be used up

3 The three Rs of saving natural resources are: Reduce, Reuse, and Recycle. What examples can you give of each of them? Do you do any yourself?

7a Water conservation

Speaking

1 Work in pairs. Why do we need to save water when over 70 percent of the Earth's surface is covered by water? Read the article and see if your answer was similar.

So what if people waste a lot of water—we've got enough, don't we? Well, we may have a lot of ocean water, but we are using fresh water faster than nature can replace it. So instead we are forced to recycle waste water, cleaning it and then piping it into people's homes. That process requires a lot of energy—running a tap for five minutes uses the same energy as burning a 60-watt light bulb for fourteen hours—and a lot of money. Also, when underground natural water reservoirs (or aquifers) get low, they can become contaminated with high concentrations of natural minerals like arsenic, or man-made chemicals from the ground. To prevent this, we need to keep these reservoirs well-stocked. Here's where our water goes:

A six minute shower	15 gallons (55 liters)
A hamburger	660 gallons (2,500 l)*
A serving of goat meat	11 gallons (42 l)
A bar of chocolate	372 gallons (1410 l)
A serving of chicken	153 gallons (580 l)*
A cup of coffee	36 gallons (135 l)
Flushing the toilet	2 gallons (8 l)
500 sheets of paper	6,000 gallons (22,500 l)
A slice of bread	11 gallons (40 l)
1 lb (½ k) of clean wool	22,500 gallons (85,000 l)

* in the case of the farm animals, only a few gallons were drunk by the animals or used in processing; the majority of the water went into the grain they were fed during their lives.

2 Look at the facts and answer the questions.

1 Are you surprised by any of the facts? Why?
2 What are the best ways to save water?

Listening

3 24 Listen to speakers from the United Kingdom, the United Arab Emirates, the United States, and Mexico talking about water. What does each say about:

1 their own attitude toward water use?
2 what will happen if water is not conserved?

4 24 Listen again and answer the questions.

Speaker 1
1 How does Liam describe Manchester?
2 What does he do when he brushes his teeth?
Speaker 2
3 What is the problem with desalinating water?
4 What is Gemal researching?
Speaker 3
5 How has the Colorado Delta changed in the last 100 years?
6 What is the river water used for?
Speaker 4
7 What practical water saving measures does Carmen do at home?
8 What does she suggest about other people's attitudes toward water use?

5 Are there similar situations in your country?

Grammar mixed conditional sentences

6 Work in pairs. Look at the *if* sentences (1–6). Answer the questions (a–c).

a Which sentences describe present situations and present consequences?
b Which describe past situations and past consequences?
c Which are a mixture of the two?

1 If we had known the facts, we would not have wasted so much water in the past.
Example:
B. *We didn't know the facts in the past, so we wasted a lot of water in the past.*
2 If I had been brought up in Saharan Africa, I would be more aware of my water use.
3 If we used less water, we wouldn't have to use so much energy treating it.
4 If not for desalination, this country would not have been able to develop.
5 If you had visited the area around the old delta in Mexico 100 years ago, you would be shocked to see it now.
6 If more people thought and acted like me, things would not have come to this point.

> **▶ MIXED CONDITIONAL SENTENCES**
>
> **First conditional (for present or future situations)**
> *If* + simple present,... *will* + base form
>
> **Second conditional**
> *If* + simple past,... *would* + base form
>
> **Third conditional**
> *If* + past perfect,... *would have* + past participle
>
> **Mixed second and third conditional**
> *If* + simple past,... *would have* + past participle
>
> **Mixed third and second conditional**
> *If* + past perfect,... *would* + base form
>
> For more information and practice, see page 165.

7 Look at the grammar box. Then make conditional sentences based on the information in these situations.

1 We bought a cheap dishwasher that wasn't very efficient so we ended up using a lot more water than we need to.
2 I don't use the dishwasher much, because no one told me that you use more water washing dishes by hand.
3 You wasted a lot of water in the past because you washed your car every week.
4 Automatic carwashes are really expensive. As a result, I haven't used them very often.
5 Our water use is way above the average because we built a big swimming pool.
6 We water the garden when the temperature is cool so that the water doesn't evaporate.
7 The United States has a water shortage because they tried to cultivate areas with a desert climate.
8 We changed our habits after we saw a TV show about how much water is wasted.

8 Finish these sentences with the correct tense.

1 If we hadn't used so much water,...
2 If you'd visited this area twenty years ago,...
3 If they don't act now,...
4 If people'd been more careful,...
5 If there's no rain,...

9 Use the conditional forms in the grammar box to make hypotheses based on these facts.

1 The Aral Sea in central Asia (a huge freshwater lake) is now one-tenth of the size it was in the 1960s because water has been used by farmers to irrigate their fields.
2 As a desert town, Las Vegas has to import a lot of water. But a lot of it goes to watering green spaces, particularly the 60 golf courses that have been built around the city.
3 Sixteen million tourists visit Greece each year, causing shortages of water on many of its islands.
4 In the 1970s, Britain found a lot of gas in the North Sea. But rather than use it carefully, they used it immediately. Now more than 50 percent of Britain's gas is imported.

The Aral Sea

Vocabulary and speaking

10 Work in pairs. Match each verb in A with as many nouns in B as you can. Then tell each other if you do any of these actions or support others who do.

A

conserve	consume	preserve	protect
run out of	save	spend	waste

B

animals	food	forests	land	money
energy	gas	time	water	

11 Think about how your country has saved or wasted resources and write conditional sentences about them. Then talk to the other students and tell each other your ideas. Choose the best idea and tell the class.

7b The minister for no oil

One thing you do not expect an oil minister to do is to block the development of his own country's oil fields. But that is exactly what Alberto Acosta did when he was appointed Ecuador's Oil Minister in 2007.

For a relatively poor country whose main income is from oil exports, this proposal seemed crazy. But if Ecuador is not rich by economic standards, in terms of biodiversity, it is one of the richest places on Earth. When scientists studied trees in the Yasuni National Park in Ecuador's unspoiled rain forest, they found over 650 different species of tree in just one hectare—more than the total number in all of the continental US and Canada combined.

Mr. Acosta said he would rather the oil companies did not destroy these natural riches. His innovative idea was to leave the oil reserves beneath Yasuni Park untouched, in return for compensation of half their value. The oil is worth more than \$7 billion, so Ecuador asked the international community to pay \$3.6 billion not to extract it.

But the plan has met with problems, both inside and outside of Ecuador. The state oil company, Petroecuador, opposes the plan and many suspect that President Correa now wishes he had never supported it. At the same time, only a few countries have shown interest, with only Germany promising \$800 million over thirteen years.

Ecuador is not the only country trying to get richer nations to pay for not exploiting their forests. Both Nigeria and Guatemala are hoping they will be able to make similar deals. A spokesperson for local environmental groups explained, "If only people in developed countries appreciated that these forests absorb a lot of the CO_2 that their industries produce. I just wish they would take a longer-term view of this problem. If we don't do something to protect biodiversity and prevent climate change, we will all be losers—with consequences I'd rather not even think about."

Vocabulary oil

1 How many of these expressions do you know? Which is shown in the photo above?

oil field oil refinery oil reserves oil rig
oil slick oil tanker oil well

▶ WORDBUILDING collocations related to one word

There are some nouns that have many words that collocate with them: *oil well, oil tanker, oil field*

2 Work in pairs. Discuss the questions.

1 How much is a gallon or liter of gas in your country?
2 Are people more careful these days about how they conserve oil or gas?

Reading

3 Read the article and choose the sentence (a–c) that best summarizes Acosta's idea.

a for Ecuador to use money from oil exports to protect its forests
b for Ecuador to be paid not to extract its oil
c for Ecuador to keep the oil underground until it really needs the money

4 Answer the questions.

1 Why did Acosta's proposal seem crazy?
2 In what way was the price Acosta asked other countries to pay a fair one?
3 What has been the reaction of the international community to the plan?
4 What has been the reaction of local environmental groups?

5 Fill in each space with a word from the article.

1 Ecuador's riches are in its ______ .
2 In Yasuni park, Ecuador has oil ______ worth $7 billion.
3 The Ecuadoran ______ opposes the plan.
4 There are other countries who would like to be paid not to ______ their natural resources.
5 People in the developed world don't ______ the forests' role, in preventing climate change.
6 People need to think about what will happen in the ______-______ .

6 Work in pairs. What do you think of Acosta's idea? Is it helpful for Ecuador? Is it unrealistic?

Grammar *wish, would rather,* and *if only*

▶ *WISH, WOULD RATHER,* and *IF ONLY*

Wish about a present situation
wish + noun/pronoun + simple past

Wish about a past situation
wish + noun/pronoun + past perfect

Wish for someone to do something about a present situation
wish + noun/pronoun + *would*
(The subject of *wish* and noun/pronoun cannot be the same.)

Strong wishes about a present or past situation
Use *if only* in place of *I wish*

Stating what you would prefer to do
would rather + base form

Stating what you would prefer someone else to do
would rather + noun/pronoun + simple past

For more information and practice, see page 166.

7 Look at the grammar box. Look at these sentences. Then choose the option that describes the actual situation.

1 Mr. Acosta said he would rather the oil companies did not destroy these natural riches.
The oil companies *destroy / don't destroy* these natural riches.
2 President Correa now wishes he had never supported it.
President Correa *supported / didn't support* it.
3 If only people in developed countries appreciated that forests absorb a lot of CO_2.
People in developed countries *appreciate / don't appreciate* that forests absorb a lot of CO_2.
4 I just wish they would take a longer-term view of this problem.
They *will / won't* take a longer-term view of this problem.

8 Choose the correct form to complete the sentences below.

1 I wish people *stopped / would stop* complaining about the price of gas these days.
2 I wish they *didn't cut down / hadn't cut down* those trees in the park to make a playground.
3 Would you rather *walk / walked* or would you prefer we *go / went* by car?
4 Most oil companies wish they *had / would have* the freedom to extract oil from wherever they wanted.
5 If only we *didn't have / wouldn't have* to rely on our cars so much out here in the countryside.
6 If only I *could speak / would speak* another language, I could work abroad.
7 Suri wishes that she *had taken / would take* a job with Exxon when she had the chance. She'd much rather *work / worked* for them than Shell.
8 I wish people *woke up / would wake up* to the problems of climate change.

Speaking

9 Look at these situations and make two sentences for each one with *wish, if only,* or *would rather*. Then read your sentences to your partner.

1 Your car is old and uses a lot of gas. You don't have enough money to buy a new one.
2 You would like to travel more, but you only get three weeks' vacation.
3 Your trip to work takes you an hour a day, so you never get home in time to do any exercise, which you would love to do.

7c A world of its own

Reading

1 Work in pairs. Look at the facts on page 87 about the island of Madagascar for two minutes and then cover the page. Get your partner to ask you three questions about these facts. Then get them to cover their books and ask them three other questions.

2 Read the article. Answer the questions.

1 Which of Madagascar's natural resources is the author most worried about?
2 How is this resource collected and used?
3 What examples of sustainable ways of making money from Madagascar's natural resources are mentioned?

3 Choose the correct option (a–c) to complete the sentences.

1 Madagascar has unusual ________ .
   a flora   b fauna   c both
2 The Madagascan people are ________ .
   a poor
   b anxious
   c wealthy
3 Cultivating crops meant ________ .
   a clearing the forest carefully
   b setting fire to forests
   c getting government permission
4 President Ravalomanana was ________ .
   a ecologically-minded
   b an inexperienced politician
   c popular with the military
5 The new government passed a law allowing people to ________ .
   a cut down hardwood trees
   b import hardwood from China
   c sell wood from fallen hardwood trees
6 For many Madagascans, cutting down hardwood trees is ________ .
   a an easy way to make money
   b necessary to make furniture
   c against their beliefs
7 Other types of trees are cut down to ________ .
   a protect the rivers
   b make medicines
   c transport the hardwoods
8 The forest offers locals other ways to make money, such as ________ .
   a developing new medicines
   b taking tourists on guided walks
   c exporting flowers

Critical thinking emotive language

4 Often, when writers feel very strongly about an issue, they will use strong or emotive language to try to make the reader feel as they do. Find emotive words or phrases that convey:

1 how individual Madagascar is (para 1)
2 how hard the lives of the local people are (para 2 and 5)
3 how strongly ecologists feel about the situation (para 3)
4 how inconsiderate the loggers are (para 4)
5 how impressive and special these hardwood trees are (para 4)
6 how hopeless the situation is (para 7)

5 Do you think that by using such language, the writer helps his argument? Or would it be better to give a more balanced argument? What facts or information would you include to do this?

Vocabulary strong feelings

6 Replace the words in bold with a word from the article to make these sentences more emotive.

1 A lot of efforts are being made to preserve this **individual** place. (para 1)
2 She was **anxious** to get the job. (para 2)
3 Li **disapproves of** logging. (para 3)
4 A number of oil companies now want to **take** oil **from** the Arctic. (para 4)
5 It is a beautiful view, with the **tall and elegant** mountains in the background. (para 4)
6 Archaeology is much more **physical and tiring** than most people think. (para 5)
7 With no prospect of a job, many young people think the future looks **hopeless**. (para 7)
8 All environmentalists seem **very interested in** climate change. (para 7)

7 Work in pairs. Think of a place that is very special and should be protected (like a local green space, a traditional community). Write a short description of it (100–150 words) using emotive language. Then read your description to the class. Vote on which description is the most persuasive.

A world *of its* own

Madagascar, the world's fourth largest island, at over 225,000 square miles, is a unique place that has been blessed with exceptional riches. Roughly 90 percent of its flora and fauna is found nowhere else on the planet. The spectacle of its carrot-shaped baobab trees and ghostly lemurs makes even the most well-traveled visitors wide-eyed with amazement and delight.

But its rare beauty hides the desperate situation of its people. The typical Madagascan lives on about a dollar a day, even though you would not guess this from the cheerful and optimistic Malagasy, the island's main ethnic group. Since the first humans arrived in Madagascar some 2,300 years ago, loggers and developers have destroyed nearly 90 percent of the island's original forest habitat, harvesting it for timber or burning it down to create room for crops and, more recently, cattle.

Considering that Madagascar's population is growing by three percent a year, this tension between rich land and poor residents is increasing daily. Alarmed ecologists have named Madagascar a biodiversity hot spot, deploring the practice of slash-and-burn agriculture. In 2002, the global environmental community rejoiced when green-friendly Marc Ravalomanana was elected president. But only seven years later, in the spring of 2009, the military replaced Ravalomanana with a former radio disc jockey who seemed to have little interest in protecting the environment.

Needing money, the new government reversed a ban on the export of precious hardwoods, making it legal to sell wood from trees which had already been cut down or had fallen during the cyclones that regularly hit the island. Yet in reality they did little to control the loggers who continued to rob the forests of new wood. The main targets of this environmental crime are the rosewood and ebony trees. The wood from these majestic trees is in high demand: in China, it is used to make exotic imperial-style furniture for the new middle class; in Europe and America, it is a valued material in the manufacture of expensive musical instruments.

The locals are caught in a trap. Poverty and the high value of rosewood—at $3,000 per cubic meter it is ten times as valuable as oak—have driven them to cut down trees that are traditionally considered sacred. It is dangerous and back-breaking work. Using hand axes, in a few hours they bring down a tree that has stood tall for many centuries. Then they cut the trees into logs and drag them several miles to the nearest river.

The rare hardwood trees are not the only casualties. In order to transport the heavy rosewood logs downriver, rafts must be built from other wood. For each raft, the loggers cut down four or five lighter trees near the river, causing the earth to erode and silt up the rivers. Animals' habitats have also been disturbed, putting their survival at risk.

In this bleak landscape, one man's work offers hope. Olivier Behra, who first came to Madagascar from France in 1987, believes that the only solution is to give local people economic alternatives. Almost single-handedly, he has stopped deforestation in the Vohimana forest by encouraging the locals instead to collect medicinal plants, which they never imagined had any monetary value, and sell them overseas. The village lemur hunter has been retrained as a guide for tourists obsessed with lemurs. The same tourists also pay to visit the wild orchid conservatory that Behra has set up. Can small-scale and sensitive initiatives like this compete with the rosewood mafia of Madagascar? Only time will tell.

MADAGASCAR IN NUMBERS

FOURTH-LARGEST island in the world after Greenland, New Guinea, and Borneo

22 MILLION people from 18 different Asian and African ethnic groups living here

90 PERCENT of its flora and fauna is found nowhere else on Earth

70 different species of lemur found only on Madagascar

300 YEARS: the time it takes a rosewood tree to reach maturity

Number 1 producer of vanilla in the world

27,000 TONS of ebony and rosewood exported in 2009, much of it illegally

7d The climate change debate

Real life making your point

1 Work in pairs. What causes climate change? Is it man-made or a natural phenomenon? Use the expressions below to help you.

CO_2 emissions	natural weather cycle
fossil fuels	the greenhouse effect
global warming	

2 25 Listen to four people discussing climate change. Which two people would change their habits to help prevent climate change?

Speaker 1: Elena ☐ Speaker 3: Jim ☐
Speaker 2: Anne ☐ Speaker 4: Rick ☐

3 25 Listen again. Complete the expressions (1–6) that the speakers use to make their points.

MAKING YOUR POINT

Giving examples
Take..., for example...
Let me give you an example...
Imagine [1] ______ hair...

Stressing a point
The point is that...
I, for one, [2] ______ in how I pollute...
Look, there's no doubt that [3] ______...
To be honest with you,...

Rejecting an argument
I don't accept that.
I used to believe [4] ______, but...
Yeah, but that's not the point.
I (don't) believe it simply because [5] ______.

Challenging the question itself
The whole starting point for this debate is wrong.
We're approaching this debate all wrong by saying [6] ______ problem.

4 25 Discuss which of the techniques (a–e) each speaker used to make a point. Listen again and check.

a humor
b challenging the question itself
c speaking clearly and slowly
d illustrating with examples/stories
e anticipating counter-arguments

5 Which technique did you find most effective? Which technique do you prefer yourself? Tell your partner.

6 Pronunication sentence stress

a 26 When making their point, each speaker uses word stress to emphasize the important words. Listen to this example.

I don't know and I'm not sure **anyone** knows for sure. (2 words)

b 27 Underline the words which you think are most stressed. Then listen and check.

1 We don't know that we're causing it, but some people say we might be... (2 words)
2 ...scraping ice off the inside of my windows rather than the outside. (2 words)
3 Regional temperatures may be lower, but average global temperatures keep on rising. (2 words)
4 Because it's not just an environmental problem. It's an economic problem, a social problem, even an ethical problem. (4 words)

7 Work in pairs. Choose one of the solutions to climate change given below. Work out arguments in favor of this solution. Think about the techniques you will use to make your point and the examples you could give. Then debate another pair who have a different solution.

The solution to climate change is:

- reducing energy use by inreasing fuel prices
- paying poor countries to protect their forests
- finding a technological solution to cool the Earth (like putting millions of tiny mirrors in space to reflect the sun's rays)
- getting all countries to sign an international agreement to limit CO_2 emissions

7e Waste of energy

Writing a letter to the editor

1 Do you ever read the letters section of newspapers, local or national? Have you ever written a letter to the editor yourself?

2 Read the letter. Answer the questions.

1 Who wrote the letter?
2 Why did they write it?
3 Do you find it persuasive? Why?

Financial News **Published: March 20**

To the Editor:

James Anderson (Travel section, March 15) writes about the waste of energy in hotels: overheated rooms, lights left on all night, towels used once and washed. He is right, but why stop with hotels? Wouldn't it be better to mention all the other mindless waste that characterizes modern life?

In the morning, I walk downtown past stores whose doors are wide open, blowing hot air into the street. At night, I walk home past fully-lit, empty office buildings, when the workers have already left; past enormous flashing screens where advertisers try to go one better than the competition. At the supermarket, I take my frozen vegetables from open freezer bins. My children leave their computers on when they go out, and their phone chargers plugged in with no phone on the other end (though they should know better).

All this waste illustrates two simple facts. First, that energy is too cheap and we had better increase its price substantially to make people more energy-conscious. Second, that no one really considers the public interest anymore.

Just as it is in the public interest that we have speed limits on our roads—though some of us may not like it—so would we be better off if we were forced by our government to conserve energy.

V. Dupeyrat
Head of Energy Services
DEF Energy, Seattle

3 Work in pairs. How is the letter organized? Match the functions (a–d) with each paragraph. Discuss whether they could be organized differently.

a Examples that illustrate the problem
b A recommendation or call to action
c The reason for writing
d A summary of the problem

4 Word focus *better*

Underline all the phrases using the word *better* and match them with the definitions (a–e) below. Compare answers with your partner.

a not be so stupid
b in an improved (often economic) situation
c more useful or desirable
d improve on the effort of another
e really ought to

5 Writing skills giving vivid examples

a What does the writer say about lights and towels to illustrate his argument?

b Find more examples of energy waste in the first two paragraphs.

6 Look at this list of things that annoy people about modern life. Expand three of them to explain what is annoying about it, as in the example. Then compare with your partner.

Example:
magazines that… *are full of news about celebrities*

airlines which…
cell phones that…
TV shows about…
supermarket food that…
computer programs which…

7 Write a short letter (150 words) to the editor, talking about one of the items in Exercise 6. Make sure you include the same elements as in the sample letter. Then exchange letters with your partner. Do they agree with the way you feel?

8 Read your partner's letter. Use these questions to check their letter. Is it correctly organized?

- Does it use enough examples?
- Does it end with a summary?
- Is it persuasive?

7f Galapagos energy
Video

Naturalist Charles Darwin once called the Galapagos "a little world within itself."

Before you watch

1 Work in groups. Look at the photo and discuss the questions.

1 What do you know about the Galapagos Islands? Make notes about:
  a their location.
  b the population.
  c what the islands are famous for.

2 What do you think Darwin meant when he called the Galapagos "a little world within itself"?

2 Complete the video summary with words from the glossary below.

The Galapagos Islands are home to many unique species of plants and animals. However, recently human beings have invaded this tropical [1] .... Tourism has [2] .... and workers from the [3] .... have followed. This has created pollution from vehicle [4] .... , the energy people use, and the trash they produce, which harms the islands. Now, [5] .... , corporations, and the government are working to minimize human impact.

While you watch

3 Watch the video and check your answers from Exercises 1 and 2.

4 Watch the first part of the video (to 02:41) and answer the questions.

1 Why did the animals on the Galapagos evolve into unique species?

....

2 What do people always say about the islands?

....

3 What do the volcanic eruptions tell scientists?

....

4 How long have humans been living on the islands?

....

5 What is one positive aspect of tourism?

....

6 What happened after the recent oil spill?

....

5 Watch the second part of the video (02:42 to the end). Mark the things you see.

a bird with a blue beak	a bicycle	boats
a bird with a red beak	black sandals	a bus
a recycling bin	a motorbike	a seal
a blue dress	a pink T-shirt	a turtle

6 Watch the second part again and answer the questions.

1 What is the goal of the program that international organizations and the Ecuadoran government are working on?

....

2 What four examples of conservation projects does the video show?
  a ....
  b ....
  c ....
  d ....

After you watch

7 Roleplay an interview with Leopoldo Bocheri More

Work in pairs.

Student A: Imagine you are going to interview Leopoldo Bocheri More. Read the information below and prepare a list of questions.

Student B: Imagine you are Leopoldo Bocheri More. A journalist is going to interview you. Look at the information below and think about what you are going to say the journalist.

- the problems the Galapagos have
- what the government is doing
- what other help is needed

Act out the interview. Then change roles.

8 Work in groups and discuss these questions.

1 What natural areas in your country have been adversely affected by human activity?
2 What can be done to protect such places?

conservationist (n) /ˌkɑnsərˈveɪʃənɪst/ a person who works to preserve nature
contaminant (n) /kənˈtæmɪnənt/ something that pollutes
emissions (n) /ɪˈmɪʃənz/ smoke and gas from machines
haven (n) /ˈheɪvən/ a place people or animals can escape to
leak (n) /lik/ liquid or gas that escapes through a hole
mainland (n) /ˈmeɪnˌlænd/ a large area of land that is not an island
oil spill (n) /ˈɔɪl ˌspɪl/ when oil accidentally escapes from the place it is stored
old-timer (n) /ˈoʊld ˈtaɪmər/ a person or animal who has lived in a place for a long time
pristine (adj) /prɪsˈtin/ in perfect condition
relic (n) /ˈrelɪk/ something left over from the past
revenue (n) /ˈrevəˌnu/ money earned
run aground (v) /ˈrʌn əˈgraʊnd/ hit rocks or the bottom of the sea
skyrocket (v) /ˈskaɪˌrɑkɪt/ to go up very quickly
wake-up call (n) /ˈweɪk ʌp ˌkɔl/ a warning to pay attention

UNIT 7 REVIEW

Grammar

1 Work in pairs. Do you think that young people are more or less aware of the need to conserve resources than their parents' generation?

2 Read part of a blog discussing young people's attitude toward resources. What kind of things are they aware of? And not aware of?

3 Complete the text with the correct form of the verbs.

The younger generation seems very aware of global problems with natural resources. If you ask them about the rain forests, for example, they [1] *will say / would say*: "Oh, I wish people [2] *stopped / would stop* cutting them down. They're destroying the planet."
But on a personal level, they don't seem to be so aware. For example, it seems they would rather [3] *leave / left* the computer in sleep mode than [4] *turn / turned* it off. If the central heating was on too high, they [5] *would be / would have been* more likely to open a window than turn it down!
We parents are partly to blame for this. If we [6] *were / had been* stricter with our children when they were young, they [7] *would know / would have known* how to act now. I wish that they [8] *had / had had* more energy-saving education at school. As parents, we'd all rather schools [9] *teach / taught* these things because when we try, our children just think we are nagging!

I CAN	
hypothesize about present and past situations using mixed second and third conditionals	☐
express wishes and preferences about the past and future with *wish, if only, would rather*	☐

Vocabulary

4 Work in pairs. Find the odd one out in each group of words. Explain why it doesn't fit.

1 conserve, waste, save, preserve
2 natural, abundant, scarce, inexhaustible
3 oil refinery, oil slick, oil rig, oil tanker
4 sunlight, minerals, air, wind
5 majestic, tall, obsessed, desperate

5 Work in small groups. Think of two natural resources that are scarce. Discuss what we can do to protect them.

I CAN	
talk about natural resources	☐
use nouns, verbs, and adjectives about using and conserving natural resources	☐

Real life

6 Work in pairs. Which speakers (1–5) agree with this sentence and which disagree?

We should force developing countries to consume resources more carefully.

1 "Worry about developing countries? I have enough trouble remembering to turn off the lights!"
2 "The point is that the developed nations have used resources as they wished, so why shouldn't developing countries do the same?"
3 "If a rich person in India wants to own four cars and a mansion, who am I to say he can't?"
4 "I know you'll say that it's *everyone's* duty not to waste resources, but I don't accept that."
5 "It's not about what's fair; it's about what's necessary. We all need to conserve."

7 Which technique (a–e) does each speaker use to make their point?

a humor
b challenging the question itself
c using emphasis
d using examples / stories
e anticipating counter-arguments

8 Choose one of the techniques in Exercise 7 and make your own point about the need to conserve resources.

I CAN	
use different techniques to make my point in a debate	☐

Speaking

9 Work in small groups. Discuss the following issues.

- a regret you have about harming the environment
- a consequence of not protecting natural resources in your area
- an action to help conserve a natural resource

Unit 8 The news

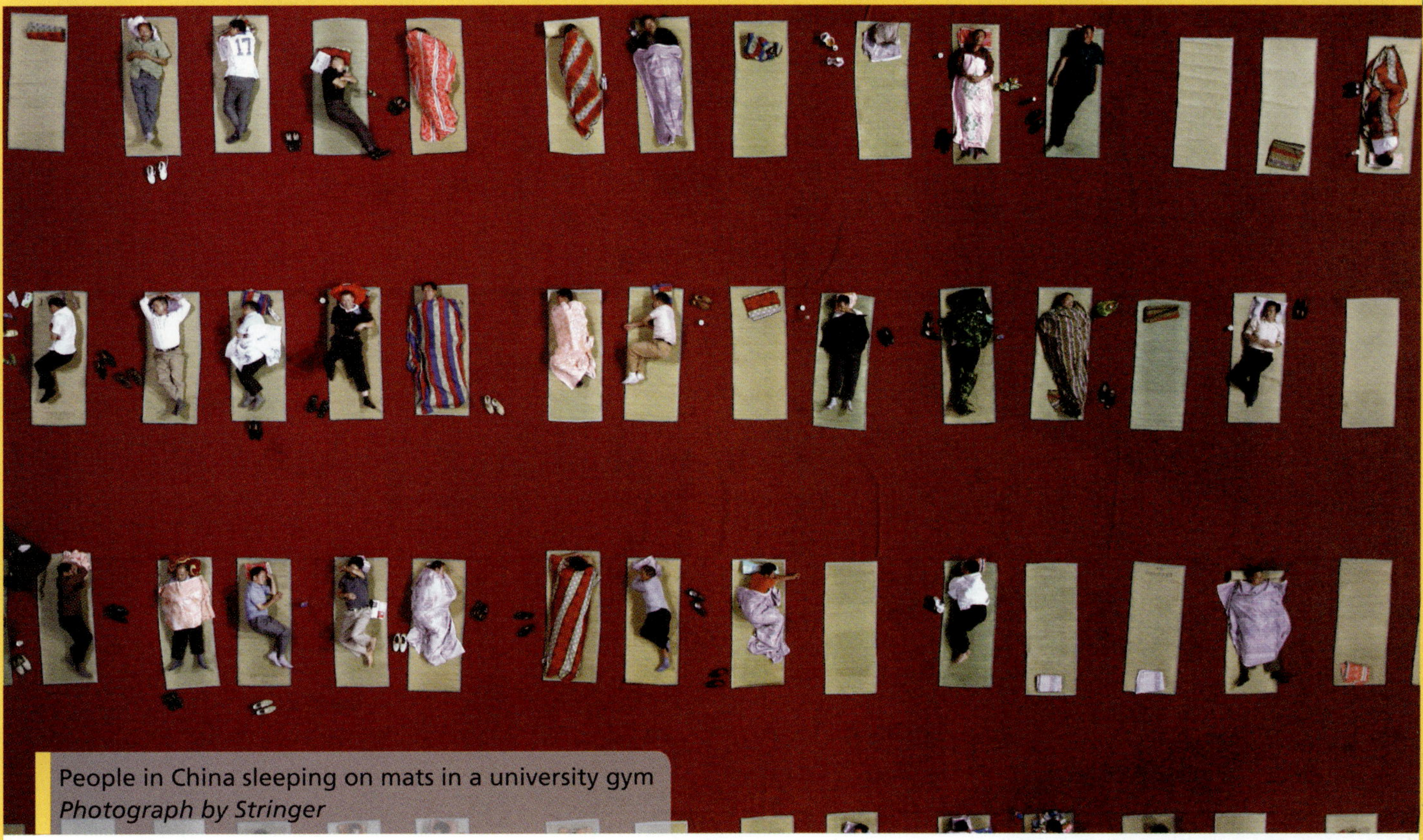

People in China sleeping on mats in a university gym
Photograph by Stringer

FEATURES

1 Match the phrases to complete these English sayings about the news. What sayings about news do you have in your language?

1 Good news… a is good news.
2 Bad news… b doesn't sell.
3 No news… c travels fast.

2 Work in pairs. Look at the photo and caption. Why do you think these people are sleeping in the gym? Think of a news story to explain the photo. Share your answers with the class.

3 Do the following fall into the category of hard news (serious, urgent) or soft news (less serious, not urgent)? Discuss.

- a column with celebrity gossip
- a local news story about a new housing development
- an editorial about a political scandal
- business news about interest rates
- a travel feature about Nicaragua
- a science news story about a cure for Alzheimer's disease

8a A life revealed

Vocabulary photography

1 Read the quotations. Find the following:

- 3 words that mean *a photograph*
- 2 words for parts of a camera
- 3 verbs that describe what a camera does with an image

2 Which is your favorite quotation? Why?

> A picture is worth a thousand words. - *Fred R. Barnard*
>
> What you have caught on film is captured forever… it remembers little things, long after you have forgotten everything. - *Aaron Siskind*
>
> There is one thing the photograph must contain: the humanity of the moment. - *Robert Frank*
>
> Look and think before opening the shutter. The heart and mind are the true lens of the camera. - *Yousuf Karsh*
>
> I see no reason to record the obvious. - *Edward Weston*
>
> A great photographer takes 100 shots and keeps just one. - *Anon*
>
> Seeing and composing the beauty is what separates the snapshot from the photograph. - *Matt Hardy*

Reading

3 Work in pairs. Look at the two photos and discuss the questions. Then read the article and check your answers.

1 Have you seen either of these photos before?
2 Where are these people from?
3 How old are they?
4 What is the relationship between them?

4 Complete these sentences by finding the contrasting facts in the article.

1 Sharbat Gula let McCurry take her picture, even though…
2 The picture became world famous, even though…
3 McCurry recognized 29-year-old Gula immediately, even though…
4 Gula does not complain about her life, even though…

A LIFE REVEALED

She remembers the moment the photographer took her picture. The man was a stranger, but he asked if he could, and she agreed to let him take it. She had never been photographed before and, until they met a second time seventeen years later, she was not photographed again.

The photographer, Steve McCurry, remembers the moment too. It was 1984 and he was recording the lives of Afghan refugees in a camp in Pakistan. She was staring out of the school tent and he admits thinking at the time that the picture would be nothing special. Yet the "Afghan girl," as the portrait is now known, became one of the most iconic images of our time. McCurry used her intense expression, so untypical of an average, carefree twelve-year-old girl, to warn us not to ignore the victims of war, especially its young victims.

In 2002 National Geographic persuaded McCurry to return to Pakistan to look for the girl. After showing her photo around the refugee camp, he found a man who had known her as a child and knew where to find her. He offered to get her from her home in the Tora Bora mountains and after three days returned with Sharbat Gula, a woman perhaps 29 years old. McCurry knew at once that this was her.

Time and hardship had erased her youth. Her skin was weathered. Yet her eyes still burned with the same intensity. Her brother explained the story of their lives, blaming the war for forcing them and many other Afghans out of their homeland. When Sharbat was six years old, they fled to the mountains, hiding in caves and begging people to give them food and blankets. She married when she was sixteen and now her time is occupied with bringing up her three children, cooking, cleaning, and caring for them. Yet she does not complain about having a hard life. More amazingly, she is not aware of the impact that the photo of the young Sharbat with her sea-green eyes had on the world.

iconic (adj) /aɪˈkɑnɪk/ well-known and admired everywhere

Grammar reporting verbs

5 Look back at the article and complete these sentences using reporting verbs. Note the form that follows the reporting verb in each case.

1 She **agreed** __________ him take her picture.
2 He **admits** __________ at the time that the picture would be nothing special.
3 McCurry used her intense expression to **warn** us __________ the victims of war.
4 In 2002 National Geographic **persuaded** McCurry __________ to Pakistan.
5 He **offered** __________ her from her home in the Tora Bora mountains.
6 Her brother **blamed** the war __________ them out of their homeland.
7 They **begged** people __________ them food and blankets.
8 She does not **complain** __________ a hard life.

6 Work in pairs. What is being reported in Exercise 5? Discuss what the person actually said at the time. Then compare answers with another pair.

1 She agreed to let him take her picture.
Yes, you can take my picture.

> **REPORTING VERBS**
>
> **Verb + infinitive**
> *She agreed to let him take her picture.*
>
> **Verb + someone + infinitive**
> *National Geographic persuaded McCurry to return to Pakistan.*
>
> **Verb + -ing**
> *He admits thinking at the time that the picture would be nothing special.*
>
> **Verb + preposition + -ing**
> *She does not complain about having a hard life.*
>
> **Verb + someone + preposition + -ing**
> *Her brother blamed war for forcing them out of their homeland.*
>
> For more information and practice, see page 167.

7 Look at the grammar box. Use the verb given to report each of these statements.

1 You've taken some amazing photos!
She __________. (complimented)
2 You should think seriously about doing this professionally.
She __________. (encouraged)
3 You are far too modest about your own talents.
She __________. (accused)
4 Why don't you take a better photograph?
She __________. (suggested)
5 I'll also introduce you to my friend, who is a wildlife photographer.
She __________. (promised)
6 In fact, I'm sorry I haven't introduced you to him sooner.
She __________. (apologized)
7 You really should enter that photo competition in National Geographic.
She __________. (urged)
8 I can lend you my camera, if you don't think yours is good enough.
She __________. (offered)

8 Complete the article about the ethics of taking photos of other people. Put the verbs in the correct form. (You may need a preposition.)

> Photographers who take pictures without their subject's knowledge are accused [1] __________ (be) sneaky or even unethical. A photographer who uses a telephoto lens to take a picture of someone at home cannot deny [2] __________ (do) wrong—they invaded someone's privacy. Newspaper reporters are often criticized [3] __________ (do) this kind of thing, not that it stops them.
>
> But isn't this the same as taking pictures of strangers without permission? They haven't said it's OK for you [4] __________ (take) their picture. Maybe they would feel uncomfortable if you asked them [5] __________ (pose) for a shot; they might even refuse [6] __________ (let) you do it.
>
> A lot of photographers insist [7] __________ (be) invisible so that their shots are more natural. They object [8] __________ (ask) their subject for permission first because this would spoil the moment. But I disagree. I always advise photographers [9] __________ (talk) to their subjects first. In fact, I strongly recommend [10] __________ (get) to know their subjects' story, because it gives the shots more meaning.

Speaking

9 Work in small groups and discuss the questions.

1 Do you like having your photo taken? Why?
2 What is the best way to get a good photo of someone?
3 Do you ever take photos of people you don't know? How do you approach this?
4 Have you ever felt uncomfortable about taking a photo of someone you didn't know?

8b And finally…

Vocabulary the feel-good factor

1 News programs often like to end with a good news story. Look at the adjectives that describe how this type of story can make people feel and match each one to a definition.

amusing	appealing	charming	encouraging
inspiring	odd	optimistic	quirky

1 ________, ________: hopeful
2 ________: makes one smile or laugh
3 ________: shows what people can achieve
4 ________, ________: unusual or strange
5 ________, ________: delightful

WORDBUILDING forming adjectives from verbs

We can add *-ing* to many verbs to form adjectives.
amuse → amusing, encourage → encouraging

2 Work in pairs. Think of an example of a good news story you have heard recently. Tell your partner. Use one of the adjectives in Exercise 1.

I saw a really inspiring local news story on TV about a five-year-old boy who raised money for his sick sister by...

Listening

3 28 Listen to four feel-good news stories and complete the summaries.

1 People thought that the ________, but they were wrong because ________. As a result in the future we will see ________.
2 Researchers believe they have found ________. When people took ________, the result was that ________.
3 The world's largest ________ says they have invented ________. But doctors ________.
4 Costa Rica is ________ because it has ________. Countries like ________ on the other hand, ________.

4 Work with a student from another group and retell the stories to each other. Which story did you find the most optimistic? Quirky? Inspiring?

Grammar passive reporting verbs

5 Look at these two examples of passive reporting verbs and answer the questions.

It *was thought* that the large blue butterfly was extinct.
It *is estimated* that 20,000 large blue butterflies will be seen this summer.

1 What do/did people actually say or think?
2 When do/did they say or think this?

PASSIVE REPORTING VERBS

Typical reporting verbs
say, think, believe, report, consider, know, estimate, expect, claim

***It* + *is* + passive reporting verb + *that* + sentence…**
It is thought that people are more healthy these days. (present report of present event)
It is thought that people were less healthy in the past. (present report of past event)
It is thought that people will be healthier in the future. (present report of future event)

***It* + *was* + passive reporting verb + *that* + sentence…**
It was thought that the butterfly was extinct. (report and event at same time in past)
It was thought that the butterfly had disappeared. (past event before past report)
It was thought that the butterfly would not return. (past report of a future event)

For more information and practice, see page 167.

6 Work in pairs. Look at the grammar box. Then look at the audioscript on page 179 and underline more sentences with passive reporting verbs. For each one decide:

- when the reporting happened
- when the reported event happened

1 ....

2 ....

3 ....

4 ....

5 ....

6 ....

7 ....

7 Transform these sentences into passive reporting sentences using *it*.

1 People report: "Large blue butterflies are everywhere now."
Example:
It is reported that large blue butterflies are everywhere now.
2 30 years ago people said: "The large blue butterfly is a common species."
3 People said: "Hunters caused the butterfly to die out."
4 The announcer said: "People thought the butterfly was extinct."
5 I said: "I take zinc and I haven't had a bad cold in a year."
6 In the past people thought: "Costa Rica is a poor country."
7 Scientists claim: "Taking zinc helps if you have a cold."
8 They said: "None of the previous experiments has been conclusive."
9 Experts claimed: "Eating the new chocolate will improve your health."
10 But people know: "Eating too much chocolate is actually bad for you."

8 Look at these other news items and facts and make sentences using the passive reporting verbs given. Tell your partner whether you think each one is true or not. Then check your answers on page 155.

1 It / believe / that chewing gum when you peel onions / prevent / you from crying.
2 It / say / Google's name / come / from "googol," a number with 100 zeros.
3 It / know / that laughing regularly / increase / life expectancy by up to ten years.
4 In 2008, it / report / that air pollution in the US / fall / by 40 percent since 1980.
5 It / claim / recently that scientists studying the zebrafish / discover / a way for the human heart to heal itself.
6 In 2011, it / report / that a man whose house had been crushed by a huge rock in the New Zealand earthquake /sell / the rock for $10,000.

Writing and speaking

9 Work in groups of three and prepare a feel-good news story. Choose a theme of your own or one from the list below. Then write the story together, using at least two passive reporting verbs. When you have finished, practice reading it aloud. Then each person should join a new group of three and read their stories to the other students.

- a person rescued by an animal
- the discovery of a valuable painting or antique
- a child's remarkable musical ability
- the invention of a new clothing fabric
- a couple who are celebrating their 90th wedding anniversary
- a dentist that people actually enjoy visiting

8c From hero to zero

Reading

1 Work in pairs. Look at the headlines below, as they appeared over several months. Discuss what you think happened.

HERO BA PILOT PETER BURKILL SPEAKS: I THOUGHT WE'D DIE IN HEATHROW CRASH

"I AM NOT A HERO"
SAYS BA CRASH PILOT CAPTAIN PETER BURKILL

REAL HERO OF BA FLIGHT 38
IS COPILOT JOHN COWARD

HERO PILOT "FORCED OUT OF BA"

FALLEN HERO: THAT DAY CHANGED MY LIFE FOREVER

OFFICIAL REPORT SAYS ICE FAULT CAUSED BA AIRPORT CRASH

2 Read the story quickly. Then check the sequence of key events with your partner. How did the story differ from your answer in Exercise 1?

3 Mark the statements true (T) or false (F).

1 Burkill's copilot was at the controls when the engines failed.
2 Some passengers were badly hurt.
3 At the time of the accident, Burkill was a single man who liked to enjoy himself.
4 Burkill's crew read BA's internal report.
5 Burkill was praised in the AAIB report.
6 He was too loyal to BA to work for another airline.

4 Complete the sentences with words from the article.

1 Burkill went from being a hero to being a (opposite of *hero*) *villain* . (para 1)
2 When the plane crash-landed, (incredibly) ________ it stayed upright. (para 2)
3 Perhaps his colleagues believed he was (no good at his job) ________ . (para 3)
4 The press portrayed Burkill as irresponsible: he (failed) ________ the people he was supposed to be responsible for. (para 4)
5 Burkill felt (completely unsupported) ________ by his colleagues. (para 5)
6 After the official report was published, Burkill was (given as a prize) ________ a medal for his actions. (para 7)

Critical thinking different perspectives

5 Each participant had a different perspective and a different motivation for acting as they did after the accident. Make notes to complete the table.

People involved	Their view of Burkill's role	Motivations for their actions
Peter Burkill	*he did what any pilot would have done*	*to clear his name and keep his job*
BA staff		
BA management		
AAIB*		
the newspapers		

*Air Accidents Investigation Branch

6 Who do you believe? Who do you think the newspapers' readers believed?

Word focus *word*

7 Find four expressions in the article with *word*. Match each one with the definitions below.

1 make the final point in an argument and win it
2 news or a rumor starts to circulate
3 no evidence other than what two sides claim to be true
4 no news about something

8 Work in pairs. What do these other expressions with *word* mean?

1 "The new gallery is amazing. But **don't take my word for it**: go see for yourself."
2 "When my husband handed me the keys to a new car for my birthday, I was at a loss **for words**."
3 "The hotel doesn't advertise at all. It just relies on **word of mouth** to get new customers."
4 "I can't believe they're closing the library. They **gave their word** that they wouldn't."

Speaking

9 Work in groups. Discuss the media in your country.
1 How respectful are reporters towards politicians?
2 How balanced is the reporting of public scandals?
3 Are people interested in reading about the private lives of famous people?

FROM HERO TO ZERO

In January 2008, hours after saving his plane from crashing at Heathrow Airport, Captain Peter Burkill was being praised as a hero. Only days later, when reports appeared in the press accusing him of freezing at the controls, he became a villain. How did this extraordinary transformation come about?

Peter Burkill was the pilot on flight 38 from Hong Kong and ultimately responsible for the lives of its 152 passengers. Seconds before landing, two of the plane's engines failed. With the plane losing height fast, Burkill let his copilot John Coward take the controls while he himself adjusted the wing flaps to help the plane reach the runway. His risky decision worked. The plane missed some houses and landed heavily on the grass just short of the runway. After skidding for a few hundred feet, it miraculously came to a stop without turning over. The passengers escaped without serious injury. As far as Burkill was concerned, he had done what any captain would have done. The rest was luck.

However, this was not the version of events that began to circulate among BA's staff in the following days, whether because they just liked to gossip or felt Burkill was incompetent. Word went around that rather than taking control of the plane, Burkill had frozen. Worse, it was reported that he had failed to issue a mayday call and had not evacuated the passengers correctly.

Some newspapers, sensing a chance to sell more copies, picked up the story, claiming that John Coward was the real hero. They published details of Burkill's colorful past, painting a picture of a well-paid pilot who had lived the life of a playboy, and—when it mattered—had let down his crew and passengers. Worse still for Burkill, it wasn't even his word against theirs. British Airways banned him from speaking about the events until the full investigation by the Air Accidents Investigations Branch (AAIB) was complete.

Overnight, Burkill's life changed. Before the accident, he had had everything: a great job, a beautiful home, a loving family, and the respect of his colleagues. Now he felt betrayed and desperate. The stress put enormous pressure on his family. In the weeks that followed, he spent more time at home helping his wife, Maria, to look after their young children. But he became depressed. He begged the company to issue a statement to clear his name, but they refused, clearly anxious to avoid bad publicity in case the official investigation found Burkill guilty. Even when they published their own internal report in May 2008, clearing him of any wrongdoing, it was only read by the senior management. No word of it reached his close colleagues, and rumors circulated that crew members were afraid to fly with him. He wrote to BA's chief executive asking for help, but got no reply.

The official AAIB report, the result of a completely independent inquiry, was finally published in February 2009. It concluded that ice had formed in the fuel system during the approach to Heathrow, cutting the fuel supply to the engines. The actions of the crew had saved the lives of all on board, it said, in particular Captain Burkill's split-second decision to reduce the flap setting.

The pilots and thirteen cabin crew were awarded the British Airways Safety Medal and the story of Peter Burkill the hero once again made the headlines. But the damage had been done. In August 2009, Peter Burkill took voluntary retirement from the company he had served for 25 years. He began applying for jobs with other airlines, but he was not invited to a single interview.

So did his critics win? No. Burkill himself had the last word. BA said that he was and always had been welcome in the company and in September 2010, BA invited him to come back and fly for them. Burkill accepted their invitation.

Captain Peter Burkill (right) and copilot John Coward

mayday call (n) /ˈmeɪdeɪ ˌkɔl/ a call for help in an emergency
runway (n) /ˈrʌnˌweɪ/ the part of an airport where planes land and take off
skid (v) /skɪd/ to slide without any control
voluntary retirement (n) /ˈvɑlənˌteri rɪˈtaɪərmənt/ to agree to leave your job in exchange for payment

8d Spreading the news

Real life reporting what you heard

1 🔊 **29** Listen to two neighbors discussing an incident. Choose the picture that best illustrates what happened.

2 🔊 **29** Work in pairs. Discuss the questions. Then listen again and check.

1 Why didn't Phil see the incident?
2 Who did Jess learn about the incident from?
3 How could the argument between the drivers have been avoided?
4 Who was one of the drivers identified as?
5 What happened in the end?

3 🔊 **29** Look at the box. Complete the phrases Jess (J) uses to report what someone said and Phil (P) uses to say how reliable this source was. Then listen again and check.

1 J: __________ that it was an argument between two drivers and __________ it got pretty nasty.
2 J: __________ one of the drivers became really aggressive.
3 P: I'd take what Tara says with __________ . She tends to __________ things __________ .
4 J: She __________ that if the police hadn't arrived, there would have been a fight.
5 J: Someone __________ they had seen one of the drivers before. __________ , he is a local politician.
6 P: I think I'd take __________ ; he's not the type to __________ .
7 J: __________ Chris, they took them both away.

> **▶ REPORTING WHAT YOU HEARD**
>
> I heard that…
> Someone said that…
> They figure that…
> According to (somebody)…,
> It seems that…
> Apparently,…
> Supposedly,…
>
> **Expressing belief and disbelief**
> I'd take his/her word for it.
> He/She generally gets his/her facts right.
> He's/She's not the type to spread gossip.
> Don't pay attention to what he/she says.
> It's been blown out of proportion.
> I'd take that with a grain of salt.

4 Pronunciation the schwa

🔊 **30** Unstressed syllables often produce the schwa sound /ə/. Listen for these examples and repeat. The stressed syllable is underlined.

/ə/ /ə/ apparently	/ə/ /ə/ generally
/ə/ /ɪ/ supposedly	/ə/ happened

5 You are going to spread news around the class. Follow these steps:

- Tell your partner two facts (one true, one false) about yourself or something you did.
- Talk to other students in the class and tell at least three people what you heard.
- Return to your partner and report the new information you heard.
- Discuss which ones you think are true or not. Use the expressions in the box.
- Tell the class what you thought and see if you were right.

8e A residents' meeting

Writing minutes from a meeting

1 Read this report of a residents' meeting on a street where a traffic incident occurred. Answer the questions.

1 What three ideas were suggested to avoid confrontations between drivers?
2 Which one was chosen as the best idea and why?

Flores Street residents' association

From: Antonia Perez

Re: Residents' meeting about road rage incident

Thanks to all of you who wrote and apologized for not being able to attend Tuesday's meeting. Here are the minutes.

We met to discuss what to do about traffic on our street following last week's incident. Various ideas were discussed about how we could prevent drivers from getting into these angry confrontations. One proposal was to make Flores a one-way street, but most people thought that this wouldn't be good for residents. Another suggestion was to reduce the number of parking spaces to allow more places for cars to pass each other. The objection to this was that it would force residents to park in neighboring streets and just move the problem to another street.

In the end, it was agreed that the best thing would be to put some signs at each end of the road asking drivers to drive with care and consideration. Terry Miles offered to write a letter to town hall asking if this would be possible. A draft copy will be posted next week for comment before it is sent.

2 Which of these elements are included in the report? In what order do they appear?

- the aim of the meeting
- what action was decided
- who said what
- who attended the meeting
- follow-up action

3 **Writing skill** impersonal language

a Underline the phrases that the writer uses to avoid naming people directly when reporting what was said. Why does she do this? Compare your answers with your partner and discuss.

b Rewrite the sentences using the words given to make them less personal.

1 Hannah suggested that we should put speed bumps on the street.
One .... (suggestion)
2 Everyone thought this was a terrible idea.
It .... (decided / good)
3 Dan thought the speed limit should be reduced to 15 mph.
Another .... (idea)
4 But several people said that probably no one would keep to this speed limit.
It .... (agreed)
5 Javi proposed having a sign with arrows giving priority to drivers from one direction.
Another .... (proposal)
6 Sofia argued that this would be impossible to enforce.
The .... (objection / difficult)

4 Read the description of a local problem. Discuss possible solutions with your partner. Look at the suggestions on page 153. Write a report of a meeting at which these solutions were discussed. Say which one was chosen and describe the follow-up action.

The city's university has recently bought four houses on your street to accommodate students, because they don't have enough rooms at their main dorm. The students are making a lot of noise at night, playing loud music and shouting in the street. This is a problem for local residents, many of whom have young children.

5 Exchange your reports with another pair. Answer these questions.

- Did they choose the same solution as you?
- Does their report seem too personal or direct?
- Does it follow the model in Exercise 1?
- Is it missing any important information?

8f Mount Fuji

Video

Climbing Mount Fuji is a mind exercise. It's mind over matter more than anything.

Before you watch

1 Work in groups. Look at the photo and discuss the questions.

1 Where are the people in the photo?
2 Why do you think they are there?
3 What do you think the caption tells us about the people in the photo?

2 Mark the things you think you are going to see in this video.

a bear	a rollercoaster
a bulldozer	snow
clouds	sunflowers
drums	a sunrise
food vendor	umbrellas

While you watch

3 Watch the video and check your answers from Exercise 2.

4 Watch the video again and describe these things.

1 Mount Fuji

....

....

2 the fire and water festivals

....

....

3 the weather when Karen Kasmauski climbs the mountain

....

....

5 Watch the first part of the video (to 02:07). Are these sentences true (T) or false (F)? Correct the false sentences.

1 Karen Kasmauski is enjoying perfect weather for her photo shoot.
2 Karen thinks Japanese people worship Mount Fuji because it is so beautiful.
3 Mount Fuji is worshipped with fire and water festivals.
4 Karen starts her photo shoot in the forest at the base of the mountain.
5 You can buy crackers and cakes at Mount Fuji.
6 Climbing Mount Fuji is seen mostly as something tourists have to do.

6 Watch the second part of the video (02:08 to the end). Make notes about these things. Then compare your notes with a partner.

1 How Karen feels when she gets to the top.

....

....

2 How Mount Fuji was different in the past.

....

....

3 Managing Mount Fuji.

....

....

4 What happens at the end of the climbing season.

....

....

After you watch

7 **Roleplay interviewing a National Geographic photographer**

Work in pairs.

Student A: Imagine you are a photographer for National Geographic. You are going to be interviewed by an amateur photographer. Make notes about the items below.

Student B: Imagine you are an amateur photographer. You are going to interview a photographer for National Geographic. Prepare questions based on these items.

- lifestyle of a photographer
- the advantages and disadvantages of the job

Act out the interview, then change roles.

8 Karen Kasmauski says that climbing Mount Fuji is "a national bonding experience." What do you think she means? Are there any symbols of national unity in your country?

9 Work in groups and discuss these questions.

1 Are there any special places in your country where people like to go and take photographs?
2 What makes an interesting photograph for you: the place, the people, or what is taking place?
3 Is there any famous place in the world you would like to photograph? Why?

appease (v) /ə'piz/ keep a person or a thing calm
bento box (n) /'bentoʊ ˌbɑks/ a wooden or metal box, divided into compartments, used in Japan for storing a meal
bonding (n) /'bɑndɪŋ/ the process of becoming emotionally close to other people
bulldozer (n) /'bʊlˌdoʊzər/ a large machine that moves earth
conical (adj) /'kɑnɪkəl/ shaped like a cone
pilgrimage (n) /'pɪlgrɪmɪʤ/ a journey to a holy place
purification (n) /pjʊərɪfɪ'keɪʃən/ the process of making something clean
typhoon (n) /taɪ'fun/ a very strong tropical storm
vending machine (n) /'vendɪŋ məˌʃin/ a machine that sells things, for example, drinks or food

UNIT 8 REVIEW

Grammar

1 Work in pairs. Look at the photo of a new development. What do you think the designers are trying to create?

2 Read the news article below and see if you were right.

3 Complete the article with the correct form of the verbs. Use prepositions where necessary. Then check your answer to Exercise 1.

Big cities are often criticized [1] ______ (be) big polluters. But it is generally considered that Singapore [2] ______ (be) an exception to this rule. For a long time the government has encouraged developers and conservationists [3] ______ (think) of ways to increase the island's green spaces. Recently green groups suggested [4] ______ (turn) the old KTM railway corridor into a nature trail. But perhaps the most striking project is Gardens by the Bay, a futuristic park which includes eighteen Supertrees. When it is complete, it is said that each of the eighteen trees [5] ______ (be covered) in more that 200 varieties of plants.

The government invited various companies [6] ______ (submit) ideas for the project and this was chosen as the most exciting. A spokesman for the government complimented the designers [7] ______ (come) up with a "truly innovative" design. The Supertrees are between 80 and 160 feet tall and mimic the function of real trees, absorbing sunlight through photovoltaic cells and collecting rainwater. The photographer who took this picture admitted [8] ______ (feel) skeptical about the project until he saw it for himself. "It looks like something from the movie *Avatar*: almost too good to be real!"

I CAN	
report speech with reporting verbs and the correct dependent verb form	☐
report what is generally said or thought with passive reporting verbs	☐

Vocabulary

4 Work in pairs. Find the odd word out in each group. Explain your choice.

1 movie, photo, snapshot, picture
2 column, feature, scandal, editorial
3 inspiring, amusing, optimistic, encouraging
4 lens, shutter, flash, camera
5 urge, promise, encourage, persuade
6 objection, suggestion, proposal, recommendation

5 Work in pairs. Describe a news photo that had a big impact on you. What was the story behind the picture?

I CAN	
talk about photography	☐
relate feel-good news stories	☐

Real life

6 Put each phrase into the right category: reporting what someone said (R), expressing belief (B), or expressing disbelief (D).

1 They figure that half a million people came to the free festival.
2 I'd take that with a grain of salt.
3 Apparently, a lot more people came than expected.
4 I think the number has been blown out of proportion.
5 According to official reports, around 250,000 attended.
6 It seems that the organizers were only expecting 150,000.
7 You can take the organizer's word for it.
8 Don't pay attention to what the promoters say. They just want publicity.

7 Work in small groups. Discuss an event, local or national, people have been talking about recently. Tell each other what you believe to be the real facts.

I CAN	
report what I heard	☐

Speaking

8 Work in pairs. Create a short news item about an event in your class or institution. Include at least two verbs reporting what people said.

Unit 9 Talented people

A mahout (elephant driver) bathes his elephant.
Photograph by Robert Harding

FEATURES

1 Work in pairs. Match the words in the box to the definitions (a–g).

background	experience	knowledge	degrees
qualities	skills	talents	

a strong natural abilities
b abilities developed by practice
c (generally positive) characteristics
d certificates which show you have learned something
e what you've done in your life
f what you know
g your past in general (birthplace, education, places lived)

2 Look at the photo and the caption. What qualities, skills, knowledge, and experience do you think a mahout needs to do their job well? Discuss.

3 Make short notes on your own background, experience, knowledge, and talents. Then ask each other questions.

9a An ordinary man

Reading

1 Work in pairs. Look at the photo and read the title of the article. Do you know who Neil Armstrong is? Tell your partner what you know.

2 Read the article and say in what ways Armstrong was an ordinary man and in what ways he was extraordinary.

3 Read the article again. Answer the questions.

1 Why is Armstrong called "the ultimate professional"?
2 Who paid for his college and what did they get in return?
3 What motivated Armstrong?
4 What does "the rest is history" mean?
5 What did Armstrong do to avoid publicity after the Apollo 11 mission? Why?
6 According to Armstrong, who was responsible for the success of the Apollo 11 mission?

An ORDINARY man

Neil Armstrong, the most famous of the astronauts on Apollo 11, has been called the ultimate professional. He was hired to do a job. He did the job and then he went home and kept quiet about it. In 40 years, he gave two interviews. He died in August 2012. But how could the man who first set foot on the Moon, a hero to millions of people, have remained such a mystery?

People like Armstrong often develop their interests at a young age. He pursued a career built on a passion for flying that he developed during his childhood in the 1930s. He learned to fly before he had graduated from high school in Wapakoneta, Ohio. He then took courses in aerospace engineering at Purdue University in Indiana, sponsored by the United States Navy. In return, Armstrong served as a naval pilot for three years. He saw action almost immediately, flying 78 missions in the war in Korea.

He left the Navy in 1952, and two years later got a job with the Lewis Flight Propulsion Laboratory, where he flew experimental aircraft. He reached speeds of 4,000 MPH and altitudes of over 200,000 feet. When he decided to become an astronaut is not clear. Certainly, it was not his ambition to be famous. An extremely talented pilot, he wanted simply to push the boundaries of flight.

He was selected for a space training program in 1960, and shortly after, news began to circulate that NASA was looking for astronauts for their Apollo program. Incredibly excited, he applied for the job and was accepted in 1962. The rest, as they say, is history.

When the astronauts returned from the Apollo 11 Moon landing of July 1969, Armstrong was a worldwide celebrity and could have done anything he wanted: TV shows, public speaking, etc. Instead, he became a professor at the University of Cincinnati. On weekends, he went flying to get away from all the attention. He subsequently worked for two private avionics companies until he retired in 2002. In 40 years he only gave two interviews. Why did Armstrong avoid publicity? Certainly he felt fortunate to have had the chance to fulfill his dream, but he did not feel any more special than the thousands of people who worked on the Apollo space program. He was just the pilot.

Astronaut Buzz Aldrin photographed on the Moon by Neil Armstrong (visible in Aldrin's visor)

Vocabulary careers

4 Work in pairs. Find verbs in the article that collocate with each of these nouns. Then identify the different steps in Armstrong's career.

1 to .... a career
2 to .... a school or college
3 to .... a course
4 to .... in the Navy
5 to .... an astronaut
6 to .... a company
7 to ...., ..., ... a job

WORDBUILDING verb (+ preposition) + noun collocations

pursue a career
graduate from a school/college

Grammar articles: *the* or no article?

5 Look at how *the* or no article are used in the paragraph. Match the words in bold (1–7) with the uses of *the* and no article (a–g).

Neil Armstrong, (1) **the most famous** of (2) **the astronauts** on Apollo 11, has been called the ultimate professional. He was hired to do a job. He did (3) **the job** and then he went (4) **home** and kept quiet about it. In 40 years, he gave two interviews. But how could (5) **the man** who first set foot on (6) **the Moon**, a hero to (7) **millions** of people, have remained such a mystery?

a to talk about an already mentioned thing
b to talk about something unique
c before a superlative adjective
d to talk about a specific thing or person
e to talk about specific things or people
f to talk about things or people in general
g before certain familiar places (like work)

6 Work in pairs. Find one more example of each use in the rest of the article.

ARTICLES: *THE* or NO ARTICLE?

definite article
the + singular/plural count nouns, noncount nouns = specific things

no article
– + plural count nouns, noncount nouns = things in general
Note: We don't use *the* with most time expressions or place names. However, there are some exceptions.

For more information and practice, see page 168.

7 Find an example in the article of the following:

1 no article with:
a) a country
b) a subject of study
c) a month
2 *the* with:
a) a country
b) a professional group
c) a period of time

8 Complete these sentences by inserting *the* where necessary.

1 While flying for .... Navy in .... Korea, Armstrong had to eject into .... sea when one of .... wings on his plane was damaged.
2 Armstrong and Aldrin only spent one day on .... surface of .... Moon.
3 Armstrong retired from .... NASA in .... 1972, but he helped with .... crash investigations in .... later years.
4 .... first investigation was in .... May 1970 following an explosion on .... Apollo 13.
5 .... other investigation involved .... space shuttle Challenger, which broke into .... pieces over .... Atlantic Ocean near .... Florida.
6 In .... nineties, Armstrong stopped signing .... autographs, because .... dealers were selling each for $1,000.

Speaking

9 Draw a path of your own (or a parent's) career. Begin with your interests as a child. Finish with future ambitions. If it is not an obvious linear progression, show how the direction changed. Then explain the path to your partner.

When I was a kid, I really liked to draw. But my parents wanted me to be a lawyer, so I started college for law in 2013.

But now you're in art school!

Yes… I hated it, so I took a year off and then dropped out!

9b Pushing the boundaries

Listening

1 31 Listen to an interview about the National Geographic Emerging Explorers program and answer the questions.

1 What is the aim of the program?
2 How does National Geographic help those selected?
3 What kind of fields do Emerging Explorers work in?

2 31 Are the sentences true (T) or false (F)? Listen again and check.

1 Emerging Explorers are people who are not yet fully established in their careers.
2 Emerging Explorers get money and publicity for their work in the magazine.
3 They generally have a scientific background.
4 Storytellers are explorers who record traditional stories from different cultures.
5 Alexandra Cousteau's father filmed other Emerging Explorers.
6 Alexandra is interested in how new technology can help to spread the environmental message.

Grammar relative clauses

3 Work in pairs. Look at the relative clauses in bold from the interview (a–e). Then discuss the questions (1–4).

a Each year, between eight and fifteen explorers, **whose work is really outstanding**, are selected.
b Emerging Explorers are generally people **who are at an early stage of their careers**.
c National Geographic awards each one of them $10,000, **which is intended to go towards further research**.
d The magazine is a place **where other interested people can read about their work**.
e There are all these people doing important work out there in the various fields **that I have described**.

1 In which sentence is the relative pronoun the subject of the relative clause?
2 In which sentences does the relative clause explain who or what is being talked about?
3 In which sentences does the relative clause give extra information and how does the punctuation help you know this?
4 In which sentence could the relative pronoun be omitted?

RELATIVE CLAUSES

Relative pronouns: *who* (*that*), *which* (*that*), *where*, *whose*
Subject: *She's the woman who won the award.*
Object: *That's the award which/that the woman won.*
OR *That's the award the woman won.*

Defining relative clause
This clause contains essential information for identification.
She's the woman who won an award for her photography.

Non-defining relative clause
This clause contains extra information, separated by one or two commas.
Her husband, who is also a photographer, accompanied her on the trip.

***that* or no pronoun**
The article (that) I read about her was good.

For more information and practice, see page 169.

4 Look at the grammar box. Then complete these sentences about Emerging Explorer Alexandra Cousteau by inserting the correct relative pronoun and any commas that are missing.

1 Alexandra Cousteau ________ is a conservationist believes water will be the most important issue of the 21st century.
2 Alexandra Cousteau ________ father was an oceanographer is a great advocate for environmental protection.
3 Cousteau says that the environmental movement uses communication tools ________ are old-fashioned.
4 She is currently planning an expedition ________ aim is to research different water ecosystems around the world.
5 She is currently working on a book ________ she hopes will teach people how to live on a "Water Planet."
6 The problem ________ she says was created by people is a problem ________ people can only solve by working together.

Grammar reduced relative clauses

5 An alternative to a relative clause is a reduced relative clause. Look at the participles in bold in these sentences. Which are active and which are passive?

1 We have so many different types of explorers, **chosen** from diverse fields.
2 There are all these people **doing** important work out there in the various fields.
3 That's the skill of the storytellers, **communicating** important facts about the planet.
4 She works as a conservationist, **trying** to persuade people to protect resources like water.
5 Alexandra Cousteau, **inspired** by her father's success as a storyteller, is researching ways in which the environmental community can use new media.

REDUCED RELATIVE CLAUSES

Present participle
researching
She works at Harvard, ~~where she is~~ researching sharks. (active)
Past participle
researched
It's a subject ~~which is~~ researched by only a few people.
(passive)

For more information and practice, see page 169.

6 Look at the grammar box. Then rewrite the reduced relative clauses in Exercise 5 as relative clauses.

7 Complete the profiles of other Emerging Explorers below by inserting the missing information as a reduced relative clause where possible and if not, as a relative clause.

1 She has been called the real-life Lara Croft by the *New York Times*.
2 She cycled a distance of 700 miles.
3 They threatened to harm her.
4 He is fascinated by the truly big questions.
5 He plays music to take his mind off problems.
6 He spends his time diving into water caves deep under the ground.
7 The caves have been undisturbed for 3.5 million years.
8 Knowledge is provided by these dark and wonderful places.

8 Work in pairs. Circle the eight adjectives in the profiles that describe people's strengths and qualities.

9 Which of these people would you most like to meet? Tell your partner.

Speaking and writing

10 Think of someone you admire for the work they do. Write a short description of their achievements and qualities. In groups, read your descriptions and ask questions.

Kira Salak, [1] ________, doesn't want to tell travel stories you have already heard. Independent and adaptable, she has traveled across Papua New Guinea on foot, and Alaska on a bicycle, [2] ________. It is not easy traveling alone as a single woman in remote and dangerous regions. In Mozambique, she escaped soldiers [3] ________. But she does not regret such experiences because she says they have helped her discover her strengths.

Stephon Alexander is a theoretical physicist [4] ________ like "how did space and time begin?" It's an unusual job because you need to be not only analytical and patient, but also daring and a risk taker, because to answer such questions you have to make guesses. Often you can be completely wrong. But when you are right, he says, the feeling is amazing. The work can be mentally tiring, but Alexander is quite an easy-going type. He is also a jazz musician, [5] ________.

Kenny Broad is an extreme explorer [6] ________. These "blue holes," [7] ________, are like time capsules, full of interesting scientific evidence about the way life on our planet has evolved. The caves are also important reservoirs of fresh water. An articulate and passionate speaker, Broad promotes the idea that by working together, scientists from different backgrounds can benefit from the knowledge [8] ________.

9c The king herself

Reading

1 Work in pairs. Look at the title of the article. What is strange about the words *king* and *herself* together?

2 Read the article and put these events about Hatshepsut's life in the correct chronological order.

a Her mummy was discovered in a minor tomb.
b The monuments she built were destroyed.
c Thutmose III became pharaoh.
d She ruled Egypt as king for 21 years.
e Her mummy was identified and put in the Royal Mummy Rooms.
f She married Thutmose II.
g She was born, the eldest daughter of Thutmose I and Queen Ahmose.

3 What were the different roles that Hatshepsut fulfilled (like pharaoh)?

4 Choose the correct option (a–c) to complete the sentences.

1 Hatshepsut's mummy was not identified at first because it:
 a was badly damaged.
 b was not in a royal tomb.
 c had another name with it.
2 Hatshepsut was very worried that people would:
 a realize she was a woman.
 b not think she was royalty.
 c not remember her.
3 Thutmose III did not want people to know that Hatshepsut had been:
 a king.
 b queen.
 c related to him.
4 Thutmose II's children consisted of:
 a one son and one daughter.
 b one son.
 c one daughter.
5 According to tradition, the queen regent was supposed to:
 a make offerings to the gods.
 b help until the king was ready.
 c be a politician.
6 In later statues and images, Hatshepsut appears male from:
 a her body shape.
 b the way she stands.
 c the dress she wears.

Critical thinking weighing the evidence

5 Find evidence that supports each sentence (1–6). If the sentence is definitely true, write 100%. If there is no evidence, write 0%. Put percentages in between if it is not clear.

1 When Hatshepsut's sarcophagus was first found in 1903, it was empty.
2 The mummy called KV60a was Hatshepsut's body.
3 Hatshepsut wanted to produce a male heir, but failed.
4 Hatshepsut had a greater claim to become pharaoh than Thutmose III.
5 Hatshepsut wanted her subjects' approval.
6 The king in waiting, Thutmose III, was angry that Hatshepsut had assumed the role of king.

6 Work in pairs. Compare your scores and your evidence.

Word focus *long*

7 In the article, find these six phrases (1–6) with the word *long* and match each one to its definition (a–f).

1	at long last	a	soon
2	as long as	b	over a long period of time
3	long for	c	after much waiting
4	long after	d	provided that
5	before long	e	much, much later
6	in the long term	f	desire very much

8 Complete the sentences using phrases with *long*.

1 Hatshepsut clearly .... people to remember her.
2 The grand monuments she built ensured she would be remembered ....
3 .... people believed she had a divine right to be pharaoh, Hatshepsut felt safe.
4 Hatshepsut died in 1458 BC and ...., Thutmose III had destroyed most references to her as king.
5 Experts in hieroglyphs .... uncovered the truth.
6 Thutmose III ruled for another 34 years, ... Hatshepsut had died.

Speaking

9 Work in small groups. Say who you would expect to find doing these jobs: mostly men, mostly women, or an equal number of men and women. Give reasons.

company director	cleaner	nurse	teacher
IT technician	doctor	plumber	
machine operator	florist	secretary	
prime minister	lawyer	senior civil servant	

10 Look at the statistics on page 154. Which job in Exercise 9 fits in which category? Compare and discuss your answers.

THE KING *Herself*

Today she is in the Royal Mummy Rooms at the Egyptian Museum in Cairo, reunited at long last with her family of fellow pharaohs, with a sign saying she is Hatshepsut, the king herself (1473–1458 BC).

But in 1903, when the archaeologist Howard Carter found Hatshepsut's sarcophagus in the Valley of the Kings, it was empty. Had her mummy been stolen or destroyed? The truth only came out a century later when Egyptian scientists positively identified a mummy called KV60a, discovered more than a century earlier in a minor tomb, as that of Hatshepsut. None of the treasures normally found with pharaohs' mummies were with it. It was not even in a coffin.

For Hatshepsut, a pharaoh who did not fear death as long as she was remembered, the irony is great. As one of the greatest builders in one of the greatest Egyptian dynasties, she raised numerous temples and shrines. She commissioned hundreds of statues of herself and left accounts in stone of her titles, her history, even her hopes and fears. Inscribed on an obelisk at Karnak are the words: "Now my heart turns this way and that, as I think what the people will say. Those who see my monuments in years to come, and who shall speak of what I have done."

But following her death, her successor and stepson Thutmose III set about erasing her memory. At Deir el Bahri, at the temple designed to be the center of Hatshepsut's cult, her statues were smashed and thrown into a pit. Images of her as queen were left undisturbed, but wherever she proclaimed herself king, the destruction was careful and precise. Why?

Hatshepsut was the eldest daughter of Thutmose I and Queen Ahmose. But Thutmose also had a son by another queen, and this son, Thutmose II, became pharaoh when his father died. As was common among Egyptian royalty, Thutmose II married his sister, Hatshepsut. They produced one daughter; another, less important wife, Isis, gave Thutmose II the male heir that he longed for, but Hatshepsut was unable to provide.

When Thutmose II died not long after from heart disease, his heir, Thutmose III, was still a young boy. As was the custom, Hatshepsut assumed control as the young pharaoh's queen regent. And so began one of the most intriguing periods of ancient Egyptian history.

At first, Hatshepsut acted on her stepson's behalf, respecting the convention that the queen should handle political affairs while the young king learned the ropes. But before long, she began performing kingly functions, like making offerings to the gods. After a few years, she assumed the role of king of Egypt, supreme power in the land. Her stepson was relegated to second-in-command and "the king herself" proceeded to rule for an amazing 21 years.

What caused Hatshepsut to break so radically with the traditional role of queen regent? A social or military crisis? A desire for power? A belief that she had the same right to rule as a man? No one really knows. Maybe she felt, as a direct descendant of the pharoah Thutmose I, she had a greater claim to the divine line of pharaohs than Thutmose III. At first she made no secret of her sex—in images her body is unmistakably a woman's—but later she is depicted as a male king, with headdress and beard, standing imposingly with legs apart.

Her hieroglyph inscriptions have frequent references to "my people" which suggest that she knew she had broken with tradition and wanted her subjects' approval. Whatever their opinion was, there is no doubting the frustration of Thutmose III. After Hapshepsut's death, he took his revenge, wiping his stepmother's reign as pharaoh out of history. But in the long term it is she, the king herself, who achieved the greater fame.

coffin (n) /ˈkɔfɪn/ a box in which a dead body is put to be buried
commission (v) /kəˈmɪʃən/ to order and pay for something to be made
divine (adj) /dɪˈvaɪn/ related to God
heir (n) /eər/ a successor

9d Right for the job

Real life describing skills, talents, and experience

Shelterbox
is a charity which sends boxes of essential items needed in an emergency—a tent, tools, cooking utensils, a water purification kit—to places where disasters, such as earthquakes and floods, have struck. Boxes are prepared in the US and delivered immediately by Shelterbox employees to anywhere in the world where they will help save lives.

1 Read the description of Shelterbox. What kind of organization is it and what service does it offer?

2 🔊 **32** Listen to someone being interviewed for a job at Shelterbox. Answer the questions.

1. What aspect of Shelterbox's work is the candidate interested in?
2. What is the interviewer concerned about?

3 🔊 **32** Look at these phrases from the interview describing the candidate's suitability for a job. Note the prepositions used in each case. Then listen to the interview again and complete each one.

▶ DESCRIBING SKILLS, TALENTS, AND EXPERIENCE

I'm familiar with your work because I have a friend who [1] ....
I'm really interested in [2] ....
I specialized in [3] ....
I think I would be well-suited for [4] ....
I'm good at coping with [5] ....
I have quite a lot of experience [6] ....
I'm pretty good with [7] ....
I'm comfortable with all [8] ....
I'm serious about wanting to [9] ....
I need to become more knowledgeable about [10] ....

4 Work in pairs. Discuss: did the candidate do a good job of selling himself to the interviewer?

5 Pronunciation difficult words

a 🔊 **33** The spelling of a word in English is not always a clear indication of its pronunciation. How confident are you that you can pronounce these words from the interview? Mark each word confident (✓), somewhat confident (?), and not confident (×). Then listen and check.

although	comfortable	environments
foreign	knowledgeable	months
specialized	suited	world

b 🔊 **34** Listen to and spell eight more words.

6 Work in pairs.

Student A: Choose one of the jobs below that interests you and think about the skills, talents, and experience you have that would help you do it. Try to convince Student B why this would be a good job for you.

Student B: Interview Student A for the job. Then swap roles.

- a travel guide for walking tours
- a sales assistant in a children's bookstore
- an outreach director for a charity that helps the homeless
- an assistant to a cameraman who makes films about plants and wildlife

9e Professional networking

Writing an online profile

1 Do you use any professional networking sites? Why?

2 Read the profile and summarize in no more than nine words what this person's main skills and qualities are. How effective was his profile in putting across the key points?

3 Read the tips on how to write a profile on a professional networking site. Put a check mark (✓) next to each tip that has been followed, a cross (×) next to those which have not, and a question mark (?) if the tip has only been partly followed.

> Tips:
> 1 Include a personal photo and recommendations from others.
> 2 Give a heading and summary so that readers can get the main idea quickly.
> 3 Say what you're doing now.
> 4 List all the places where you have worked or studied; someone from there may be looking at your profile!
> 5 Job titles may mean nothing to others, so always describe what you did in each job.

Profile

Tom Vasquez
Managing Director of EverReady Learning

Location: Chicago, IL
Industry: Online learning
Current: Developing innovative e-learning program for the car industry

Past
- Head of development, Faheys Educational; responsible for new products
- Editorial Director, York Books; published *Learning in the 21st Century*
- Director of Business Studies, Carston University

Education: Stanford University

Summary
Learning is my passion. I specialize in the design and management of online learning programs for industry, but I am also a writer, editor, blogger, educator, and business consultant. My work has brought me into contact with many companies and I am now skilled at identifying and responding to the learning needs of any business sector, from cosmetics to car-making. If my experience has taught me one thing, it's that learning is the key to improvement for all of us.

4 Writing skill writing in note form

a Look at these four phrases from the profile. Which are proper sentences? Which are written in note or shortened form? Why is this?

1 responsible for new products
2 Learning is my passion.
3 published *Learning in the 21st Century*
4 Developing innovative e-learning program for the car industry

b Insert the necessary words (pronouns, articles, auxiliary verbs) to show what the phrases in note form would look like as full sentences.

c Convert these statements from other profiles into a shorter, more concise form by deleting the unnecessary words.

1 I worked as a personal assistant to the Marketing Director.
2 I am currently writing an article for *National Geographic* magazine.
3 I was in charge of organizing corporate social events.
4 I took the official photos for the Boston Ballet.
5 I am working for various charities.
6 I was hired to raise money for a local college.

5 Write your own short professional profile, similar to the one above. Think about the message you would most like the reader to be left with. When you have finished, exchange profiles with another member of the class. Read them once quickly and tell each other your main impression.

6 Read your partner's profile again. Check the following points:

- Has the profile been laid out correctly?
- Have the tips in Exercise 3 been followed?
- Has note form been used in places to make the profile more concise?

9f Queen of Egypt
Video

She has a reputation for beauty, power, controversy, and ultimately, tragedy.

Before you watch

1 Work in pairs. Make notes about what you know of Cleopatra.

- who she was
- when and where she ruled
- important events in her life

2 You are going to watch a video about the story of Cleopatra. Write down three kinds of images you think you might see which help to tell this story.

While you watch

3 Watch the video and check your ideas from Exercises 1 and 2.

4 Watch the video again and answer the questions.

1 Why was Cleopatra forced from power?

....

2 How did she first meet Julius Caesar?

....

3 How did Cleopatra's relationship with Caesar help her?

....

4 Why did Octavian go to war with Mark Antony and Cleopatra?

....

5 In what year and what battle was Mark Antony beaten?

....

6 How did Mark Antony die?

....

7 How did Cleopatra die?

....

5 Match the sentence beginnings (1–7) with the endings (a–g). Then watch the video again to check.

1 Julius Caesar arrived in Alexandria
2 Cleopatra's relationship with Caesar kept Rome
3 After Caesar's murder
4 Cleopatra and Antony shared
5 Mark Antony's Roman rival, Octavian
6 Cleopatra spread numerous
7 Antony's followers carried him to Cleopatra

a from taking direct control of Egypt.
b false rumors of her death.
c where he died in her arms.
d in pursuit of a rival Roman general.
e her position became uncertain.
f went to war against them.
g a hunger for power.

After you watch

6 Roleplay first meeting with Caesar

Work in pairs.

Student A: Imagine you are Cleopatra. You arrive in Caesar's court hidden in a rug. You need to charm Caesar so that he will help you become queen again. Read the information below and make notes.

Student B: Imagine you are Caesar. Cleopatra arrives in your court hidden in a rug. Read the information below and make notes.

- how you feel (surprised, excited, curious)
- what you want from the other person
- how you can help the other person
- what you decide to do

Act out your meeting, then change roles and act out the meeting again.

7 At the end of the video, the narrator says: "Cleopatra lives on in history through her personal story of love and tragedy." Why do you think her story has lasted for so long? Do you think her story teaches us anything about love and power today?

8 Work in groups and discuss these questions.

1 Do you think Cleopatra was an admirable woman? Why?
2 Are there any similar characters in the history of your country?
3 Would you like to have lived in Cleopatra's time? Why?

charmed (adj) /ʧɑrmd/ fascinated by
controversy (n) /ˈkɑntrəˌvɜrsi/ disagreement about something
court (n) /kɔrt/ the place where a ruler lives and works
distort (v) /dɪsˈtɔrtt/ change something from its normal shape
dynasty (n) /ˈdaɪnəsti/ a family that rules a country for several generations
grief (n) /grif/ great sadness
infuriate (v) /ɪnˈfjʊriˌeɪt/ make very angry
overjoyed (adj) /ˌoʊvərˈʤɔɪd/ extremely happy
pursuit (n) /pərˈsut/ the act of chasing someone or something
rival (n) /ˈraɪvəl/ a person or group that competes with another
rug (n) /rʌg/ a small carpet
seize (v) /siz/ take by force

UNIT 9 REVIEW

Grammar

1 Complete this text with *the* where necessary.

Constance Adams has had an unusual career path. She studied [1] ______ architecture at [2] ______ Yale University before working as an architect in [3] ______ Berlin and [4] ______ Japan. She then joined [5] ______ Johnson Space Center in [6] ______ US, where she helped design TransHab, a module for [7] ______ International Space Station. The idea of [8] ______ module was to provide [9] ______ living quarters for [10] ______ astronauts during their stay in [11] ______ space. In [12] ______ 2005 she became a National Geographic Emerging Explorer.

2 Complete the text with relative pronouns in 1–5 and present and past participles in 6–10.

Adams explains that the TransHab module was intended to be a habitat for a crew of six astronauts, [1] ______ mission was to reach Mars. The team had to design a module [2] ______ would be only 14 feet in diameter when it was launched. But once in space it needed to be three times that size to house the six astronauts [3] ______ lived there. So they made a structure [4] ______ could inflate and unfold in space to become a three-level "house" [5] ______ astronauts could eat, sleep, and work.

The outer shell of the module, [6] ______ (compose) of over twenty layers of different materials, had to resist the space debris [7] ______ (hit) the spaceship all the time. This debris can hit the spaceship seven times faster than a bullet, [8] ______ (cause) great damage. The outer layers were made of a kind of foam [9] ______ (use) in chairs and cushions. The inner shell was made of Kevlar, a material [10] ______ (wear) by soldiers and police for body protection.

3 Work in pairs. Discuss what was special about the module's size, shape, and materials.

I CAN	
use *the* and no article	☐
use relative clauses and reduced relative clauses	☐

Vocabulary

4 Complete the sentences with these nouns and the correct form of the verbs.

background	become	do	experience
pursue	graduate	knowledge	degree
quality	serve	skills	take

1 My main academic ______ is in physics and I got it when I ______ from Duke University.
2 I have a lot of ______ organizing things. I ______ in the army for four years.
3 I think my main ______ is that I'm adaptable. I can ______ many different jobs.
4 I have good computer ______ . I ______ a course in advanced computing last year.
5 My ______—both my parents are scientists—meant scientific research was a natural career for me to ______ .
6 My ______ of astrophysics helped me to ______ a space scientist.

5 Work in pairs. Use the nouns and verbs to describe your own skills and experience.

I CAN	
talk about my experience and skills	☐
describe my career path	☐

Real life

6 Put the correct preposition into each space.

1 I'm familiar ______ most design software.
2 I specialized ______ mechanical engineering.
3 I think I am well-suited ______ working abroad.
4 I'm good ______ people.
5 I'm good ______ persuading people.
6 I'm serious ______ pursuing a career in art.
7 I'm not very interested ______ sitting all day.
8 I am pretty knowledgeable ______ mechanics.

7 Work in pairs. Tell each other about a job that would be right for you and one that wouldn't.

I CAN	
describe what kind of work I am suited for	☐

Speaking

8 Work in small groups. Describe the work of someone you admire. Include these points:

- a description of their qualities and talents
- what they have achieved

Unit 10 Customs and behavior

Two generations of Chinese visitors visit Beijing's Forbidden City.
Photograph by Nigel Swinn

FEATURES

1 Work in pairs. Look at the photo. What is it about the behavior of the younger tourists that surprises the older pair?

2 Look at the quotation below. Discuss what you think it means. Do manners make you a better person, or more socially acceptable—or both?

"Manners maketh man." *William of Wykeham (1324–1404)*

3 Complete these phrases about manners with words from the box. Check your answers with your teacher. Then discuss whether you think these things are important to teach children. What would you add?

chew	courtesy	inappropriate	interrupt
offensive	point	well-behaved	stare
talk	slouch		

1 Don't ________ with your mouth full.
2 Don't ________ when grown-ups are speaking.
3 Don't ________ or ________ at people.
4 Don't ________ gum.
5 Don't wear clothes that are ________ or ________ .
6 Be polite, ________-________, and show ________ to others.

10a Cruel to be kind

Reading

1 Work in pairs. Answer the questions.

1 What is happening in the photo?
2 How would you describe the mother's attitude: strict, intense, something else?
3 How strict were your parents? Are you happy that they were this way or not?

2 Work in small groups. Which of these things should parents control strongly? A little? Which should the child decide?

- watching TV
- playing computer games
- practicing a musical instrument
- going out to play with friends
- doing homework
- choosing what subjects to study at high school
- choosing extracurricular activities

3 Read the article and find out who "tiger mothers" are. How do their attitudes to the first five items in Exercise 2 compare to Western attitudes?

4 Does the writer approve of the "tiger mother" approach to child-rearing? Do you?

Vocabulary raising children: verbs

5 Work in pairs. Look at the pairs of verbs below and discuss the difference between them. You will find the first verb in each pair in the article.

1 *bring up* and *educate* children
2 *praise* and *reward* good behavior
3 *rebel against* and *disobey* your parents
4 *push* and *discipline* yourself
5 *give in to* and *spoil* your children
6 *nag* and *pester* someone
7 *shame* and *punish* someone

CRUEL TO BE KIND

Is there a right way to bring up children? Some parents read guides to find an answer, many just follow their instinct. Whatever they do, a doubt always remains: could I have done a better job?

A recent contribution to the subject is Amy Chua's controversial book *Battle Hymn of the Tiger Mother*, which describes the approach to child-rearing of an ambitious Chinese parent living in the West. According to Chua, Western mothers are far too soft on their children. She says they are always praising their children for every effort they make, even if the result is coming last in a race or playing a piano piece badly. These are the kind of parents who will give in to their children's demands to go out and play rather than do their homework, if they protest loudly enough.

The "tiger mother" method is very different and the key is total control. Tiger mothers will accept nothing less than perfect grades in every subject—failure to achieve these is just proof that children have not worked hard enough. They will encourage not with praise and reward, but by punishing and shaming. Chua told her daughter that she would give her doll's house to charity if she failed to master a difficult piano piece. She even rejected a homemade birthday card because her daughter had drawn it in a hurry.

But that highlights another difference, says Chua, which is directness and honesty. A tiger mother will not hesitate to tell her children that they are lazy, whereas Western parents are always telling their children not to worry, that they will do better next time, even if they think they have been lazy.

The constant nagging of the tiger mother, the banning of TV and computer games, seems harsh, but perhaps it works. Chua's children have not rebelled, and they don't resent their strict upbringing. They regularly get the top grades at school and are proficient at violin and piano—stereotypical symbols of success, critics would say. By contrast, children with more freedom and more laid-back parents will often lack self-discipline and will fail to push themselves to achieve more.

Grammar habitual actions: present tenses, *will*

> **▶ SIMPLE PRESENT, PRESENT CONTINUOUS, and *WILL* FOR REPEATED ACTIONS**
>
> **Simple present**
> *Some parents read guides to find an answer.*
>
> **Present continuous with *always***
> *She says they are always praising their children for every effort they make.*
>
> ***will***
> *These are the kind of parents who will give in to their children's demands.*
>
> For more information and practice, see page 169.

6 Work in pairs. Look at the sentences in the grammar box. Which tense is used to describe:

1 typical behavior?
2 a habit which the speaker finds annoying?
3 a simple fact or general truth?

7 Find and underline:

1 an example of tiger mothers' typical behavior; an example of typical behavior of Western mothers' children.
2 a simple fact about Chua's children.
3 something Chua finds annoying about Western mothers.

8 Complete these comments by underlining the correct verb forms. Sometimes there is more than one possibility. Then discuss which ones you sympathize with and which you don't.

1 My parents *will always tell / are always telling* me to practice the piano and it just makes it a chore.
2 In my experience, children *will do / do* as little work as they can. So you have to make them do it.
3 Children *will want / want* to be loved. It's also true that they *will perform / perform* much better in a loving and secure environment.
4 All parents *will hope / hope* that their children will be successful, but they *won't always admit / aren't always admitting* it to their children or even themselves.
5 You have to have a different approach with different children. Some *will respond / respond* better to gentle encouragement; others *will need / need* to be pushed and challenged.
6 I don't like parents who *will always try / are always trying* to be friends with their children. There are too many parents who *will buy / buy* their children presents and let them do what they want just to get on their good side.

9 Read the anecdotes below and put the verb in the right form. Then check your answers with your teacher.

I've seen this kind of situation so many times in Mexico when children [1] ______ (beg) their parents for some candy. At first the parent [2] ______ (say) no. So then the child [3] ______ (pester) and pester until the parent finally gives in—which they always do. It's against all the rules of parenting.

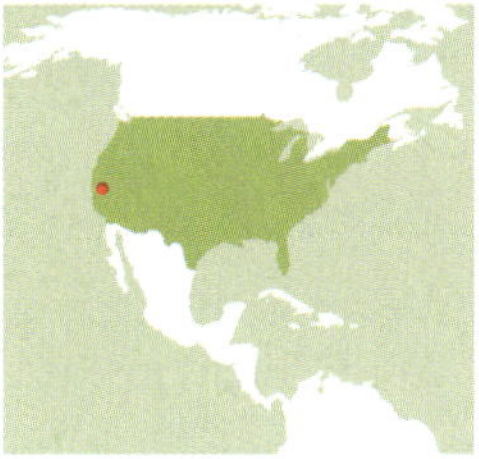

I teach in a school in San Francisco where we have quite a lot of ethnic Chinese and Japanese kids. By and large, they [4] ______ (do) what you tell them. But the other kids [5] ______ (always / misbehave). You have to tell them ten times to sit down.

Where I live in India, it is common for young children to work. Kids still [6] ______ (depend) on their parents, but they have a different attitude toward responsibility. Just as children in every culture [7] ______ (play) naturally, so children in India naturally [8] ______ (assume) responsibility for working and earning money.

Speaking

10 Work in pairs. Discuss the situations in Exercise 9. How familiar is each one to you? Does the behavior seem right or wrong?

11 Think of three more examples of children's and parents' behavior in your country: a simple fact about the way children or parents behave; an example of typical behavior; an example of behavior that annoys you or seems wrong.

12 Describe your examples to another pair. Are they similar to theirs?

10b A matter of taste

Listening

1 What is the strangest thing you have ever eaten? Why did you eat it? What did it taste like?

2 🔊 **35** Listen and answer the questions.

1 Where is the Nochmani tribe from?
2 What do they eat mostly?
3 How do they make sure there is enough of this food?

3 🔊 **35** Listen again and choose the correct word or phrase to complete the statements.

1 We live in an age when people are very .... what they eat.
   a nervous about   b conscious of
   c careless about
2 In the past it was thought that the Nicobar Islands contained ....
   a no inhabitants   b no fresh water
   c no fish
3 The Nochmani didn't want to eat ....
   a sweets and cakes   b meat
   c any of the food they were offered
4 Insects have a lot of .... in them.
   a carbohydrates   b vitamins
   c protein
5 The speaker thinks we could all benefit from eating ....
   a less meat   b more insects
   c alternative types of food

4 What do you think of the diet of the Nochmani? Do you think what we eat is just a matter of habit? Why? Can we learn to eat anything if we have to, or are there some things we can never eat?

Grammar *used to, usually, be used to,* and *get used to*

5 Match each verb form in bold (1–5) to the meaning (a–e).

1 We **didn't use to worry** so much about food.
2 People **usually need** mammals in order to live.
3 The Nochmani **were not used to eating** meat.
4 If you **are used to** something, you prefer it.
5 We should **get used to eating** insects.

a refers to something that was strange or abnormal for someone
b refers to something that happens regularly or is generally the case
c refers to learning to cope with something difficult or unfamiliar
d refers to what someone did regularly in the past, but doesn't do anymore
e refers to something that is normal and not strange

▶ *USED TO, USUALLY, BE USED TO,* and *GET USED TO*

Past habits	**Present habits**
used to + infinitive	*(not) usually* + simple present
I used to eat…	*I usually eat…*
I didn't use to eat…	*I don't usually eat…*
Did you use to eat?	*Do you usually eat?*
Familiar (and unfamiliar) habits	**Habits that are becoming familiar**
be used to + noun or *-ing* form	*get used to* + noun or *–ing* form
I am used to (eating) Italian food.	*I am getting used to (eating) American food.*
I am not used to…	*I am not getting used to…*
Are you used to… ?	*Are you getting used to… ?*

For more information and practice, see page 170.

6 Look at the grammar box and then choose the right form to complete sentences 1–9 in A, B, and C. Note that we use *be used to* and *get used to* for things that are not strange or difficult to do.

A In China, people [1] *do not usually finish / didn't use to finish* everything on their plate, because it is a sign that they have not had enough to eat. Visitors from the West find it difficult to [2] *be used to / get used to* this, because they [3] *usually eat / are used to eating* everything to show that they like it. When a Chinese host sees their empty plates, he [4] *usually assumes / is used to assuming* that they want more.

B Fifty years ago, people in the US [5] *used to sitting / used to sit* down for meals with their families each evening. Families nowadays [6] *usually eat / used to eat* together only three times a week, because busy lives and TV get in the way. But it is believed that if more families could [7] *be used to dining / get used to dining* together, it would strengthen family relationships.

C Eating a traditional English breakfast of eggs, bacon, and sausages [8] *used to be / was used to being* a common thing in the UK. A big breakfast was important because people [9] *didn't use to eat / weren't used to eating* so many snacks during the day.

7 Put the verb in the most appropriate form to complete these sentences.

1 We .... (eat) out a lot, but restaurants are so expensive that we don't anymore.
2 I .... (have) a tuna salad sandwich for my lunch.
3 I .... (take) sugar in my coffee, but now I have a sweetener. It took a little while to .... (get used to) the taste, but now I can't tell the difference.
4 When I was staying with my friends in Iowa, we ate at six o'clock in the evening. It was strange, because I .... (eat) much later.

8 Are any of the sentences in Exercise 7 true for you? Have you had similar experiences? Discuss with a partner.

I also used to eat out a lot, but now I try to get home for lunch.

Not me, I usually buy a sandwich... not tuna, though!

9 In pairs, ask each other these questions.

1 What is something you have gotten used to doing recently?
2 Do you usually do your homework in the mornings or the evenings?
3 Are you used to eating dinner with your family or do you usually eat on the go?
4 What is the best way to get used to a new place?
5 What is something that you used to do that you don't do anymore? Why did you stop?
6 What is something that you are used to doing that you wish you could change? Why?

Vocabulary and speaking

10 Work in pairs. Place these four items of food into the correct category. Think of two more items for each category. Then compare your list with another pair.

breakfast cereal chocolate bars
rice yogurt

dairy products (like milk)	processed food (like frozen peas)	staple foods (like potatoes)	snacks (like potato chips)

11 Complete these sentences with information about eating habits in your country. Go around the class and exchange your information with at least three other people. Then work with your partner. Tell each other the two most memorable statements you heard.

1 When I was growing up, a lot of families used to...
2 The main staple food is... People aren't used to eating...
3 For breakfast, people usually...
4 I think visitors find some of our eating customs strange, because they are not used to...
5 People in my country don't usually eat...
6 Young people find it difficult to get used to...

10c A universal language

Reading

1 Work in pairs. Put the actions in the box into the correct category of body language. Then demonstrate the actions to each other. What is the meaning of each?

a handshake	standing with arms crossed
biting your bottom lip	waving
sitting back in your chair	
smiling	

posture: ....

gesture: ....

facial expression: ....

2 Read the article. Which sentence best summarizes the author's view?

a We need to learn how people from different cultures use body language.
b The differences in body language between cultures are small but important.
c There are more similarities than differences in body language between cultures.

3 According to the writer…

1 Making comparisons between cultures can be:
  a fun. b useful.
  c dangerous.
2 Standing too close to someone of another culture can:
  a cause arguments. b cause discomfort.
  c be a serious insult.
3 A lot of the facts given in travel guides are:
  a very important. b wrong.
  c not of much practical help.
4 Looking away from the speaker is a sign of:
  a sadness. b boredom.
  c both.
5 To avoid making mistakes in body language with other cultures, people need to be:
  a sensible. b sensitive.
  c both.
6 Differences in body language between people start at:
  a an individual level. b a cultural level.
  c an emotional level.

4 With your partner, demonstrate to each other:

- the two gestures described in paragraph 3
- the two greetings mentioned in paragraph 4
- the body language associated with boredom and anger described in paragraph 6

5 Do you agree with the writer's view about cross-cultural communication? Is your culture one that generally shows its emotions or not?

Critical thinking sources

6 The article gives a lot of information about body language and customs. But how do you know how reliable this information is? Underline the examples of different cultures' body language and customs in the article.

7 Work in pairs. Find the author's source for each example. Mark the source according to this scale:
3 = very credible; 2 = quite credible;
1 = incredible; and 0 = no source.

Word focus *common*

8 Match the meanings of the word *common* (1–2) with the sentences (a–d).

common (adj)
1 something usual or normal
2 something that is shared by two or more people

a It is quite common in European countries to sit with your legs crossed.
b The things that we all have in common…
c There are also common factors when people are bored.
d If we all just apply a little sensitivity and common sense,…

9 Now do the same for these expressions.

e In a negotiation, always try to find common ground between you and the other party.
f It is a common misconception that English people drink only tea, not coffee.
g Don't worry about mispronouncing my name; it's a common mistake that everyone makes.
h It's common knowledge that many Asian cultures use chopsticks, not knives and forks.

Speaking

10 Work in pairs. Describe the following customs in your country. Then compare your answers with another pair. How similar were they?

- The most common form of greeting
- Common gestures that visitors are not used to
- Common eating customs
- Common misconceptions foreigners have about your country

A universal language

People love to compare and contrast. In most parts of England, you buy your bus ticket on the bus. In France, you buy it at a metro station. In Australia, you can buy it at a newsstand. We all find this kind of comparison entertaining. Books on cross-cultural communication exploit our curiosity by focusing on differences between people around the world, including the significance of their body language.

Proxemics, the study of different standards of personal space, is one example. How close I stand when speaking to people depends not only on my relationship to them, but also on my culture. This is important because if people are not used to standing as close as I do when we are talking, they might feel uncomfortable. Statistics tell us that the average distance at which two people stand in a social context—neighbors chatting, for example—is somewhere between 4 and 11 feet. In Latin cultures (like South America and Italy), and also in China, this distance tends to be smaller, while in Nordic cultures (like Sweden and Denmark), people usually stand farther apart.

The messages sent by your posture and gestures is another case in point. For example, it is quite common in European countries to sit with your legs crossed and the top foot outstretched. But, as I know from personal experience, people in Arab countries hardly ever sit this way because they might show you the bottom of their shoe, which is a serious insult. It is said that in the Philippines, people often greet each other by raising their eyebrows quickly. In the US, this is a sign of surprise.

Such information fills the pages of guide books, but I would really question the usefulness of what are presented as must-know facts. Clearly it is important to know a little about eating customs, tipping, and the rules concerning basic greetings—whether you should bow or shake someone's hand. But beneath the surface, we are not so different. Many signs are universal in the emotions that they communicate. Focusing on them is a much more profitable route than focusing on our differences.

Smiling is the best known sign, but not the only one. Behaviorists have proven that all over the world, people show sadness in a similar way. The face falls, the mouth becomes downturned and the eyes begin to look glassy. The person will probably look down or away and seem distracted.

There are also common factors when people are bored. They will look at other things, their feet will begin to move restlessly indicating that they want to escape, and they will tap their fingers or scratch their heads. Anger can also be read quite easily: the facial muscles tense up, often causing people to frown; the eyes stare, fixing themselves on the target of their anger; blood rushes to the face, turning it red. If the anger is great, the body will also tense up as if preparing itself for a physical fight.

Understanding these universal signals and reacting appropriately is the real key to cross-cultural communication. If we all apply just a little sensitivity and common sense, we are unlikely to cause lasting offense by making the wrong gesture or invading a stranger's personal space. Of course, some cultures show their emotions more openly and others prefer to keep them more hidden. But isn't that also the case within cultures, from one individual to another?

frown (v) /fraʊn/ to lower your eyebrows, causing lines to appear on your forehead
scratch (v) /skrætʃ/ to move your fingernails backwards and forwards across your skin
stare (v) /steər/ to look intensely and for a long time at something
tap (v) /tæp/ to hit something lightly with a finger or hand

10d A pre-wedding ritual

Vocabulary weddings

1 What pre-wedding customs or events are traditional for the bride-to-be in your country?

2 Work in pairs. Look at the words related to weddings and answer the questions.

bride	groom	bachelorette party
bachelor party	veil	

1 Which word means a pre-wedding party for the man? And for the woman?
2 Which word means the woman on her wedding day? And the man on his?
3 Which word means a piece of fine cloth that covers the woman's face?

▶ WORDBUILDING word pairs

Some words have a natural partner or make a matching pair.
bride and *groom*, *host* and *guest*

Real life describing traditions

3 **36** Listen to the description of a traditional pre-wedding henna night in eastern Turkey. Then complete the first four phrases in the box below.

▶ DESCRIBING TRADITIONS

[1] It takes place ______________ .
[2] It marks the ______________ .
[3] It is an occasion for ______________ .
[4] It symbolizes the ______________ .

It's traditional / customary for this to be done by...
Typically / As a rule / Usually the women from...

Describing the sequence of events
The ceremony begins with the...
Then,... / After that,... / Next,... / Finally,...

While this is happening / During this part, the guests...
After / Once the bride's head has been...
On the morning of the wedding, a...

4 **37** Listen to the rest of the description. Number the items in the order they occur.

a A child presents the hennaed coin to the groom.
b The bride's head is covered with a red veil.
c The guests sing separation songs.
d The bride's hands and feet are hennaed.
e A gold coin is put into the remaining henna.
f The henna is prepared by the daughter of another couple.

5 **38** Retell the events to each other using the linking words in the box to help you. Then listen and compare.

6 **Pronunciation the letter *s***

a **39** Listen to these words and for each one say if the letter *s* is pronounced /s/ or /z/. Note the spellings that produce each sound.

custom	dress	friends
music	suppose	weddings

b **40** Work in pairs. Practice saying the words, then listen and check. Think of three more words for each sound. Then compare words with another pair.

across	eastern	lose	place
rings	single	spends	surprise

Speaking

7 What special events take place before or after a wedding in your country? Describe one using the box to help you. Think about:

- when it takes place
- the sequence of the events
- its significance
- any special symbols used

8 Working in small groups, describe these customs to each other. When each person has finished their description, ask them questions.

10e Business customs

Writing an informal email (2)

1 Imagine you are about to go on a business trip to a country you haven't visited before. What would you want to know about the customs there?

2 Read the first email. What is Paul asking for? What is he worried about?

3 Read Dominic's reply. Which pieces of advice should calm Paul's worries?

> Hi Dominic
>
> Good to see you briefly the other day. Forgot to tell you I'm going to China next week. Not sure what to expect. I know you have experience doing business there. Don't want to make any mistakes with any potential business partners. Could you let me know what I should be particularly aware of?
>
> Thanks,
> Paul

> Hi Paul,
>
> Glad to hear you're going to China. Think you'll enjoy it. Is it Shanghai? Let me know. Maybe I can fix you up with a couple of contacts. Anyway, my advice:
>
> - Take plenty of business cards; Chinese people will always give you theirs (make sure you read them carefully). It's embarrassing not to give one in return.
> - Keep the name and address of your hotel on you at all times. Visitors are always getting into trouble because they can't remember where they're staying.
> - The Chinese love their food and are very proud of it. They'll offer you some unusual dishes. Be adventurous and be grateful!
>
> Good luck and talk to you soon,
> Dominic

4 Writing skill elision in informal writing

a Look at the two emails again. Underline four phrases in the first email and four in the second email where words have been omitted to save time.

b Rewrite the sentences and phrases by inserting the missing words to make them more formal.

Example:

It was good to see you the other day.

c Convert these sentences into a more economical style by removing unnecessary pronouns, auxiliary verbs, or the verb *be*.

1 I hope we can meet up soon.
2 It was too bad that you didn't get the job.
3 I'll be back next Tuesday night.
4 This is my address in New York…
5 I will look forward to hearing all about it.
6 It went pretty well, didn't it?

5 Write a response to this email.

> Hi there,
>
> Wondered if you could help. I'm flying over next week to meet some clients. Will have to take them out to dinner and talk to them a little socially. Can you give me some advice about how things are done over there? Eating customs, what to talk about, etc. Sorry to ask, but very grateful for any information you can provide.
>
> Thanks!
> Sara

6 Work in pairs. Exchange emails. Read your partner's reply and answer the questions.

- Is it written in an informal style?
- Has the writer given some useful tips?
- Is the content short and to the point?
- Has the writer used some elision?

10f Eating insects

Video

Larry Peterman is a candy man on a mission.

Before you watch

1 Work in groups. Look at the photo and discuss the questions.

1 What do you think a candy man is?
2 How does the photo make you feel? Do you think most people would feel the same as you?
3 What do you think Larry Peterman's mission is?

2 Work in pairs. Think about the candy you used to eat when you were a child. Describe them to your partner.

3 You are going to watch a video about eating insects. Answer these questions.

1 Which countries include insects in their diets?
2 Do you think eating insects is a new habit?
3 Are insects good for you?
4 Is producing insects better for the environment than producing meat?

While you watch

4 Watch the video and check your answers from Exercise 3.

5 Watch the video again. Number the foods in the order you see them.

a banana, cream, and cockroach dessert
b salt-water taffy
c lollipop with cricket
d cricket cocktail
e mealworm-covered apples
f stir-fry
g caramels
h caterpillars

6 Answer the questions.

1 Where is Hotlix?

....

2 How long has Larry been trying to get Americans to eat insects?

....

3 According to Larry, why do most Americans not like eating insects?

....

4 How many species of insects are eaten around the world?

....

5 How does Larry compare insects to wine?

....

After you watch

7 Roleplay a meal at Larry's restaurant

Work in groups of three.

Student A: Imagine you are Larry. Prepare an interesting insect menu. Then give the menu to your customers. Explain what each dish is and answer their questions.

Student B: You don't like the idea of eating insects but are prepared to try. Ask Larry about the menu and order your meal. Also ask Larry why he is so interested in promoting insect foods.

Student C: You love the idea of eating insects. Order a meal.

Act out the conversation, then change roles. Prepare a different menu.

8 At the end of the video, Larry predicts that gourmet insects will have "snob appeal." What do you think that means?

9 Do you think Larry will eventually win people over to eating insects? Why?

10 Work in groups and discuss these questions.

1 Are there any unusual dishes or foods in your country?
2 What types of foods do people in your country avoid eating generally? Why?
3 Are there any foods you don't like? Why?

advocate (n) /'ædvəkɪt/ a person who supports something
brim (v) /brɪm/ be full of
bug (n) /bʌg/ insect
munch (v) /mʌntʃ/ eat
niche (n) /niʃ/ a specialized business opportunity
revolting (adj) /rɪ'voultɪŋ/ disgusting
snob (n) /snab/ a person who thinks he or she is better than other people
swat (v) /swat/ hit

UNIT 10 REVIEW

Grammar

1 Work in pairs. Look at the photo. What do you know about the eating habits of the Spanish: when they eat, what they eat?

2 Read the paragraph from a travel guide. What times are Spanish meals?

3 Underline the correct forms.

People visiting Spain for the first time can find it difficult to [1] *be used to / get used to* the eating customs of the Spanish. It's not so much the food itself, but the timing of the meals that visitors [2] *aren't used to / don't get used to*. I [3] *was used to living / used to live* in Cadiz, and I actually liked the way they did things. Breakfast is a light continental affair—just a roll and some coffee usually—eaten between 8 and 9:30 a.m. The main meal of the day is lunch, which people [4] *are used to eating / usually eat* sometime between 1 and 3:30 p.m. Quite a few of the shops, museums, and galleries [5] *close / are closing* around this time, because the locals like to take time over lunch. They [6] *are always resting / will rest* for a short time afterwards, although the traditional afternoon siesta is not as common as it [7] *was used to being / used to be*. People eat late in the evening—rarely before 9 p.m.—and on the weekend, the locals often [8] *aren't eating / won't eat* before 11 p.m. or even midnight.

I CAN	
use *used to, be used to,* and *get used to* correctly	☐
talk about habits and typical behavior with simple present, present continuous, and *will*	☐

Vocabulary

4 Work in pairs. Which word doesn't belong in each group? Explain your choices.

1 punish, discipline, nag, spoil
2 educate, bring up, look after, raise
3 encourage, shame, praise, reward
4 bread, cheese, rice, pasta
5 sit back, shake hands, wave, point
6 interrupt, stare, smile, chew gum
7 well-behaved, offensive, polite, courteous

5 Tell each other what postures, gestures, or facial expressions you often use and in what situations.

I CAN	
talk about bringing up children	☐
talk about eating habits	☐
talk about body language	☐

Real life

6 Work in pairs. Find the correct ending from list B for each phrase in list A.

A	B
It marks	people give adult presents to the child.
It takes place	the moment when a child becomes an adult.
It is an occasion	the child to stand up and give a short speech.
It symbolizes	the parent walking into the hall with the child.
It's customary for	people in the audience can also say some words.
Typically the ceremony begins with	on the child's 16th birthday.
	for celebration.
After the child's speech	leaving childish things behind.

7 Tell your partner about a special celebration in your country and the traditions that surround it.

I CAN	
describe traditions and customs at special events	☐

Speaking

8 Work in small groups. How is children's upbringing these days different from when you were a child? Look at the quote. Do you agree with this speaker?

My parents were quite strict. They used to expect us to do jobs around the house. I think children these days have it much easier, although they are always complaining that their parents expect a lot from them.

Unit 11 Knowledge and learning

Students processing their DNA at a museum learning lab
Photograph by Rajat Bansal

FEATURES

1 Work in pairs. Match each technique of acquiring knowledge or learning (1–4) to a definition (a–d). Which technique are the students using in the photo?

1 by authority
2 by observation
3 by reasoning
4 by trial and error

a experimenting
b using logic
c judging from what you see or hear
d reading or listening to an expert

2 Match these phrases with their definitions.

1 You have **a basic grasp** of chemistry.
2 You need **to find out** when the paper is due.
3 You're working with a tutor **to pick up** some test-taking tips.
4 You need to read through your notes and **process** them before writing your paper.
5 You're not sure what the right answer is, but you chose A because of a **gut feeling**.

a You are going to learn some strategies from an expert.
b You need to learn the date.
c You understand the fundamental principles.
d You need to internalize and reflect on the information.
e You picked an answer based on instinct.

3 Intuition is something we know without having to learn it. Tell a partner about a time when you used your intuition to make a decision.

11a Knowledge conservation

Reading

1 Work in pairs. Look at the photo in the article below of a botanist in the field. What does a botanist do?

2 List the plants or plant products you use on a daily basis. Then compare your list with another pair. Which uses did your lists have in common?

Example: *cotton in my clothes*

3 Read the article and answer the questions.

1. How is Maria Fadiman's interest in plants different from that of a traditional botanist?
2. Where does she work?
3. What two uses of plants are mentioned in the article?

4 What does the article say about:

1. the way Fadiman collects knowledge from local people?
2. the way that local people often pass their knowledge on?
3. the way Fadiman passes her knowledge on to her students?

5 Do you think that Fadiman's idea of recording traditional plant knowledge is useful? Why? What knowledge has been passed down to you by your parents or grandparents? Tell your partner.

WORDBUILDING IDIOMATIC EXPRESSIONS

Often there are idiomatic expressions that can replace basic verbs like *think, realize*

It struck me that... = I realized that...

KNOWLEDGE CONSERVATION

Dr. Maria Fadiman is an ethnobotanist: she studies how people use plants. "Looking at plant conservation without including people is a fantasy," she says. "The focus of my work is finding a balance where people use resources in a sustainable way."

It struck Fadiman early on that this was what she wanted to do. "I was born with a passion for conservation and a fascination with indigenous cultures," she explains. "Ethnobotany lets me bring it all together. On my first trip to the rain forest, I met a woman who was in terrible pain because the people in her village weren't able to remember which plant would cure her. I saw that traditional plant knowledge was being lost, and at that moment I knew conserving this kind of knowledge was what I wanted to do with my life."

Visiting the Ecuadoran rain forest, Dr. Fadiman was amazed at the variety of plants. "It looked like one big, green mish-mash," she says. "But the people who lived there were able to pick out the right plants for medicine and could distinguish not only the plants that were safe to eat, but also the right part of each plant."

The problem often is that such knowledge is stored only in local people's minds and it is passed down from generation to generation. Fadiman managed to persuade inhabitants of the Ecuadoran rain forest to let her record the information in written form. "They are excited by this idea because suddenly their knowledge is valued."

But conservation doesn't just mean protecting indigenous plants. If bringing in non-native plants, including cash crops like coffee, is beneficial to people and the environment, then that's fine too. In the Galapagos Islands, where overfishing was a real problem, environmentalists like Fadiman succeeded in getting local people to think about alternatives, like growing coffee.

By forming close relationships with local people and joining in with their way of life, Fadiman has inspired her own students at Florida Atlantic University. Students who couldn't easily absorb facts and statistics said they were able to engage much more easily with the subject when they heard her stories of going to the river to brush her teeth or sitting around a cooking fire.

indigenous (adj) /ɪn'dɪdʒənəs/ native to a particular country or area

mish-mash (n) /'mɪʃ,mæʃ/ a confusing mixture or collection of things

Grammar *could, was able to, manage to,* and *succeed in*

6 Work in pairs. Underline the sentences in the article where the following forms (1–6) are used. Then match each form to the uses (a–c). Note that some forms can have more than one use.

1 *could*
2 *was / were able to (do)*
3 *couldn't*
4 *wasn't / weren't able to*
5 *managed to (do)*
6 *succeeded in (doing)*

a to describe success in a task on a particular occasion in the past
b to describe a general ability in the past
c to describe an inability to do something in the past

> ▶ ***COULD, WAS ABLE TO, MANAGE TO,* AND *SUCCEED IN***
>
> ***could*** **+ base form**
> *He could tell which plants were safe.*
>
> ***couldn't*** **+ base form**
> *I couldn't remember the name of the plant.*
>
> ***was / were able*** **+ infinitive**
> *We were able to learn a lot from the local people.*
> *He wasn't able to explain how he knew it was right.*
>
> ***manage*** **+ infinitive**
> *After two hours climbing, we managed to reach the top.*
>
> ***succeed in*** **+ *-ing***
> *We succeeded in finding a guide to take us.*
>
> For more information and practice, see page 171.

7 Look at the grammar box. Then complete the sentences.

1 In the past, people could ________ (distinguish) plants more than they can now.
2 Recently, a group of children who were asked where cotton came from weren't able ________ (say) whether it was from an animal or a plant.
3 People were able ________ (use) this knowledge to find food and medicines.
4 They also managed ________ (work) out which plants were good for certain purposes.
5 But they didn't always succeed ________ (pass) this knowledge on to the next generation.
6 So people couldn't ________ (keep) some of this knowledge from being lost.

8 Underline the correct form in each of these sentences. Sometimes both forms are possible.

1 By specializing in ethnobotany, Fadiman *was able to combine / succeeded in combining* an interest in plants with her interest in people.
2 She also studied geography, which meant she *could look at / managed to look at* people and the land.
3 In Ecuador, Fadiman *could record / managed to record* plant data that hadn't been written down before.
4 In Yucatan, Mexico, local women taught Fadiman how to weave, something that she *wasn't able to do / didn't manage to do* before.
5 On a recent trip to Ecuador, she *could visit / was able to visit* a lot of places in a short time by using a helicopter rather than buses and canoes.
6 Fadiman was impressed by how indigenous people *were able to make / succeeded in making* use of the plants around them.

Vocabulary learning

9 Work in pairs. Find pairs of words in this group with the same meaning.

absorb	acquire	be ignorant of
connect with	engage with	grasp
inspire	motivate	not know
pick up	take in	understand

10 Complete these sentences about your own learning at school using one of the forms in the grammar box. Ask and answer these questions.

1 Which teachers ________ (inspire) you at school?
2 What kind of facts ________ (absorb) most easily?
3 Which subjects ________ (engage with)?
4 ________ (pass) all your exams?
5 What knowledge ________ (acquire) that has been useful in later life?
6 Was there anything that ________ (not / grasp) that you wished you did now?

Speaking

11 Work in pairs. Think of a subject you know a lot about. How did you acquire that knowledge? Have you managed to record or pass it on in any way?

11b Memory

Speaking

1 Work in pairs. Look at the picture below for ten seconds. Then turn your book over and list the objects you can remember.

2 Compare your results with another pair. What techniques did you use to remember the items?

Items left at the Vietnam Memorial, Landover, Maryland

Listening

3 What things do you commonly forget? Which failures of memory annoy you the most?

4 **41** Listen to the first part of a talk on memory by a psychologist and note the common failures of memory that he mentions. Were any of them the same as yours?

5 **42** Listen to the rest of the talk and answer the questions.

1 What is AJ good at remembering?
2 How does she feel about her good memory?
3 Why are people's memories not as good as they used to be?

6 **43** Complete each statement with the missing word. Then listen and check.

1 AJ's memory is stimulated by ________ in the same way that our memories can be stimulated by certain ________ .
2 Having a good memory should make people feel more ________ .
3 Our memories are selective: they remember mostly ________ things and ________ things.
4 We should be ________ for all the things that our memories hide.
5 Technology has become "our ________ memory."
6 Now medical science is trying to address the problem of ________ memory.

7 Work in pairs. Discuss how much you rely on your internal memory to remember things as compared to aids such as Post-it notes, your computer, or diaries. Do you agree with the speaker that our memories are getting worse?

Grammar future in the past

8 44 Listen to the first part of the talk again and complete the first half of these sentences with the correct verb forms.

1 You ______ to make a comment at a meeting and then...
2 You ______ to send a friend a card for his birthday, but then...
3 You recognized someone in the street and ______ spoken to her, but...
4 You promised you ______ mail a letter for someone and two days later...
5 You ______ to write down a great idea you had, but when you found a pen and paper,...

9 Work in pairs. What happened next in each case? Were any of these actions completed? Why?

10 Choose the right verb form to complete this description of another memory patient.

One interesting patient couldn't form new memories. He could only remember events before 1960. I [1] *was going to interview / would interview* his doctor about how someone with no memory managed to cope with daily life, but she suggested I interview him instead.
Our appointment [2] *was supposed to be / would be* at 2 p.m., but it made no difference since he lived only in the present. I [3] *would tell / would have told* him my name and why I was there, but I realized there was no point: [4] *it was going to mean / it would have meant* nothing to him. So I began by asking him about his past and he talked about his time as a child during the Second World War. Then the telephone rang. When he came back, I [5] *was about to ask / would ask* him to continue, but I realized he had completely forgotten our earlier conversation. I thought he [6] *was about to be / would be* frustrated by this but not at all. He seemed happy for not being burdened by memory.

FUTURE IN THE PAST

going to* and *about to
I was going to call you, but I forgot.
I was about to call you, but I was interrupted.

would* and *would have
He said he would call me.
I would have called you, but I didn't have your number.

supposed to
He was supposed to call you. Did he forget?

For more information and practice, see page 172.

11 45 Look at the grammar box. Transform these original plans into future in-the-past forms. Then listen and check your answers.

1 "I'm going to ask Sanjip to come."
I ______, but I asked Kumar instead.
2 "She's supposed to be in Cairo this week."
She ______ in Cairo this week, but she's sick.
3 "I'll definitely send you the original."
He promised he ______ me the original, but he sent me a copy.
4 "We will be there by ten o'clock."
We ______ there by ten o'clock, but the train didn't get in until eleven fifteen.
5 He's about to announce that he will retire.
He ______, but now he thinks he'll stay another year.
6 "The city planners will build a new shopping mall downtown."
The city planners ______ a new shopping mall downtown, but residents opposed it.

12 **Pronunciation contrastive sentence stress**

a 45 Work in pairs. Underline the words in each sentence in Exercise 11 that highlight the contrasting facts. Listen again and check. Then practice saying each sentence.

b Complete each of these sentences with a contrasting idea. Underline the words in the sentence that highlight the contrast. Then say your sentences to your partner. Ask them which words they thought were stressed.

1 I was going to order a steak, but…
2 They were supposed to be going on vacation, but…
3 I would have driven, but…
4 He said he would wait for me, but…
5 We were about to buy a new TV, but…

Speaking

13 Work in pairs. Choose a situation below. Think of a good excuse to explain why it happened. Then change pairs and explain your excuse again.

- You were 30 minutes late for an important business meeting and didn't call to say so.
- You borrowed someone's car and were supposed to return it the following day, but they had to call you to find out where you were.
- It was a close friend's birthday two days ago. You didn't send a card or get them a present.

11c A clever bird

Reading

1 Work in pairs. Do you know a domestic animal which is particularly intelligent? How does this intelligence show itself?

2 Read the article and say how Alex the parrot's intelligence showed itself.

3 Mark the sentences true (T), false (F), or not answered (NA).

1. People are right to believe that animals have thoughts and emotions.
2. Pepperberg's idea was to let Alex communicate to her how he saw the world.
3. Pepperberg didn't want people to think she had chosen Alex for his intelligence.
4. Alex showed that he could distinguish between colors and shapes but not numbers.
5. Pepperberg concluded that cognitive skills were necessary for survival in the wild.
6. Alex felt very proud of his ability to communicate in English.

4 In pairs, discuss if you were surprised by Pepperberg's results, and why.

Critical thinking reinforcing ideas

5 Often when writers express an idea, they reinforce it, to make sure the reader understands, by:

- saying the same thing in other words
- giving examples
- quoting someone who also made this point

Find and underline the ideas expressed below by the author. Note how each one is reinforced.

1. How can we find out if animals can think?
2. Pepperberg's idea was to ask the parrot for his thoughts.
3. Researchers had no confidence in her idea.
4. She wanted to get inside the parrot's head.
5. Alex's cognitive abilities are not typical of all animals.
6. Alex's cognitive abilities are necessary to cope with his environment.
7. Alex worked through various mental tests.
8. Alex behaved like a bored teenager.

6 Which method of reinforcing an idea did you find the most effective?

Word focus *learn*

7 Work in pairs. Find these three expressions in the article with the word *learn*. Discuss what each one means.

1. learn as you go along
2. learn by heart
3. learn the hard way

8 Look at the expressions in bold with *learn* in the sentences below and figure out what each one means from its context. Which one means the same as "learn the hard way"?

1. If you work with an experienced chef, you can **learn some tricks of the trade**.
2. You're not ready to design the new brochure. You have to **learn to walk before you can run**.
3. It's **never too late to learn**. My grandfather took up the piano when he was 73.
4. I've **learned my lesson**. I'm never going to try to build a piece of furniture again without reading the instructions first.
5. I hate it too, but we're going to have to **learn to live with it**.
6. You'd think that the government would **learn from its mistakes**, but it never does.

9 Choose two of the expressions from Exercise 8 and use them in sentences about your own learning experiences. Read your sentences to your partner, omitting the expressions with *learn*. Can your partner figure out the missing expressions?

Speaking

10 Work in pairs. Take the quiz on page 154 to find out what type of learner you are. The answers are on page 155.

11 Work in small groups. Discuss how your learning style affects your language learning. What things can you do to learn more effectively? Look at the ideas below and add any others you can think of:

- watching English-language movies with subtitles
- reading stories (in English newspapers, books, magazines) and retelling them
- keeping a vocabulary book and drawing illustrations of each new word

How does a scientist find out to what extent an animal is capable of thinking? What evidence is there that it is able to acquire information about the world and act on it, learning as it goes along?

In 1977, Irene Pepperberg, a recent graduate of Harvard University, decided to investigate the thought processes of another creature by talking to it. In order to do this, she would teach a one-year-old African gray parrot named Alex to reproduce the sounds of the English language. "I thought if he learned to communicate, I could ask him questions about how he sees the world."

Pepperberg bought Alex in a Chicago pet store. She let the store's assistant choose him because she didn't want other scientists to say that she had deliberately chosen an especially smart bird. Given that Alex's brain was the size of a walnut, most researchers thought Pepperberg's communication study would be futile. "Some people actually called me crazy for trying this," she said.

But with Pepperberg's patient teaching, Alex learned how to imitate almost 100 English words, including the names of food. He could count to six and had learned the sounds for seven and eight. But the point was not to see if Alex could learn words by heart. Pepperberg wanted to get inside his mind and learn more about a bird's understanding of the world. She couldn't ask him what he was thinking about, but she could ask him about his knowledge of numbers, shapes, and colors.

In one demonstration, Pepperberg placed Alex on a wooden perch in the middle of the room. She then held up a green key and a small green cup for him to look at.

"What's the same?" she asked.

Without hesitation, Alex's beak opened: "Co-lor."

"What's different?" Pepperberg asked.

"Shape," Alex said. His voice had the sound of a cartoon character. But the words—and what can only be called the thoughts—were entirely his. Many of Alex's cognitive skills, such as his ability to understand the concepts of "same" and "different," are rare in the animal world. Very few animals share these skills. But parrots, like humans, live a long time in complex societies. And like humans, these birds must keep track of the dynamics of changing relationships and environments.

"They need to be able to distinguish colors to know when a fruit is ripe or unripe," Pepperberg explained. "They need to categorize things—what's edible, what isn't—and to know the shapes of predators. And it helps to have a concept of numbers if you need to keep track of your flock. For a long-lived bird, you can't do all of this with instinct; cognition must be involved."

In the demonstration, Alex then ran through various tests, distinguishing colors, shapes, sizes, and materials (wool versus wood versus metal). He did some simple arithmetic, such as counting the yellow toy blocks among a pile of mixed colored blocks. And then, as if to offer final proof of the mind inside his bird's brain, Alex spoke up. "Talk clearly!" he commanded, when one of the younger birds Pepperberg was also teaching mispronounced the word "green." "Talk clearly!"

Alex knew all the answers himself and was getting bored. "He's moody," said Pepperberg, "so he interrupts the others, or he gives the wrong answer just to be difficult." Pepperberg was certainly learning more about the mind of a parrot, but like the parent of a troublesome teenager, she was learning the hard way.

A clever bird

11d Keep learning

Real life getting clarification

1 Look at the list of short courses offered by an adult education college. Use a dictionary if you need to. Which of the courses interest you and why?

2 46 Listen and answer the questions.

1 What kind of course is Ahmad interested in taking?
2 What course does Liz suggest for him instead? Why?
3 What does Ahmad decide to do?

3 Look at the expressions used by Ahmad. Which are used for repetition (R) and which are used for explanation (E)?

GETTING CLARIFICATION

What do you mean by... ?
Can you speak up a little?
Can you explain what...?
I'm not really with you.
Are you saying that... ?
Could you give me an example of... ?
What was... again?
Hang on a second. That's too much to take in all at once.
I didn't catch...
Did you say... ?

4 46 Listen again. Complete the unfinished sentences in the box.

5 **Pronunciation linking in question forms**

a 47 In certain commonly used combinations (*did you, could you, what do you*) the words are strongly linked together. Listen to these examples.

Are you saying the course is full?
Can you speak up a little?
Could you give me an example?
Did you say Tuesday?
What do you mean?

b Work in pairs. Practice saying these sentences.

Can you explain what you mean?
Could you repeat that?
Did you mean September?
What are you trying to say?
What do you think?

6 Work in pairs. Act out a conversation, inquiring about the course. Then change roles.

Student A: You are a prospective student. Choose one of the courses in Exercise 1 or another course you would like to take. Ask Student B about your choice.

Student B: You are a college administrator. Prepare what you are going to say about Student A's chosen course.

ROUSHAM
ADULT EDUCATION CENTER

COURSE TITLE	FREQUENCY	EXAM COURSE
Basic car mechanics *Apr 5, 10 wks*	1 x 2hrs	✗
Psychology of human behavior *Jan 22, 18 wks*	1 x 2hrs	✓
Public speaking *Apr 11, 8 wks*	1 x 1.5hrs	✗
First aid *Apr 12, 4 wks*	2 x 1.5hrs	✓
Desert and jungle survival *Mar 1, 12 wks*	1 x 1.5hrs	✓
Ikebana: Japanese flower arranging *Jan 22, 18 wks*	1 x 2hrs	✗
Art appreciation *Apr 5, 10 wks*	1 x 2hrs	✗
Screenwriting *Jan 21, 18 wks*	1 x 2hrs	✗
Surfing *Apr 12, 6 wks*	1 x 3hrs	✓
Investing in stocks and buying shares *Apr 11, 8 wks*	1 x 1.5hrs	✗

11e The wrong course

Writing an email about a misunderstanding

1 Work in pairs. Read the email from a student to an adult education college. Answer the questions.

1 What is the misunderstanding about the course?
   a the timing b the level c the subject
2 How would you describe the student's feelings?
   a angry b offended c frustrated
3 How would you describe the tone of the email?
   a complaining b reasonable c apologetic

> Dear Sir or Madam:
>
> I enrolled in your course "car mechanics 1" in August and have attended three sessions. When I originally inquired about the course, I was told that it was suitable for people with no previous knowledge of car mechanics. But in fact, everyone else in the course seems to know a lot already. So despite the fact that the lessons generally start with a basic concept, they move very quickly onto more complicated ideas.
>
> I don't blame the teacher. On the contrary, he does his best to explain concepts to me. But I feel that I am just holding everyone else back. They know how an engine works already, whereas I have no background at all in mechanics.
>
> I was going to wait a couple of weeks more before saying anything, but in the last session I felt so out of my depth that I have decided to write now and ask for a refund. While I understand this isn't really anyone's fault, I hope you will appreciate how frustrating the situation is for me.
>
> I look forward to hearing from you.
> Karen Redman

2 If you were an administrator at the college, how would you react to this email?

3 Writing skill linking contrasting ideas

a Find the words or phrases in the email that link these contrasting ideas.

1 The course should be for beginners. No one else is a beginner.
2 Each lesson starts with a simple idea. It progresses quickly to difficult ideas.
3 The teacher is not at fault. He helps me as much as he can.
4 The other students know a lot. I know nothing.
5 No one is to blame for this. I still feel it is unfair.

b Match these words and phrases to the ones in the email that they could replace.

1 although
2 in actual fact
3 but on the other hand
4 but in reality

c Complete these sentences with appropriate linking phrases.

1 .... the brochure says the start date is September 12, the first real class is a week later, on the 19th.
2 The course is advertised as "practical," .... you learn a lot of theory as well.
3 .... the course fee is quite high, it's a great investment in your future.
4 The course isn't much fun, ... , you would expect a course in lifesaving to be serious.
5 The French conversation class focuses on everyday French, ... in the advanced French class you cover literature.
6 Surfing is not an easy skill to learn. .... , you need to have a lot of perseverance.

4 Imagine you enrolled in one of the other courses on page 136. Think of a misunderstanding that occurred with the course. Write an email to the college explaining the misunderstanding and asking for a refund.

5 Exchange letters with your partner and check the following items:

- Does the email make clear what the misunderstanding was?
- Is the tone reasonable?
- Has the writer used linking words and phrases correctly?
- Do you think the email will get the desired response?

11f Paraguay shaman

Video

Paraguay's renowned healers, called "shamans," have a deep knowledge of local medicinal plants.

Before you watch

1 Work in groups. Look at the photo and discuss the questions.

1 What do you know about shamans?
2 What techniques do you think they use?

2 You are going to watch a video about medicinal plants. Answer these questions.

1 What problem do you think faces these plants?
2 What solution to the problem might the video suggest?
3 Write down three kinds of people you're going to see in the video.

While you watch

3 Watch the video and check your answers from Exercise 2.

4 Cross out the wrong information in these sentences. Then rewrite the sentences correctly.

1 When the scientists arrive, Gervasio, the local shaman, is collecting plants in the forest.

....

2 Gervasio and the team set off to look for an insect the scientists are interested in.

....

3 The local people eat the root raw.

....

4 Later, back in the village, Gervasio shows the team a book he has written.

....

5 Watch the video again and answer the questions.

1 What illnesses are mentioned in the video?

....

2 How do traditional folk healers in Paraguay help scientists?

....

3 Why is it important to record shamans' knowledge urgently?

....

4 Why does Gervasio use chants and prayers before going into the forest?

....

5 Why are the scientists interested in the suruvi root?

....

6 What does the scientists' book set out to do?

....

6 Number these in the order you hear them.

a Recording and analyzing Paraguayan plants for possible medical cures is urgent business.
b To reach Gervasio, a group of researchers set out on a long journey through the reserve.
c Somewhere in this forest, maybe in this plant or that herb, there might be a cure for an illness.
d When he feels ready, Gervasio and his wife lead the group on the search.
e The rain forests of Paraguay have long been a source of medicinal cures.

After you watch

7 Roleplay interviewing a scientist

Work in pairs.

Student A: Imagine you are a National Geographic reporter. You are going to interview the scientist who made the documentary about Gervasio. Use the information below to prepare questions.

Student B: Imagine you are the scientist who made the documentary about Gervasio. Look at the information below and think about what you are going to say to the reporter.

- the journey to the reserve
- the journey to Tekoha Ryapu
- what it feels like to work with Gervasio
- the importance of Gervasio's knowledge
- what they were able to achieve on this trip
- how the book might help

Act out the interview, then change roles.

8 Work in groups and discuss these questions.

1 Do you know of any modern medicines that originated from rain forest plants?
2 Do you think traditional medicines from plants are effective?
3 What do you think about other forms of traditional medicine, for example acupuncture, massage therapy, and homeopathy?

chant (n) /tʃænt/ a kind of rhythmic song that uses only one or two notes
deforestation (n) /dɪˌfɔrɪˈsteɪʃən/ cutting down trees
folk healer (n) /ˈfoʊk ˌhilər/ a person who uses traditional methods to cure illnesses
multiply (v) /ˈmʌltɪˌplaɪ/ reproduce quickly
renowned (adj) /rɪˈnaʊnd/ famous
reserve (n) /rɪˈzɜrv/ an area of land where plants or animals are officially protected

UNIT 11 REVIEW

Grammar

1 Work in pairs. What is the maximum number of languages someone can speak fluently? Does speaking one language help you to learn another?

2 Underline the correct option below.

When police in Brazil arrested an illegal immigrant speaking an unrecognizable language, they immediately called Ziad Fazah, the world's greatest linguist. Fazah realized quickly that the man was speaking a dialect used in Afghanistan. With Fazah's help, the man [1] *explain / was able to explain* that he had escaped Afghanistan and was seeking asylum in Brazil. At that time, Fazah, originally from the Lebanon, [2] *could speak / managed to speak* 54 languages. He also [3] *could get / succeeded in getting* his name into the Brazilian *Guinness World Book of Records* as the world's greatest living polyglot. Fazah had done a lot of interpreting for the police, but unfortunately they [4] *couldn't pay / didn't manage to pay* him.
When Fazah was 17, his talents were recognized by the Lebanese government, who [5] *were going to use / would use* him as an interpreter, but soon after, he moved to Brazil. Eventually he began giving private language lessons. Fazah [6] *would remain / would have remained* unknown, but in 2006 his language abilities were tested on a Spanish television show and he got international attention. Then people began to question his abilities. [7] *Was he really able / Did he really manage* to speak over 50 languages? The show [8] *was supposed to show / would have shown* that he could, but the evidence was not convincing.

3 Answer the questions.

1 What is a polyglot?
2 What is Fazah's regular job?
3 How many languages is he really fluent in?

I CAN
- describe past abilities with *could, was able to, managed to,* and *succeeded in*
- talk about past intentions and predictions with the future in the past

Vocabulary

4 Work in pairs. Complete the paragraph. The first letter of each missing word is given.

There are many ways to [1] a________ knowledge: by [2] t________ and error, from an authority, by reasoning, and by [3] o________ (in other words, just by watching). Some things, like bringing up children, are more instinctive; you have a gut [4] f________ about the right way to do things. Some things, like playing a musical instrument, you can [5] p________ up as you go along. But other things need to be taught. For example, you might have a basic [6] g________ of mathematics, but still be completely [7] i________ of how calculus works. For this type of learning, you need an authority like a book or a teacher that can help you to [8] e________ with the subject and understand it.

5 Tell each other how you learned to do two things (like cook or play an instrument).

I CAN
- talk about learning and knowledge

Real life

6 Work in pairs. Match 1–5 to a–e.

1 What do you mean by that?
2 Could you give me an example?
3 Can you speak up a little?
4 What was that again?
5 I'm not really with you.

a I didn't catch that.
b I don't really understand.
c For instance?
d Can you explain that?
e I can't hear you very clearly.

7 Think of something you can do, but your partner probably can't. Give your partner some instructions. As you receive the instructions ask for clarification and repetition.

I CAN
- get clarification by asking someone to repeat or explain

Speaking

8 Work in small groups. Tell each other about a good or bad learning experience.

At school we had a great art teacher who could inspire anyone. He had really good ideas, such as…

Unit 12 The economy

A woman in a pink mink coat next to her pink Rolls Royce, Hong Kong
Photo by Jodi Cobb

FEATURES

1 Work in pairs. Look at the photo. What does a matching luxury car and fur coat say about a person? Do rich people in your country like to show off their wealth?

2 Match the word (1–7) with its synonym (a–g).

1 afford	a poor
2 hard up	b have enough money
3 income	c expensive
4 loaded	d a good price
5 pricey	e very rich
6 reasonable	f comfortable
7 well-off	g earnings

3 Work in small groups. What is the definition of "poor" in your country? How would you define *rich* and *poor*? Can you be rich without having a lot of money?

12a Saving for a rainy day

Reading

1 Work in pairs. What do you know about Norway: its landscape, its people, its industry? Look at the photo for ideas.

2 Read the article. In what ways is Norway a "rich" country?

3 Complete these summaries of each paragraph. Then compare answers with another pair.

1 For a long time, Norway has had a better .... than other countries.
2 The three reasons for Norway's success are: big oil reserves, ..., and ....
3 For Norwegians, being rich means ....
4 Norway is saving money for ....

4 Do you think that the Norwegians are right to save their money? Why?

Grammar focusing adverbs *only, just, even*

> **FOCUSING ADVERBS *ONLY, JUST, EVEN***
>
> ***only***
> *Only Luxembourg and a couple of other countries are richer.*
>
> ***just***
> *Just 80 years ago, Norwegians were emigrating to the US.*
>
> ***even***
> *This isn't even a competition anymore.*
>
> For more information and practice, see page 172.

5 Work in pairs. Look at the grammar box. Which of these statements (a–c) is true of *only, just,* and *even*?

a they always come directly after the word they are emphasizing.
b they always come directly after the main verb.
c they always come directly before the word they are emphasizing.

6 Find other examples of these words in the article. Do they follow the same rule?

SAVING FOR A RAINY DAY

Come on, Norway; this isn't even a competition anymore! For the last eight years, Norway has registered the highest quality of life among the world's nations. It is one of the wealthiest countries in the world; only Luxembourg and a couple of others are richer. Norwegians can also expect to get a good education, find the job they want (unemployment is only 2.5 perect), enjoy good health, and live a long life. People say the prisons are quite comfortable too!

Norway has not always been a rich country. Just 80 years ago, Norwegians were emigrating to the US by the thousands, in search of a better life. The rise in oil prices in the 1970s changed all that. But Norway's success is not only the result of its huge reserves of oil. Other countries have had such riches and squandered them. It is also due to the Norwegians' thrift and their strong work ethic.

When you arrive in Oslo for the first time, don't expect to be met with Dubai-style skyscrapers, entrepreneurs in designer suits, and rows of Ferraris and Porsches. Norway may be rich, but it is modest in its wealth. Norwegians also work hard and are always near the top in surveys of global worker productivity rates. But in today's high-tech world, where work seems to follow us wherever we go, the people of Norway are redefining what wealth means. Laws just recently passed by the government emphasize the importance of family and time off, offering generous maternity and paternity leave, subsidized childcare, and long vacations as well.

Also, the country is saving for the future. Every dollar earned from oil is put straight into what is now the world's biggest pension fund, worth over $200 billion. Extraordinarily, none of this money is allowed to be spent on state infrastructure projects. It is not even invested in new schools and hospitals. But at a time when most other countries are wondering how they will finance the pensions of a growing retired population, Norway is sitting pretty.

leave (n) /liv/ time off from work
sitting pretty (v) /ˈsɪtɪŋ ˈprɪti/ in a good or comfortable situation
squander (v) /ˈskwɑndər/ waste
thrift (n) /θrɪft/ carefulness when spending money

7 Discuss the meaning of each sentence (1–8), then match it to what follows logically (a–h).

1 Only visitors think Norway is expensive.
2 Visitors only think Norway is expensive.
3 Visitors think only Norway is expensive.
4 Among the Scandinavian countries, I have visited Norway just once.
5 Among the Scandinavian countries, I have visited just Norway.
6 Even fathers are given time off to be with their new babies.
7 Fathers are even given time off to be with their new babies.
8 Fathers are given time off even to be with their new babies.

a Of course mothers are given a lot of time off too.
b I have visited the others several times.
c They are also given time off to move and to look after elderly parents.
d ...but all the Scandinavian countries are.
e ...but actually it's quite reasonable.
f I haven't visited the others at all.
g The residents themselves find it reasonable.
h ...in addition to extra money.

8 Complete these sentences by putting a focusing adverb in the right place. Then compare answers with your partner. Tell them whether these facts are true of your country.

1 Many people work long hours during the week, so they see their children on weekends.
2 People with college degrees are finding it difficult to get jobs these days.
3 For most people, a job is a way to make money, not something they particularly enjoy.
4 The rich represent about five percent of the population.
5 You don't see extreme poverty. Poor people usually have food and somewhere to live.
6 The state pension gives you enough to live on, but not to live very comfortably.

Grammar focusing adverbs *too, as well, also*

9 Work in pairs. Look at the position of *too* and *as well* in these sentences. Find the same sentences in the article, but with the word *also*. What do you notice about the position of *also*?

1 Norwegians can expect to get a good education too.
2 It is due to the Norwegians' thrift as well.
3 Norwegians work hard too.
4 The country is saving for the future too.

▶ FOCUSING ADVERBS *TOO, AS WELL, ALSO*

sentence + *too*	*also* + main verb
sentence + *as well*	*be* + *also*
Also, + sentence	auxiliary verb + *also* + main verb

For more information and practice, see page 172.

10 Look at the grammar box. Which patterns from the box can you find in the article? Underline them. Then compare your answers with your partner.

11 Rewrite the sentences using the focusing adverbs given. Compare your answers with another pair.

1 Norwegians like their secure pensions, but they would like to see the government increase spending on healthcare. (*as well / also*)
2 Most countries have high public borrowing and a lot of debt. Norway has neither. (*too / also*)
3 Teachers in Norway receive a good salary and if they teach "heavy" subjects, they get extra payments. (*also / too*)
4 Artists can get a grant—not a loan—from the government of around $20,000 a year and support with childcare. (*also / as well*)
5 Food prices seem very high to outsiders and fuel is expensive. However, house prices are relatively low and so property is a good investment. (*too / also*)
6 Nurses in Norway get 42 weeks' maternity leave at full pay. They can use the hospital's day care when they return to work. (*as well / also*)

Vocabulary money

12 Look at the verbs below and find the right noun in Exercise 11 to make phrases with the same meaning.

1 pay money = make a ....
2 invest money = make an ....
3 borrow more money = increase your ....
4 spend less money = reduce your ....
5 be lent money = take out a ....
6 owe money = have a ....
7 earn money = receive a ....
8 be given money (by the government) = receive a ....

Speaking

13 Work in pairs. Prepare questions to ask each other about the economy in your country or countries (the cost of living, work-life balance, government spending, government grants for certain professions). Use the items in Exercise 11 to help you get ideas.

14 Now change partners with another pair and ask and answer your questions.

12b Don't do it yourself

Vocabulary domestic help

1 Work in pairs. Which of the domestic workers listed below is the person in the photo? What do the other jobs involve?

au pair	babysitter
cleaner	cook
dog walker	gardener
handyman	maid
nanny	personal shopper

2 Discuss these questions about the jobs in Exercise 1.

1 Have you done any yourself?
2 Have you (or your family) employed anyone in these roles?
3 Which jobs involve the greatest skill?
4 Would you like to do any of them? Why?

Listening

3 48 Listen to the interview with the author of a book called *The Servant Economy*. Answer the questions.

1 How many domestic workers are there in the US today? Who are they?
2 Does the author think the growth of the servant economy is good or bad?

4 48 Listen again and identify:

1 which jobs from Exercise 1 the speakers mention.
2 what other jobs are mentioned.
3 whether many people or only the rich employ such workers.

WORDBUILDING *the* + adjective

We can refer to a group of people using *the* + adjective.
the rich, the poor

5 Work in pairs. What did the interviewer find strange about hiring someone to install a Christmas tree? Do you agree?

6 Complete Hilaire Belloc's quotation. Do you agree with it? Why?

"It is the duty of the .... man to give .... to the artisan." *Hilaire Belloc*

Grammar causative *have* and *get*

7 Look at the forms in bold (a–d). Answer the questions (1 and 2). Then look at the transcript on page 181 and find one more example of each type of phrase.

a Thirty years ago, the idea of **getting a worker to hand wash** your car was unthinkable.
b Nowadays, you can **have it washed** for $6.
c You don't have to be rich **to have a cleaner come** once a week.
d Another example would be **getting your windows cleaned** every few months.

1 Which phrases mean someone does a job for you?
2 Which phrases tell you who actually does the job?

CAUSATIVE *HAVE* and *GET*

have/get **+ something + past participle**
I had/got the fence fixed yesterday.

have **+ someone + base form**
I had the gardener fix the fence.

get **+ someone + infinitive**
I got the gardener to fix the fence.

For more information and practice, see page 173.

8 Look at the grammar box. Then complete the paragraph.

Nearly half of all homes in Britain get outside staff [1] __________ (do) their domestic chores for an average of six hours per week. The most common reasons that people gave for having someone [2] __________ (help) around the house were their own long working hours and to avoid arguments with their partner. A third of people said if they didn't have help, nothing would get [3] __________ (do). The most popular domestic jobs are having the house [4] __________ (clean) regularly, getting someone [5] __________ (do) the gardening and having a handyman [6] __________ (fix) things when they are broken. Some of these services do not come cheap either. People pay up to $800 per week to have a personal assistant [7] __________ (organize) their appointments or have their young baby [8] __________ (care) for.

9 Look at these things that a rich couple gets other people to do for them. Complete the sentences with causative forms. Note that you can complete the sentences in two different ways.

1 When they had a party last month, someone organized everything for them.
They __________ everything for them. (get)
2 A personal trainer takes their children to the park to play.
They __________ to the park to play. (have)
3 A driver picks their children up from school.
They __________ from school. (have)
4 A travel agent plans their vacations for them.
They __________ for them. (have)
5 A nanny looks after their children.
They __________. (get)
6 Someone even packs their bags for them.
They even __________ for them. (get)

10 Write down one thing that you would never consider getting someone else to do and one thing you would always get someone else to do. Compare lists with your partner.

11 Pronunciation the sounds /ʃ/, /tʃ/, /ʒ/, and /dʒ/

a **49** Listen carefully to how the underlined letters are pronounced in the following words. Then practice saying them with your partner.

/ʃ/	/tʃ/	/ʒ/	/dʒ/
carwa<u>sh</u>	<u>ch</u>ores	deci<u>s</u>ion	chan<u>ge</u>
<u>sh</u>elves	ri<u>ch</u>er	gara<u>ge</u>	colle<u>ge</u>
<u>sh</u>opper	wat<u>ch</u>	plea<u>s</u>ure	fri<u>dge</u>

b **50** Listen to these words. Discuss which of the four sounds above each one contains. Then practice saying them.

agent	arrange	champagne	cheese
choice	fashion	general	January
sugar	television	usual	

Vocabulary and speaking

12 Work in pairs. How many DIY (do-it-yourself) jobs can you make by matching verbs in A with nouns in B?

A

assemble	clean
decorate	fix
hang	plaster
put up	tile

B

a bed	the bathroom
a carpet	some curtains
a picture	the roof
a tap	some shelves
a wall	

13 Look at the room in the photo. First make a list of all the things that need to be done before you can live in it. Then decide what you will do yourself and what you will get professional help to do. Explain your plans to another pair.

12c The gift economy

Reading

1 How do you think a gift economy works?

2 Read the article and see if you were right. Then find three examples of the gift economy.

3 Choose the correct option (a–c).

1 The false understanding of human nature mentioned is that we are all trying to:
 a compete to get as much as we can.
 b be individuals.
 c keep from being hungry.
2 Hunter-gatherers:
 a had plenty and needed plenty.
 b had little and needed little.
 c had plenty and needed little.
3 American companies found it difficult to recruit Japanese employees because they:
 a couldn't offer good conditions.
 b couldn't offer job security.
 c didn't understand Japanese culture.
4 The message of the 4th paragraph is that Japanese employers are involved in:
 a organizing employees' vacations.
 b their employees' lives.
 c the quality of employees' work.
5 According to the author, the Internet has made it easier for people to:
 a get to know each other.
 b discuss problems.
 c give and receive help.
6 The message of the last paragraph is that big organizations need to:
 a be made smaller.
 b think about the common good.
 c give more of their profits back.

4 Look at these pairs of words from the article. Which definition (a or b) matches each word?

1 gain / reward
 a profit b compensation
2 strive / thrive
 a do well b do your best
3 common / mutual
 a shared by two b shared by many
4 abundance / excess
 a too much b plenty
5 prospects / aspects
 a future possibilities b characteristics
6 accuracy / promptness
 a being precise b being on time

5 Work in small groups. Tell each other what kind of relationship exists between employer and employees in your country. Is it more like the American system or the Japanese relationship?

Critical thinking signposts to key information

6 There are certain phrases that act as signposts to key information (just given or about to follow). Find the following phrases in the article and then draw out the key information they refer to.

at the heart of… not only… rather…
the main… the real…

7 Work in pairs. Compare your answers. Did you agree on what the key information was?

Word focus *hard*

8 Work in pairs. Find three expressions in the article containing the word *hard*. Discuss their meaning.

9 With a partner, try to guess the meaning of each expression with *hard* from its context. Then compare your answers with another pair.

1 I'm sorry the boss didn't like your idea and preferred mine. **No hard feelings**, I hope.
2 Fran and Chris are pretty **hard up** these days. They've been unemployed for a year.
3 Did you hear that **hard-luck** story about the people who lost all their savings?
4 Don't **be hard on** Jake. It's not his fault he was late. His car broke down.
5 I tried to get him to sympathize with our situation because we're newly established, but he's a pretty **hard-headed** businessman.

Speaking

10 Work in groups of three. Discuss the customs of gift giving and exchange that you are familiar with. Think about:

- specific occasions (like weddings, dinner parties)
- visiting people
- help and favors
- business gifts
- returning home after a trip abroad

The Gift Economy

The banking crisis of 2008 again raised concerns that our economy is based too much on individual greed. Such an economic model, critics say, comes from a false understanding of human nature. Human society is not made up of individuals pursuing private gain through competition with each other. The real essence of human nature lies in the social bonds that we make through family, friendships, professional associations, and local communities. These bonds produce a sense of common purpose and shared values, in which groups of people strive for the common good: a sound education, a pleasant environment to live in, a healthy population. It is this idea of shared social interests that is at the heart of the gift economy.

Gift economies thrived in earlier times when people lived in a world of greater abundance and when their wants were fewer. Stone Age hunter-gatherers had shelter and enough food, and did not need many possessions, just a few weapons for hunting and clothing for warmth. They shared food and tools without any expectation of payment or immediate reward. But this is not only an idea that applies to a more primitive way of life. There are also many recent examples of the gift economy at work.

In the past, American companies operating in Japan found it difficult to attract Japanese recruits, even though, compared with Japanese employers, they offered more generous wages, shorter work hours, and better promotion prospects. But these factors were traditionally not so important to Japanese employees, who did not think of their services as being "bought." Rather, they felt they were entering into a long-term "gift exchange" relationship with their employer, which was of mutual benefit.

This relationship had many aspects. At its most basic it involves the simple exchange of physical gifts. For example, if an employee gets married, the company sends a gift and even a departmental manager to represent it at the wedding. Or the company gives its employees a yearly company vacation. On these organized weekends, coworkers share dormitories, eat together, and visit the same attractions, largely at the company's expense. For their part, the main gift employees give their company is their hard work, and this is why each Japanese employee pays such great attention to accuracy, quality in their work, and promptness in its delivery. Even the simplest tasks are carried out with extraordinary care.

Elsewhere, the Internet is facilitating the re-emergence of the gift economy. Neighborhood groups use online networks to share tools and skills. If you need a long ladder to repair your roof, you don't have to go out and buy one; simply put a message on the neighborhood discussion board and soon a neighbor will offer one. You probably will even get help with the repair, because helping and giving is part of human nature. On the Internet, knowledge and advice about almost everything are shared, from how a nuclear reactor works to building your own canoe.

"Fine," I hear you say, "but these are hard times. Helping our neighbor with his roof isn't going to pay the bills." But in an indirect way it is. The point is that by stressing the cooperative side of human nature, the gift economy helps us all. It keeps in check the excesses of big commercial organizations that seek to exploit situations for their own gain. So the big supermarket chains must understand that it is in the common interest not to force small shopkeepers out of business. Big industrial farms must realize that they cannot go on intensively farming the land until there is nothing left in it. Large companies should not always seek to drive the hardest bargain possible with their suppliers, but just pay them fairly. That is the real lesson of the gift economy.

12d The bottom line

Real life negotiating

1 Read this advice about negotiating. Do you agree with it? How does it relate to your own experience?

> A famous negotiator's advice was to "Care, really care… but not that much." In other words, don't let the other person see how much you want the thing or you will be at a disadvantage.

2 51 Listen, and answer the questions.

1 How much does each person seem to care about agreeing on the lease?
2 On what point do they have trouble agreeing?
3 What does the woman suggest to get around this problem?
4 How does the negotiation end?

3 51 Work in pairs. Listen again and complete the expressions in the box.

NEGOTIATING

To be honest, it's absolutely [1] ....
A key thing for us is how long we'd be [2] .... the lease.
I was hoping we could [3] ....
If you look at it from our point of view, we're a [4] ....
Let's face it, fifteen years is [5] ....

If your client could [6] .... on that…
I think what you have to appreciate is that our client's main concern is…
At the end of the day, it gives them some security.
To tell you the truth, that's why the rent [7] ....
That's somewhat of a sticking point.
Is there no way around that?
Maybe if we signed… , then we could pay…
If I were in your shoes, I think I'd just [8] ....
When all's said and done, it has to [9] ....

4 Work in pairs. Look at the expressions in the box and discuss which are used to:

- say what the important thing is
- be direct
- talk about an obstacle to the agreement
- ask the other person to see your side

5 How do you think each person could have done better in the negotiation? Tell your partner.

6 **Pronunciation** **sentence stress in idiomatic phrases**

a 52 Listen to these phrases and underline the one or two words that are most stressed in each phrase.

1 To be honest…
2 A key thing for us is…
3 Let's face it…
4 At the end of the day,…
5 To tell you the truth…

b 53 Work in pairs. Look at these other phrases. Mark the words where you think the stress falls. Then listen and check.

1 The bottom line for us is…
2 The long and the short of it is…
3 The fact of the matter is…
4 One thing that's bothering me is…
5 To be frank,…
6 Am I right in thinking that… ?

7 You are spending eight months in a foreign country and want to get a car to use while you are there. You see a second-hand one advertised in the newspaper. It seems to be exactly what you are looking for. Work in pairs and negotiate the sale of the car. Student A look at page 153; Student B look at page 155.

12e This is what I propose

Writing a report

1 Work in pairs. Look at this quotation by the French mathematician Blaise Pascal. Discuss what he was saying about the art of writing.

> “I'm sorry I wrote you such a long letter; I didn't have time to write a short one.”

2 Look at these elements of a good report. Which is the one referred to by Blaise Pascal?

clear aims   clear recommendation   conciseness   good organization

3 Read the report below. What is the aim of the report? What is the recommendation? Tell your partner.

Summary

I visited our potential new offices at 1 Paradise Square yesterday, May 4, and was very impressed. They seem ideal for our needs, but the lease is for fifteen years, much longer than the six or seven we agreed on at our last meeting. These are the details:

Advantages

- Space – 2,000 ft^2 of flexible office space
- Low rent: only $67,000 per year
- Central location: close to stores and train station
- Maintained: cleaning, repairs are included

Disadvantages

- Long lease: fifteen years
- Maintenance fee is high: $17,000 annually

Recommendation

I propose taking these offices. We have been looking for five months and these are the best offices I have seen at a reasonable rent. If we have to leave before the end of the lease, I am confident that the remaining part of the lease can be sold to a new tenant.

---

4 **Writing skill** subheadings and bullet points

a The writer of the report has organized it into sections using subheadings and bullet points. What do you notice about the language after each bullet point?

b Read this first paragraph of a report on a language training course. Rewrite the report, dividing it into two sections with subheadings. Then break the points in the second section into bullet points.

> Last month the company sent me to a two-week “professional English” course at Falcon Business Language Training in Chicago. I stayed with a host family. Although the course did not focus on my particular job as an engineer very much, it was well organized. On the positive side, I was made to speak English all the time, both in the school and with my host family. The teachers were very professional and had a good knowledge of the business world. We were put in small groups of three to four students, which meant that we got a lot of individual attention.

c Work in pairs. Compare your answers. Did you organize your reports in the same way?

5 Now write the second half of the report including any negative comments and a recommendation. When you have finished, exchange your report with your partner.

6 Read your partner's report. Check the following:

- Is the report concise and clear?
- Has it been broken down into clear sections using subheadings and bullet points?
- Does it end with a clear recommendation?

12f Japan

Video

It is a land of dual identities.

Before you watch

1 Work in groups. Discuss the questions.

1 What do the photos show? Describe each one.
2 What two identities do you think the caption refers to?

2 Work in pairs. Write down things you associate with Japan.

While you watch

3 Watch the video and check your ideas from Exercise 2. Which of the things that you wrote down appeared in the video?

4 Watch the first part of the video (to 02:04). What do these numbers and dates refer to?

1 127 million ....
2 4 ....
3 35 million ....
4 1868 ....
5 1941 ....
6 1945 ....

5 Watch the second part of the video (02:05 to the end). Answer the questions.

1 What gave Japan political stability after the war?
....
2 What has helped it become a world leader in technology, manufacturing, and finance?
....
3 What does the tea ceremony emphasize?
a ....
b ....
c ....
4 Who did painters like Hiroshige influence?
....

6 Match the sentence beginnings (1–5) with the endings (a–e).

1 Japan is a country that harmonizes the forces of what is Western and modern
2 The bustling urban area of greater Tokyo is
3 It looked to the West for a new, more modern
4 Although it is a land of few natural resources, Japan has become
5 Beyond the bullet trains and neon of Tokyo,

a with those that are traditional Japanese.
b political and industrial model.
c there lies a rich cultural tradition.
d the largest metropolitan area on Earth.
e one of the most industrialized countries in the world.

7 Work in pairs. Describe the snow scene painting by Hiroshige.

....
....

After you watch

8 Roleplay a conversation between two different generations

Work in pairs.

Student A: Imagine you grew up in a small village in pre-war Japan. Look at the information below and think about what you are going to say to your grandchild.

- what life was like (the work you did, how you got around, the food you ate)
- the differences between life then and now
- the war years

Student B: Imagine you are a young Japanese business person talking to one of your grandparents. Look at the information below and think about what you are going to say to him/her.

- what life is like in the city (the work you do, how you travel to work, the food you eat)
- how you combine modern and traditional life in the city

Act out the conversation. Compare life in Japan pre- and post-war. Then change roles.

9 Work in groups and discuss the questions.

1 How has your country changed culturally and economically in the last 100 years?
2 Do cultural traditions always support economic innovation?
3 Are economic advances always beneficial? Why?

bustling (adj) /'bʌslɪŋ/ busy
feudal (adj) /'fjud(ə)l/ relating to a social system where most people work and fight for more powerful people who own the land
forge (v) /fɔrdʒ/ make something under difficult conditions
glitz (n) /glɪts/ the quality of being shiny and superficially attractive
neon (n) /'niɑn/ a kind of brightly colored artificial light
raid (n) /reɪd/ an unexpected attack
shrine (n) /ʃraɪn/ a place where people go to meditate or pray
ubiquitous (adj) /ju'bɪkwɪtəs/ present everywhere
wrestling (n) /'reslɪŋ/ a sport where the contestants try to throw each other on the ground

UNIT 12 REVIEW

Grammar

1 Read the article and say why Japan has had a problem of relative poverty in recent years.

2 Insert the focus adverb into the right place in each sentence.

When we picture poverty we often think of people in under-developed countries without food or shelter. [1] But the so-called advanced economies of the world have their share of poverty (even). [2] Japan, for example, a few decades ago was enjoying an economic boom (just). [3] Yet by 2000, it had one of the highest rates of relative poverty among developed countries, with the US having a higher rate (only). [4] One reason was that Japan had one of the highest rates of non-regular workers (also). This means people who are working without proper social protection. [5] An increasingly elderly population—people who were not actively working—contributed to the problem (as well). [6] Making savings last when you live to be over 90 is a problem that people in developed countries will face in the coming years (even).

3 Put the verbs in the right form to complete this advice to people who are long-term unemployed.

1 The first thing to do is rewrite your resume and then get it ______ (check) by an expert.
2 Practice your interview technique. Have a friend ______ (play) the part of the interviewer and get them ______ (ask) you tricky questions.
3 Try to look professional when you go for an interview. Get your hair ______ (cut) and make sure your clothes are suitable. Again, get a friend ______ (help) you with this.
4 Call employers and go to see them in person. Show enthusiasm and get them ______ (see) that you are eager to work.

I CAN
- use focus adverbs to add emphasis ☐
- talk about things that others do for me with *have* and *get* ☐

Vocabulary

4 Find a synonym or close synonym in B for each word/expression in A.

A	B
hard up	paint
hang	au pair
decorate	earnings
borrow from the bank	reasonable
cheap	take out a loan
income	put up
nanny	poor
owe money	be in debt

5 Work in pairs. Make a list of domestic help that you think most people can afford now and again.

I CAN
- talk about money and the economy ☐
- talk about getting domestic jobs done ☐

Real life

6 Work in pairs. Put this conversation between a travel agent (TA) and customer (C) in order.

TA: To tell you the truth, they're not the kind of hotels you can negotiate with.
TA: So we're suggesting one week in the north of the island and one week in the south. Is this the kind of vacation you were looking for?
TA: OK, I'll give them a call and see what I can do.
TA: I understand that, and if I were in your shoes, I think I'd just go for it. At the end of the day, you only get one honeymoon.
TA: What you have to appreciate is that you've chosen two top hotels which aren't cheap.
C: I was hoping we could negotiate the price.
C: I know they aren't, but the key thing for us is to have nice accommodations.
C: Perhaps if we stayed at just one of them for the full two weeks we could get a better deal.
C: Yes it is, but to be honest, it's much more expensive than we expected.

7 Take the roles of travel agent and customer and finish the negotiation.

I CAN
- state my position and negotiate from it ☐

Speaking

8 Work in small groups. Do you think the idea below for a domestic service would work? Think of another idea. Then tell it to others in the class.

What about offering a cooking service where busy couples can have a meal prepared for them at home rather than eating out or getting takeout?

NATIONAL GEOGRAPHIC LEARNING | CENGAGE Learning

Life

5b
Combo Split
Workbook

Paul Dummett
John Hughes
Helen Stephenson

Contents

Unit 7 Natural resources

7a Solving the water problem

Solving the water problem

Conservation
This is perhaps the simplest and most cost-effective solution. Moreover, everyone can contribute, from the water companies to the end-user. The water companies can make sure that they minimize waste by repairing cracked pipes and by imposing restrictions on water usage—not allowing people to use hoses is one method. But more significantly, they can also limit water consumption by making people pay for what they use, rather than for their connection to the water supply. If everyone had a water meter, they would think more carefully when they turned on the tap. With metered water, the market for water-saving devices—low-flush toilets, efficient washing machines and dishwashers—will grow by itself.

Reading water

1 Read the paragraph and choose the best option (a–c).

1 Probably the most effective way for water companies to reduce water consumption is:
   a to fix broken water pipes.
   b to limit how much water people can use.
   c to charge for water comsumption.

2 According to the author, people will buy water-saving devices:
   a if the devices are more efficient.
   b if they see there is financial benefit.
   c whether they have a meter or not.

2 Read the paragraph again and find words that mean:

a a consumer ....
b something you use to water the garden or wash the car ....
c something that measures the amount of water you consume ....

Grammar mixed conditional sentences

3 Complete the sentences. Put the verbs in the correct form. Use first, second, third, and mixed conditionals.

1 If the water companies .... (not / impose) restrictions on water use in the past, there .... (be) water shortages now.
2 If people .... (have) to pay according to how much water they used, they .... (use) less water.
3 If companies .... (introduce) water meters, then people .... (buy) more water-saving devices.
4 If someone .... (think) of a better idea than conservation, it .... (be) in use by now.

Vocabulary conservation verbs

4 Complete the sentences about resources using these verbs. Two verbs are extra.

conserve consume preserve protect run out of save

1 We've .... milk. Can you go and buy some from the store?
2 It's very important to .... money in good times, so that you have some for the bad times.
3 Using salt to .... food is a very old practice.
4 The WWF has launched a campaign to .... the tiger from the threat of extinction.

7b Oil

Vocabulary oil

1 Label the pictures using these words.

oil barrel oil field oil pipeline oil refinery
oil rig oil slick oil tanker oil well

1 ....

2 ....

3 ....

4 ....

5 ....

6 ....

7 ....

8 ....

Grammar *wish, would rather, and if only*

2 Complete these sentences by putting the verb in the correct form.

1 We wish oil .... (go) on forever.

2 I wish I .... (be able) to give you a straight answer.

3 A lot of people wish that we .... (not / start) to go down this route.

4 I'm sure people would rather .... (have) a cheaper and cleaner alternative.

5 If only there .... (be) a cheaper, cleaner, and more efficient alternative.

6 Would you rather we .... (run) out of oil or lithium?

3 Complete the short conversations using the correct form of the verbs given.

1 **A:** Would you like to drive or will I?
B: I'd rather you .... (drive).

2 **A:** Are you going to buy that new electric car?
B: If only I .... (have) enough money, then I'd get it tomorrow, but it's over $30,000!

3 **A:** Some people think that cheap gas is a basic human right.
B: I know. I wish people .... (stop) complaining and use their cars less.

4 **A:** Your new car is amazing. Doesn't it use a lot of gas though?
B: Yes, it does. I wish I .... (buy) one with a smaller engine.

5 **A:** The oil spill was terrible. What do you think happened to all the oil in the sea?
B: I'd rather .... (not / think) about it. It's probably still out there.

6 **A:** We all depend too much on the countries who produce oil.
B: I know. I wish each country .... (become) more independent in its energy needs.

7c An emotive subject

Reading conservation stories

Story 1

In the 1970s, Cancún was just a small fishing village—a few huts on the edge of a mangrove forest. Today that forest is buried and rotting underneath 500 hotels. Only a few inhabitants remember the forest and the seven million tourists that visit each year don't know it ever existed. This place is a classic example of how not to build a tourist resort. Nature is for sale here. The mangroves are not the only victims. The coral reef all along the coast is also slowly being destroyed by all the tourists' pollution. Very little waste water is treated: it's either pumped into the sea or injected into the land, from where in time it returns to the surface. Up to now, conservationists have failed to stop this development or the pollution it's caused.

Story 2

The story of the West African giraffe is a conservation success story. A heroic effort on the part of conservationists has saved the giraffe from extinction—from numbers as low as 50 giraffes 20 years ago to over 200 today. The main job was to track the giraffe's movements, since they travel huge distances looking for food. This was done by fitting them with GPS satellite collars—easy with their long necks, you'd think, but actually it's a delicate operation because the giraffes have to be anesthetized first. Once they knew where the giraffes were going, the conservationists could then begin to educate local people about the dangers facing these wonderful creatures, and to compensate farmers when their land had been damaged by them.

1 Complete the table.

	What needs to be protected?	Has the conservation work been successful?
1	The mangrove .... in	....
2	The West African	....

2 Are the sentences true (T) or false (F)? Or is there not enough information (N) to say if the statements are true or false?

1 Every inhabitant of Cancún misses the beautiful mangrove forest.
2 Waste water has badly damaged the coral reef along this part of the coast.
3 In West Africa, conservationists needed to find out where the giraffe went for food.
4 Farmers were killing the giraffes who fed on their land.

3 Complete the sentences about the conservation projects using these words.

classic heroic rarest rotting sale small wonderful victims

1 Today that forest is buried and .... underneath 500 hotels.
2 This place is a .... example of how not to build a tourist resort.
3 Nature is for .... here.
4 The mangroves are not the only ....
5 A .... effort on the part of conservationists has saved the giraffe.
6 The conservationists could then begin to educate local people about the dangers facing these .... creatures.

4 Find words and expressions in Exercise 3 that have these meanings:

1 very typical ....
2 a person or thing against which a crime is committed ....
3 placed under the ground ....
4 you can buy it ....
5 decaying or going bad ....

7d Is globalization good?

Real life making your point

1 Globalization is a force for good. It brings us all closer together. You'll say, "Yes, it makes us all watch the same TV shows and want to buy the same brands," but that's not the point. The point is that it helps us to understand each other better: our differences and our similarities, our hopes and our fears.

2 Sorry, I just don't accept that. All it helps is people in rich countries to have cheaper goods and also goods out of season. To be honest with you, I could live without flowers that are imported from Africa in December or my computer technical support team being based in India.

3 We're approaching this debate all wrong. Globalization is just a natural economic phenomenon. It gives countries a much bigger market so that they can concentrate on producing the things they're good at producing.

4 Think of people in China making cheap toys for us to give to our children. These people would be much better off making things that were really useful to them. There's no doubt that it's helped the rich countries, but overall globalization has just increased the gap between the world's rich and poor.

1 Read what four people think about globalization and complete the summaries.

Person 1: Globalization helps us all to ______________________

Person 2: Globalization just helps people ______________________

Person 3: Globalization is just a ______________________

Person 4: Globalization has just increased ______________________

2 Complete these phrases used in the reading.

1 That's ____________ the ____________ .

2 Sorry, I ____________ don't ____________ that.

3 To ____________________ , I could live without flowers that are imported from Africa.

4 We're ____________________ this debate all ____________________ .

5 There's no ____________________ that it has helped the rich.

Vocabulary review strong feelings

3 Look at these words. Check the emotive words.

back-breaking criticize deplore desperate interested in keen on majestic obsessed with tall tiring

7e Waste

Writing a letter to the press

1 Read the letter below and answer the questions

1 What caused the writer to send the letter?

....

....

2 What does she say will happen if nothing is done?

....

....

Daily Times

Published: January 12

To the editor:

I am very tired of seeing so much waste in a world where many people [1] .... suffer shortages of food, energy, and other basic necessities.

Each day at my local supermarket, enormous quantities of food [2] .... are thrown away when it could easily be given to charities for the homeless. People often throw away electronic equipment, [3] ...., when the item is only four or five years old. Cars [4] .... sit in traffic jams with their engines running, burning fuel unnecessarily. Clothes, [5] ...., are so cheap nowadays that people think nothing of wearing something once or twice and then throwing it away.

How have we allowed ourselves to become so careless about precious resources? Are we simply too rich to care? If we do not change the way we behave, a change of behavior will be forced upon us because there will be no more resources left for us to waste.

H. Patel, Oakland

2 Writing skills giving vivid examples

a Use these words and one of the details (a–e) to add information that makes the letter more vivid. Insert the information in the spaces (1–5).

such as | with | especially | which | who

a items of fashion clothing
b flat-screen TVs, computers, or cell phones
c is near its sell-by date
d live in more difficult circumstances than us
e only one driver in them

b Make the short letter below more vivid by giving more information or examples in the spaces (1–5). Use these notes to help you.

- give more details of the building
- give examples
- describe what people do here
- give examples
- give reasons

To the editor:

I agree totally with James Needham (*Daily Times*, May 4). The decision to build a new apartment complex [1] .... on part of what is now Summerdine Park is shocking. This park not only contains many species of trees [2] ...., it is also one of the few green spaces in the area, [3] .... There are certainly other places to build new housing [4] .... It would be better to develop areas like this [5] ....

Word focus *better*

3 Match the beginning of the sentences (1–5) with their endings (a–e).

1 You had better
2 We would be better off
3 I think it would be better
4 He always tries to go one better
5 He should know better

a than me.
b if we kept this car until it gets too expensive to maintain.
c not mention the question of waste to him. He gets very emotional.
d than to cut down a tree in a conservation area.
e to send a letter to the local paper.

Wordbuilding collocations related to one word

1 Look at these noun + noun collocations. Match them to the definitions below.

air: air bridge air force air vent
water: water jug water leak water lily
wind: wind chill wind farm wind instrument

1 e.g., clarinet, oboe, flute ....
2 used for getting from the airport terminal to the plane ....
3 a place where renewable energy is generated ....
4 the drop in temperature cause by a cold wind ....
5 an escape of water from a pipe or tank ....
6 part of the military, along with the army and navy ....
7 used for serving water at the dinner table ....
8 a place (e.g., in a wall) where air can enter or exit ....
9 a flower that grows in lakes and ponds ....

2 Some noun + noun collocations become one compound noun. Look at these collocations with *sun*. Which two words are opposites?

sunglasses sunlight sunrise sunset suntan

Learning skills improving your listening

3 A key to understanding fast native speech is to understand stress and linking in English pronunciation. Read this sentence aloud and note the stress and linking in it.

1 **Stress:** Sorry I just don't accept that.
2 **Linking:** Sorry‿I just don't‿accept that.

4 Look at these sentences. Read them aloud. Underline the stressed syllables and indicate where the sounds are linked.

1 Globalization helps people in rich countries.
2 They can have goods out of season.
3 But to be honest, I don't need flowers imported from Africa in December.

5 Read these steps for improving your listening skills.

1 Write down the words you hear.
2 Read your transcript back. Does it make grammatical sense?
3 Compare your transcript with the audioscript.
4 Note the words and sounds which have the strongest stress. These should be the key words that convey the meaning.
5 Note which words are clearly linked. This will help you to distinguish them the next time you hear them.

Check!

6 Complete the crossword using phrases about natural resources. All the answers are in Student Book Unit 10.

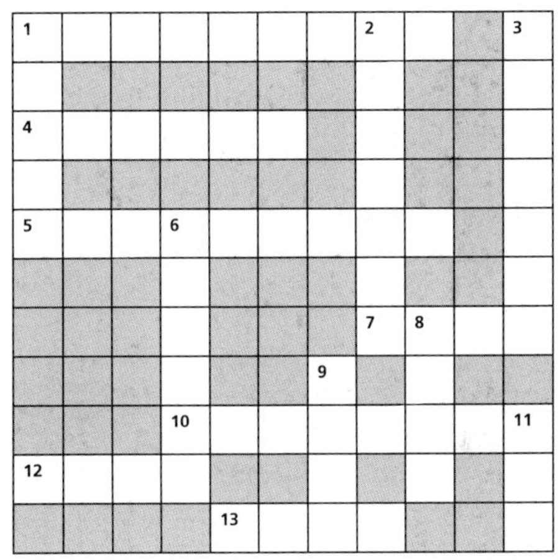

Across

1 resources which can be replaced in nature (9)
4 and 5 with its special plants and wildlife, Madagascar has one of these (6, 9)
5 see 4 Across
7 the substance which is removed from water in the desalination process (4)
10 this American river does not reach the sea anymore (8)
12 another word for "conserve" (4)
13 see 11 Down

Down

1 the three Rs in conservation: reduce, ..., recycle (5)
2 people whose job it is to cut down trees (7)
3 Ecuador wanted to be paid not to do this with its oil (7)
6 the opposite of abundant (6)
8 this sea is a tenth of the size it was in the 1960s (4)
9 producing a pound of this uses 22,500 gallons of water (4)
11 and 13 Across the point where oil is taken from the ground (3, 4)

Unit 8 The news

8a Photojournalism

Vocabulary the news

1 Complete the crossword with words related to news reporting.

Across

1 and 8 a story that is both serious and urgent (4, 4)

3 news that is less serious and not urgent (4)

7 a piece expressing the opinion of the newspaper (9)

Down

2 any piece written in a newspaper or magazine (7)

4 a special or prominent piece in a magazine or newspaper (8)

5 the title of the main news story, written in big letters (8)

6 a section of the newspaper dedicated to a particular writer (6)

	1 H	2 A						
					3 S		4 F	
5 H				6 C				
7 E								
8 N								

Grammar reporting verbs

2 Rewrite these sentences using the reporting verbs given.

1 People said that the magazine had manipulated reality.
People **accused** the magazine ....

2 The editor said they had altered the image.
The editor **admitted** ....

3 But he said they hadn't done anything wrong.
But he **denied** ....

4 He said modern technology made it easy to alter images.
He **blamed** ....

5 Some editors tell their designers that it is OK to alter images for covers.
Some editors **persuade** ....

6 People complained, saying that they had been given a false impression.
People **complained** ....

7 Some people say, "Don't trust a photo if there's anything important riding on it."
Some people **warn** you ....

3 Complete the text using the correct form of the verbs. Use prepositions where necessary.

In the past, photographers have been criticized [1] .... (invade) people's privacy or [2] .... (take) pictures that did not reflect the reality of a situation. But nowadays, in the age of digital photography, there is a new problem. How do we know that the photo has not been altered after it has been taken? It would be wrong to blame the photographer [3] .... (manipulate) some of the photos that appear in our newspapers and magazines. A photo editor might be asked [4] .... (alter) a photo digitally in order to make a good story. For example, someone might suggest [5] .... (touch) up the photo of a film star's face to make them look more attractive. Or they might urge the photo editor [6] .... (add) an image of a frightened child into a photo of a street protest. That is a practice people should possibly refuse [7] .... (accept).

8b News in brief

Grammar passive reporting verbs

1 Grammar extra **tenses in passive reporting verbs**

> **▶ TENSES IN PASSIVE REPORTING VERBS**
>
> Note how these tenses are transformed from active to passive.
>
> *People say...* → *It is said that...*
> *People have said...* → *It has been said that...*
> *People said...* → *It was said that...*
> *People had said...* → *It had been said that...*

Look at the grammar box. Rewrite these phrases using passive reporting verbs.

1 People say that... → It *is said that...*
2 Everyone understands that...
It ....
3 Everyone knew that...
It ....
4 People believed that...
It ....
5 People have estimated that...
It ....
6 People think that...
It ....
7 People had hoped that...
It ....
8 Everyone supposes that...
It ....

2 Rewrite the sentences using passive reporting verbs.

1 People say that for every negative, there is always a positive.
It is said that for every negative, there is always a positive.
2 People expect Mr. Gomez to continue doing what he loves.
It .... that Mr. Gomez .... what he loves.
3 People used to think that a glass of red wine a day helped you to live longer.
In the past, ...
4 Most people don't recommend eating fast food if you want to live longer.
It .... that you ....
5 People hoped that secret gifts would brighten up someone's day.
It .... that secret gifts ....
6 People supposed that the tree prevented the car falling further.
It ....
7 People considered the man lucky to survive the accident.
It .... that the man ....
8 People have reported great success with the idea.
It .... the idea .... very successful

Vocabulary the feel-good factor

3 Match the adjectives describing good news stories in box A with the words that have the opposite or a near opposite meaning in box B.

A	B
amusing	ordinary
charming	depressing
inspiring	pessimistic
quirky	serious
encouraging	dreary
optimistic	uninspiring

Vocabulary review photography

4 Match the verbs in Box A with the nouns in Box B and write the collocations.

A	B
capture	events
open	the lens
record	the moment
see through	a photo
take	a snaphot
take	the shutter

8c Balanced reporting

Reading news reports

The difficulty with journalism is trying always to make sure that you give a balanced view, to get your facts right, and at the same time tell a good story. National Geographic tries to find places where we can marvel at the wonders of nature and places where it thinks that natural ecosystems are in danger.

In the August 2011 issue, the magazine brought the world's attention to such a place, the Great Bear Rainforest in Canada. The main article was a full feature entitled "The Wildest Place in North America, Land of the Spirit Bear" and described the beauty of the white Kermode Spirit Bear. A smaller article, called "Pipeline through Paradise," described the building of a gas pipeline through "Great Bear" country to a gas terminal on the coast at a place called Kitimat. Here huge tanker ships were to be be loaded up with liquefied natural gas. The article stated that, "The government has already approved a fleet of liquefied natural gas tankers to call at nearby Kitimat in 2015."

Strictly speaking, this was factually inaccurate and it upset the company building the pipeline a great deal. Building of the terminal had in fact already begun, and the local government had given its verbal approval to the pipeline. But the company had not received an official license at the time of publication of the article. Even though it was likely that a license would be be granted, the journalists and editors in question clearly jumped the gun in order to make their point.

The article highlights the dilemma for journalists. They want to write an interesting article that gives definite, not probable, news. They also want to get the story first, before it appears in other newspapers or magazines. The people involved, on the other hand—in this case the company representatives who were interviewed for the article—want all the facts to be presented, not only the ones that interest the journalist. They also want any comment to be balanced: in other words, for the same amount of space to be given to their own views as to the journalist's. Ideally, they'd like to have the last word, but of course no journalist should allow that.

1 Are the sentences true (T) or false (F)?

1. National Geographic likes to report on endangered environments.
2. The main article was about a gas pipeline.
3. The speaker thinks that journalists should give equal space to both sides in a debate.

2 Read the report again and choose the correct option.

1. Journalists have to try to give a balanced *view / opinion* and tell a good story.
2. National Geographic tries to find places where we can marvel at the *joys / wonders* of nature.
3. The main article described the *beauty / nature* of the white Kermode Spirit Bear.
4. A smaller article described the building of a gas *platform / pipeline.*
5. *Technically / Strictly* speaking, it was inaccurate to say the government had given its approval.
6. The journalists and editors in question *shot / jumped* the gun in order to make their point.
7. The article highlights the *dilemma / problem* for journalists.
8. Ideally the people involved would like to have *the say-so / the last word.*

Word focus *word*

3 Complete the sentences using the expressions with *word.*

> don't take my word for it   eat my words
> gave his word
> one person's word against another's
> word of mouth

1. Our magazine gets most of its new readers by ______ or because someone has read a copy in a doctor's waiting room.
2. I assured them that it would be easy to find a good wildlife photographer. I hope I don't have to ______ .
3. It is just ______ . In the end, the reader will have to decide who they believe.
4. If you don't believe what I'm telling you, then ______ . Go and check the facts for yourself.
5. He ______ that he would not publish the story before I had read it.

8d Guess what

Real life reporting what you heard

1 Complete the sentences. Use a verb in each space. Do the sentences express belief (B) or disbelief (D)?

	B	D
1 I think I'd ________ her word for it.	☐	☐
2 He generally ________ his facts right.	☐	☐
3 He's not the type to ________ gossip.	☐	☐
4 ________ no notice of what she says.	☐	☐
5 It's been ________ out of proportion.	☐	☐
6 I'd ________ that with a grain of salt.	☐	☐

2 Read a conversation between two friends, Jane and Annie, and answer the questions.

A = Annie, J = Jane

J: Hi Annie.

A: Hi Jane. Did you hear the good news about Patrick? Guess what?

J: What?

A: Well, you know he was doing a comedy routine...

J: You mean that show that he and his friends took to the Talent Festival.

A: Yes. Well, apparently he was spotted by someone from a big theatrical agency and they want him to sign a contract with them.

J: Really? Who told you about it?

A: Kate. She figures that it won't be long before we see him on TV.

J: Hmm... Well, I'd take that with a grain of salt if I were you. It could just mean he gets a bit of advertising work or something.

A: No, according to Kate, it's more than that. They talked about him getting acting parts on TV.

J: Really? Well, that'd be fantastic. I heard that it was really difficult to get that kind of work.

A: I think it is, which shows he must have really impressed them. But don't tell anyone just yet. I think he wants to keep quiet about it.

J: Don't worry. I'm not the type to spread gossip.

A: I know you're not.

J: Well, that's great news. Thanks for telling me.

1 What is the news about Patrick that Annie wants to share?

____

____

____

2 Who did she hear this news from?

____

3 What does Annie ask Jane to do with the news? Why?

____

____

3 Complete the sentences from the conversation.

verbs: guesses heard figures seems
prepositions: about according to
adverbs: apparently supposedly
nouns: gossip grain

1 Did you hear the good news ________ (*preposition*) Patrick? ________ (*verb*) what?

2 Well, ________ (*adverb*) he was spotted by someone from a big theatrical agency.

3 She ________ (*verb*) that it won't be long before we see him on TV.

4 Well, I'd take that with a ________ (*noun*) of salt if I were you.

5 No, ________ (*preposition*) Kate, it's more than that.

6 That'd be fantastic. I ________ (*verb*) that it was really difficult to get that kind of work.

7 Don't worry. I'm not the type to spread ________ (*noun*).

8e Group action

Vocabulary meetings

1 Write two verbs that collocate with each noun.

attend discuss draft hold make (x2)
put forward reach weigh write

1 ________, ________ a meeting
2 ________, ________ a suggestion
3 ________, ________ a decision
4 ________, ________ the options
5 ________, ________ a letter

2 Writing skill **impersonal language**

Rewrite the sentences using impersonal language. Use the words given.

1 We all got together to discuss how to raise the money.
A ________ (held)
2 We discussed all the things that we could do.
All ________ (options)
3 Julian suggested that we should ask the local businesses for help.
One ________ (suggestion)
4 Pete said it was better to have some fun events.
Another ________ (idea)
5 Several people said organizing events would take too long.
It ________ (agreed)
6 No one could decide what to do about funding the project.
________ (decision)

Writing minutes from a meeting

3 Read the minutes from a local meeting about a waste incinerator (a plant where trash is burned) in the area. Answer the questions.

1 What are the main advantages and disadvantages of the incinerator? ________
2 What action was decided on? ________
3 What action was rejected? ________

Playa Grande Residents' Association

From: Kathy Barbosa

Re: New waste incinerator

Here are the minutes from the meeting which was held on September 3.

- Following the government's decision to build a new waste incinerator on the old factory site in Quibble Street, we met to decide what action residents could take to oppose this new source of pollution.
- Karen suggested that we should get everyone in the area to sign a petition against the proposal. Everyone agreed that this was a good first step.
- Tom thought we should present the government with some alternative locations, but no one at the meeting was able to suggest any so the action was rejected.
- Jo made the point that the government wanted to use the incinerator to generate electricity for the area, which was a good thing for the community.
- Kevin proposed that we could have another kind of plant which sorted the waste for recycling. Harry said he would research this option and discuss it at the next meeting.

Next meeting date: **September 26**

4 Replace the underlined phrases with more impersonal ones.

1 *a meeting was held to decide*
2 ________
3 ________
4 ________
5 ________
6 ________
7 ________

Wordbuilding forming adjectives from verbs

1 Complete the sentences using the verbs + *-ing*.

charm confuse depress inspire
refresh tire touch worry

1 It is ______________ that she is so late—she's normally very punctual.
2 The article was rather ______________ . You couldn't work out why the daughter had left her family.
3 It's very ______________ to hear a story about a business which doesn't just do things to make money.
4 He is a really ______________ man—polite, interesting, and kind.
5 The story about two friends overcoming their difficulties was very ______________ .
6 Environmental news is often ______________ , but in this case the story offered hope.
7 The news featured the ______________ story of a 14-year-old girl who got a part-time job to help support her family.
8 It's very ______________ to follow movie with subtitles for three hours.

2 Make adjectives using verbs + *-ive*.

1 good at **inventing** *inventive* (from *invent*)
2 good at **persuading** ______________
3 good at **creating** ______________
4 liking to **compete** ______________
5 **producing** a lot ______________
6 **talking** a lot ______________
7 wanting to **protect** ______________
8 not **responding** ______________

Learning skills keeping a learning journal

3 What is a learning journal and why is it a good idea to keep one? Look at these reasons and compare them with your own ideas.

- To learn from your mistakes and successes
- To track your progress
- To set goals for your learning
- To record what you have learned

4 Read the following actions which can help you to evaluate and personalize your learning.

Actions

1 Write down your experiences of learning after each lesson: what you found easy, what you found difficult, what was the most important thing you learned.

2 Note mistakes that you have made before.

3 Make a note of an excerpt, even a sentence, that you particularly liked and try to memorize it.

4 Set yourself a small task based on the language you learned in your last lesson, e.g., describe a good news story, report what someone said to you, or describe a situation where somebody's reputation was questioned.

5 Apply the actions (1–4) for Unit 8. Then remember to do it for your next lesson!

Check!

6 Do the quiz. You can find all the answers in Student Book Unit 8.

Quiz Time

1 Complete these sentences about the characters in Unit 8.
a The pilot Peter Burkill went from hero to z______________ .
b Sharbat Gula's photo is one of the most i______________ images of our time.
c It was believed that the large blue butterfly was e______________ in Britain.

2 Complete the phrases about the news.
a The best form of advertising is when news travels by word of m______________ .
b Good news stories generate a f______________ factor among people.
c It's not a good thing to s______________ gossip.
d There was an amazing f______________ about India in *National Geographic* this month.

Unit 9 Talented people

9a The great communicator

Reading

As a young man Ronald Reagan moved to Los Angeles to begin a career as an actor in films and television. After joining the Republican Party in 1962, his skills as an orator were noticed and he was persuaded to run for governor of California. He then went on to become the president of the United States between 1981 and 1989. He was often ridiculed for not being very clever—a second-rate actor, who could only read the lines he was given by his advisors—but he remains one of the most popular American presidents of the past 50 years.

Some historians say that Ronald Reagan understood the fundamental essence of leadership: that is, that a leader to be able to communicate. Reagan always gave the impression that he was listening when he was speaking to you. It was almost as if it didn't matter what his political views were. He made people feel that they mattered. That is a fantastic quality to have. Reagan's style of communication stands out as a model for all leaders. If the president can connect with the ordinary person, there's very little he can do wrong.

1 Look at the words and phrases in bold from the description of Ronald Reagan. Choose the correct meaning (a or b).

1 His skills as **an orator** were noticed and he was persuaded to run for governor of California.
   a a politician
   b a public speaker

2 He understood the **fundamental essence** of leadership.
   a real meaning
   b basic problem

3 He made people feel that they **mattered**.
   a were lucky
   b were important

4 Reagan's style of communication **stands out**.
   a is noticeable
   b is old-fashioned

Grammar **articles: *the* or zero article?**

2 Complete with *the* or zero article (–).

Countries: ____ Japan, ____ United Arab Emirates, ____ Netherlands, ____ Thailand

Places: ____ Amazon River, ____ countryside, ____ Moon, ____ Mount Everest

Times: ____ weekend, ____ Saturday, ____ April, ____ spring

Other: ____ breakfast, ____ police, ____ poor, ____ biology

Vocabulary **qualifications**

3 Complete the job interview between an interviewer (I) and an applicant (A) using these words.

background experience qualifications talents

I: So can you tell me first a little bit about your [1] ____?

A: Sure. My mother's French and my father's English. I was brought up in France and…

I: And do you have any previous [2] ____ in journalism?

A: Yes. In college I was editor of the student magazine and after that I worked for a local radio station…

I: What [3] ____ do you have?

A: I have a bachelor's degree in media studies...

I: What would you say are your [4] ____?

A: I'm good at learning languages and I'm a good photographer.

9b An inspirational scientist

Reading positive results

Something the size of a postage stamp, costing just a penny apiece, could be a medical breakthrough that will save millions of lives. According to biotechnology scientist Hayat Sindi, this tiny piece of paper has the same power as an entire diagnostic laboratory. "My mission is to find simple, inexpensive ways to monitor health," Sindi says. She believes technology pioneered by a team at Harvard University will make it possible, and she co-founded the charity "Diagnostics For All" to produce and distribute the innovation.

The small piece of paper is a low-tech tool that detects disease by analyzing bodily fluids. Positive results, which show up in less than a minute, are indicated by a change in color on the paper.

Grammar relative clauses and reduced relative clauses

1 Write sentences using relative clauses. Use the relative pronouns *who, which, whose, where,* and *when*. Use commas where necessary.

1 The piece of paper is the size of a postage stamp. It could save thousands of lives.

....

....

2 The charity "Diagnostics for All" produces the tool. It was co-founded by Sindi.

....

....

3 The tool will be used in developing countries. It is difficult to find clinics there.

....

....

4 The results show up on the paper. The paper's color changes if there is a problem.

....

....

5 Sindi later went to Harvard. She was the first Saudi woman to study biotechnology at Cambridge.

....

....

6 Sindi has become a role model for other women. They want to follow her example.

....

....

2 Replace the relative clauses in these sentences with reduced relative clauses. Number 4 has two clauses.

1 People who live far away from hospitals and clinics will benefit from this technology.

....

2 Sindi, who was determined to succeed, studied up to twenty hours a day.

....

3 Sindi uses her own experience to inspire other women who wish to become scientists.

....

4 A new foundation, which was launched recently by Sindi, offers help to young women who want to follow a career in science.

....

....

Vocabulary personal qualities

3 Complete the summary with these adjectives.

analytical articulate passionate patient

Hayat Sindi is [1] .... about helping people in developing countries. She also is an [2] .... speaker and supporter of women's right to education. To be a scientist, you have to have an [3] .... mind and to be very [4] .... , as it can take a long time to get positive results from an experiment.

9c Women leaders

Reading an interview

Interviewer: What are the particular qualities that men and women bring to leadership? Does it in fact make any difference to an organization if its leader is a man or a woman? I have with me Virginia Stanton, author of *Women Who Lead*. Virginia, surely in this day and age it doesn't matter that much, does it, what gender a leader is, as long as they're a good leader?

Virgnia: Well, if you say that, you're actually ignoring the differences that a number of studies have identified between male and female leaders. It's statistically proven that women are a) more adventurous—they're happy to take risks, and b) more effective—they focus harder on getting the job done.

Interviewer: That is a little surprising, yes.

Virgnia: Less surprising perhaps is that they tend to be more sensitive and caring—that is to say, they listen better than men and try to take other people's views into account before making a decision. That's because they seem to care more about their relationships with those around them.

Interviewer: And I suppose you're going to say, then, that men are more assertive and dominant. That's a stereotype, isn't it?

Virginia: Well, I think the important thing here is that whereas in the past, leaders—male leaders, that is—were more autocratic—"just do what I tell you to do and don't answer back"—these days you need to be more inclusive and gentler in your dealings with people. It's long been recognized that women, who traditionally have been the ones to organize and manage families or groups of volunteers in charity organizations, have these qualities. More and more, these are qualities that are needed today in the world of business and politics.

1 Based on the interview, are the sentences true (T) or false (F)?

1 The interviewer thinks that whether a leader is male or female is not the issue.
2 The author says that her claims are supported by research.
3 The author is surprised that women, not men, take more risks.
4 According to the author, men care more about what others around them think.
5 The interviewer thinks that the author is stereotyping women.
6 The author thinks that people want a more cooperative style of leadership than in the past.

Word focus *long*

2 Look at the sentence from the interview and its definition. Then match the sentences (1–10) with the correct definition (a–j).

It doesn't matter what gender a leader is, **as long as** they are a good leader. = It doesn't matter what gender a leader is, **if/provided that** they are a good leader.

1 "It's been great to see you. I hope we can meet up again **before long**."
2 He stood there for what seemed like hours and **at long last** someone opened the door.
3 She wasn't angry that the company paid her poorly, but she **longed for** recognition.
4 They arrived **long after** they had intended to.
5 Jake and I **go back a long way**.
6 **The long and short of it** is that we need to reduce our spending or we'll be in trouble.
7 He **put on a long face**, so I asked him what the matter was.
8 He **has come a long way** since he was working as a dishwasher in a café.
9 "**So long**," she said, "I'll write to you soon."
10 **In the long term,** I think we will see benefits from all these efficiencies.

a after much waiting
b are old friends
c desired very much
d goodbye
e the main message
f looked sad
g made a lot of progress
h much later than
i over a long period of time
j soon

9d Your own talents

Real life describing skills, talents, and experience

1 Complete these expressions using the correct preposition.

1 In college I majored .... photojournalism.
2 I'm very familiar .... your magazine.
3 I'm good .... spotting an interesting story.
4 I have some experience .... news photography.
5 I think I'd be suited .... working in this kind of environment.
6 I feel quite comfortable .... tight deadlines.
7 I'm very interested .... the idea of working closely with other journalists.
8 I'm serious .... wanting to become a full-time news photographer.

2 Read three people's descriptions of their skills at a job interview. What job are they applying for?

....

....

Speaker 1

Well, I'd like to know more about the job, because I'm very interested in the idea of working with young people—people are always telling me that I'm very good with children—but I don't have much direct experience with this age group.

Speaker 2

I specialize in canoeing and various other water sports, but I feel comfortable with most outdoor activities really—as long as you're not going to expect me to lead a climbing expedition up a glacier or anything. I haven't done mountaineering. But I have led groups before, so I have good organizational skills.

Speaker 3

I think I am very well qualified for this job, actually. Although I haven't led expeditions, I've been working as a physical education teacher at my local high school for the last four years. I'm good at a number of sports, in fact. But when I saw your advertisement, I thought, "This could be just the thing for me." I'm familiar with your organization and I really like the fact that you run these activities for kids from underprivileged backgrounds.

3 Answer the questions about each of the applicants.

1 What are the skills or talents of each applicant?

Applicant 1

....

....

Applicant 2

....

....

Applicant 3

....

....

2 What does each speaker lack experience of?

Applicant 1

....

....

Applicant 2

....

....

Applicant 3

....

....

4 Grammar extra adjective + *-ing* or *to* + infinitive

▶ ADJECTIVE + *ING* or *TO* + INFINITIVE

Some adjectives can be followed by a preposition + *-ing* or by an infinitive.

*I'm interested **in learning** French.*
*I'm happy **to show** you how it works.*

Look at the grammar box. Complete the sentences. Use the correct form of the verb: *-ing* form or *to* + infinitive.

1 I'd like to .... (participate) in one of your trial days.
2 I'll be sad .... (leave) this place.
3 I'm interested in .... (travel) to new places.
4 I'm excited about .... (do) field research in India.
5 I'm very interested .... (work) abroad.
6 I'd be interested .... (find out) more about the job.

9e Networking

Writing an online profile

1 Complete the personal profile using the information below (a–f).

a Current
b Freelance marketing consultant and translator
c School of Management, UMass Amherst
d Media and food
e Summary
f Past

Mitsuko Uchida

1 ……………………

Location: Tokyo
Industry: 2 ……………………
3 …………………… : Advising US supermarket on market plan for Japan

4 …………………… :

- Marketing Manager, Disney, Japan – responsible for "Winnie the Pooh" account;
- Marketing assistant, Coca-Cola, Japan;
- Translated marketing documents for various British and US companies.

Education:
Seisen International School; Tokyo University;
5 ……………………
Currently doing an online MBA.

6 ……………………
I love projects that combine my language skills with my experience in marketing. I am interested in cross-cultural issues and in fun or exciting marketing projects. You can see some examples of my work by clicking on the links below.

2 Answer the questions.

1 What kind of work is Mitsuko interested in? ……………………

2 What languages can she speak? ……………………

3 How would you describe her level of education? ……………………

3 Writing skill writing in note form

a Look at these shortened phrases from the profile and put them into full sentences.

1 advising US supermarket on market plan for Japan
……………………

2 responsible for "Winnie the Pooh" account
……………………

3 translated marketing documents for various British and US companies
……………………

4 currently doing an online MBA
……………………

b The personal profile below has no shortened phrases. Find the places where it would be appropriate to use them and rewrite the sentences in a shortened form.

Harry Ross

I am a specialist website designer
……………………

Current: I am designing an interactive website for a local sports and recreation center.
……………………

Work history: I used to work for a large telecommunications company as a computer programmer. Afterwards I worked for a local hospital designing their patient communications website. I set up my own company in 2010.
……………………
……………………
……………………

Education: I went to the University of California Davis.
……………………
……………………

Wordbuilding verb (+ preposition) + noun collocations

1 In each of these groups, one of the verbs does NOT collocate with the noun on the right. Put a line through this verb.

1	follow/do/have	a career
2	make/take/attend	a class
3	acquire/learn/get	a skill
4	take/make/pass	an exam
5	get/earn/acquire	promotion
6	gain/win/get	experience
7	own/have/nurture	a talent
8	do/work/get	a job
9	gain/earn/get	a qualification
10	join/set up/take on	a company

2 Complete the description of someone's career by putting an appropriate verb in each space.

When I was 19 I [1] .... a test to get into a drama school in New York, but I was unsuccessful. At that point, I had to decide whether to try to [2] .... a career in acting or just abandon the idea and [3] .... a completely different kind of job. All my friends told me that I [4] .... a natural talent for acting and that I didn't need to [5] .... a qualification to prove it. So instead, I [6] .... a small theater company and [7] .... experience acting that way. Just by working with other actors I was able to [8] .... new skills and two years ago I was asked by the National Theater to perform in a production of Shakespeare's *The Tempest*. I have never looked back!

Learning skills the language of learning

3 When you learn a language, you often need to ask questions about it. Look at the terms (1–8). Then match the terms with the definitions (a–h).

1 a part of speech
2 past participle
3 an idiom
4 a colloquial expression
5 a false friend
6 a collocation
7 register
8 a euphemism

a two words that naturally go together
b a phrase whose meaning is not clear from the individual words it is composed of
c the level of formality
d e.g., noun, verb, adjective, adverb, preposition
e a word that looks similar in two languages but has different meanings
f the third form of the verb, e.g., go, went, gone
g a word or phrase that expresses an idea more politely or gently
h a phrase used in everyday informal speech

4 Answer these questions about words from Unit 9.

1 What is the past participle of *feel*? ....
2 What part of speech is *the*? ....
3 What verb collocates with *knowledge*? ....
4 Is *grab someone's attention* an idiom? ....
5 What register is the online profile on page 56 of the Workbook? ....

Check!

5 Answer these questions. You can find all the answers in Student Book Unit 9.

1 What are these people's jobs?

 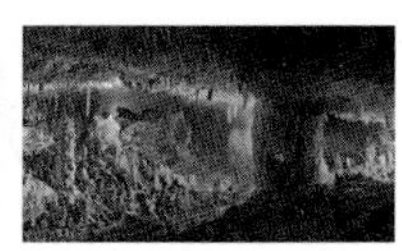

a .... b ....

2 Complete this famous quote by Neil Armstrong.

"That's one small .... for man, one giant .... for ...."

3 Which of these places have *the* in front of them?

a .... Atlantic Ocean
b .... Korea
c .... Florida
d .... USA
e .... Moon

4 What type of clause is the underlined clause in the quotation?

a a defining relative clause
b a non-defining relative clause
c a reduced relative clause

"Kira Salak, known as the real-life Lara Croft, doesn't want to tell travel stories you have already heard."

Unit 10 Customs and behavior

10a Child behavior

Grammar habitual actions: present tenses, *will*

1 Complete the short passages about growing up and child behavior. Use the present simple, present continuous, and *will*.

1
Some parents [1] ________ (take) their children out of school because they [2] ________ (think) that they are not being challenged enough. These parents then [3] ________ (teach) their children at home, giving them structured lessons each day. Some [4] ________ (follow) a curriculum specially written for home schooling, others [5] ________ (design) their own curriculum of lessons and activities.

2
Parents complain that their children [6] ________ (always / fight) and [7] ________ (squabble). It is of course the case that most children do this when they are young. Even older siblings [8] ________ (argue) and fight as they struggle for their parents' approval. But psychologists [9] ________ (say) that this is normal behavior and it [10] ________ (help) to prepare them for other relationships later in life.

3
There is quite a lot of literature written about the personality traits of children according to their birth order. First-borns [11] ________ (tend) to be model children: conscientious and reliable and high-achievers. They [12] ________ (generally / follow) a career that their parents approve of and [13] ________ (be) successful at it. Middle children are more difficult to catergorize, but they [14] ________ (always / follow) a different path from their elder brother or sister. Last-borns are sociable and fun-loving and [15] ________ (often / get) all the attention when in a group.

2 Look at these examples of annoying behavior. Complete the sentences using the present continuous with *always* of the verbs.

ask leave play spend ~~talk~~ talk

1 A girl is on her cell phone all the time.
She*'s always talking* to her friends on the phone.

2 In the car, a young boy says: "Are we nearly there yet?"
He ________ we're nearly there yet.

3 A teenage girl spends ages in the bathroom so no one else in the family can get in.
She ________ in the bathroom.

4 At mealtimes, a young boy never swallows his food before speaking.
He ________ with his mouth full.

5 A teenage boy is obsessed with computer games.
He ________ computer games.

6 A young girl never tidies her bedroom up.
She ________ her room in a mess.

10b Globalization of the food market

Grammar *used to, usually, be used to,* and *get used to*

1 Read about a person living 100 years ago. Which of the underlined verbs can be replaced with *used to, would,* or *was/were used to*? Write the alternative.

"We [1] didn't cook on a stove, because we didn't have one. We [2] cooked everything over a fire. For example, if we [3] wanted to cook sausages, we [4] hung them on hooks over the fire. But if it [5] was a special occasion and we had a lot of things to cook, then we had to take it down the road to the hotel that [6] had a proper oven and for a few pennies they [7] cooked it for us. It seems strange now, but we [8] did that whenever all the family got around the table."

1 *didn't use to cook*
2 ....
3 ....
4 ....
5 ....
6 ....
7 ....
8 ....

Vocabulary food types

2 Look at what these people ate for lunch. Which of the following did they have? Write staple food (S), dairy product (D), processed food (P), and fresh fruit and vegetables (F).

1 **Simone**
cheese sandwich ....
bag of chips ....

2 **Pilar**
mixed salad ....
grapes ....
can of soda ....

3 **David**
rice and stir-fried vegetables ....
instant coffee with milk ....

4 **Ivan**
hamburger and French fries ....
strawberry milkshake ....

Vocabulary review raising children: verbs

3 Complete the sentences using the correct verbs. The first letter has been given for you.

My father worked overseas for most of my childhood so we were [1] **b**.......... up by my mother. When he came home, he used to [2] **s**.......... us, buying us presents and taking us out. He never [3] **p**.......... us if we were naughty, because he wanted enjoy to his time with us. He left it to my mom to [4] **d**.......... us. That was tough on her, because we used to [5] **d**.......... her often—playing outside when she had told us not to.

It's difficult to be a single parent raising your children alone. You are always [6] **n**.......... them to do things, when really you want to enjoy the time you have with them.

It isn't easy being a parent. My own kids are always [8] **p**.......... me to buy them things that other children have, but I try not to [9] **g**.......... in to these demands. Of course when they do something good, I might [10] **r**.......... them with a present, but I don't want them to be spoiled!

10c Body language

Reading Desmond Morris

Desmond Morris studied to be a zoologist and in that capacity, he observed the behavior of many different species of animals. However, his lifelong interest has been human rather than animal behavior, and unlike the traditional experts in human behavior—the psychologist, the sociologist, and the anthropologist—he is not so interested in what people say, but rather in what they do. In fact, he gives little attention to human speech because he feels that human actions tell us far more about people than anything they might say. Indeed, it is said that in human communication, as much as 90% is non-verbal.

In an interview, Morris gave a fascinating example of this. The non-verbal communication that he described was called "postural echo" and this is how he explained it. Morris and the journalist were sitting discussing Morris's work in a radio studio. They were both sitting down facing each other across a table. Both had one forearm resting on the table and the other forearm upright with their chin resting on one hand. Both were leaning forward interestedly as they talked to each other. They had adopted what Morris called postural echo: that is to say, because they had a common interest, they were imitating each other's posture. This particular posture I've just described is typical when people are showing interest in what they are hearing.

In another situation, though, such postural echo might be totally inappropriate. The example Morris gave was that of a job interview. Imagine you are being interviewed for a job and the boss who is interviewing you sits back in his chair and puts his feet up on a stool. His posture is showing that he is in a relaxed and dominant position. Your posture, on the other hand, should show that you are in a subordinate position: in other words you should be sitting upright, perhaps leaning forward a little to show interest, with your hands on your lap. If you were to echo his posture, it would send the message that you felt as relaxed as him and he is not hiring another boss—he is looking for a subordinate. At best, you would not get the job; at worst, the boss would find it very insulting and end the interview immediately.

1 Based on the article about the work of Desmond Morris, are the sentences true (T) or false (F)?

1 Desmond Morris studied as a zoologist and a psychologist.
2 More than 90% of human communication is made using speech.
3 The first example describes the body language of Desmond Morris and journalist.
4 Postural echo involves imitating someone's facial expressions.
5 In the second situation, it would be right to use postural echo.
6 Leaning back in your chair shows that you feel in control.

2 Look at the diagrams and answer the questions.

1 In the first situation, how are Desmond Morris and the journalist sitting? Choose the correct diagram.
2 How should the boss and the interviewee be sitting? Choose the correct diagram.

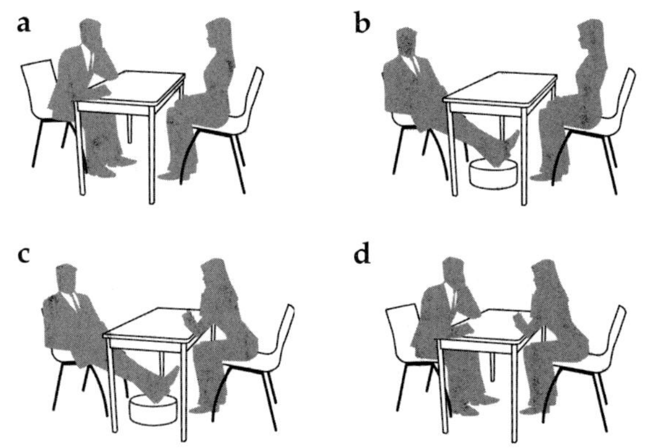

3 Choose the correct option to complete the sentences. Then read the article again and check.

1 Morris's lifelong interest has been human *more / rather* than animal behavior.
2 *Unlike / As* the traditional experts in human behavior, he is not so interested in what people say, but rather in what they do.
3 In fact, he gives *few / little* attention to human speech.
4 In another situation, though, *that / such* postural echo might be inappropriate.
5 *The worst / At worst*, the boss would find it deeply insulting.

10d Wedding customs

Vocabulary weddings

1 Write the words for these definitions.

1 a post-wedding vacation ....
2 promises the couple make to each other ....
3 a pre-wedding party for men only is a ".......... party"
4 a covering for the bride's face ....
5 what you hear when a wedding is approaching ....
6 the man on his wedding day ....
7 an offer of marriage ....

Real life describing traditions

2 Read the description of the custom of dowry-giving and answer the questions.

Dowry-giving, the gift of money from one family to another on the occasion of a marriage, is still common in certain parts of the world. It symbolizes different things. For example, it can be a sign of wealth and increase social status. It can have a historical and practical meaning: as a rule, in the past, brides did not work, so this was her financial contribution to the marriage. It's customary for a dowry to be given by the bride's family to the groom's family, but it can work the other way around, as in Nigeria, where a small dowry is given by the groom's family.

The engagement ceremony in Nigeria marks the beginning of the wedding celebrations and is an occasion for people to celebrate and have fun before the official ceremony, and also to give gifts to the couple. It takes place on the evening or a couple of nights before the wedding itself. During the party, there's a lot of music, often played by a live band, and dancing. It used to be traditional for money to be thrown at the couple's feet while they danced, but now people usually bring regular wedding gifts. After the party, the groom's family delivers a kind of dowry to the bride's family's house in the form of a gift of traditional clothes and jewelry. It's not the last time the groom has to visit the bride's house. On the night of the wedding, after the reception party is finished, the bride goes back to her own house where she waits until she's claimed by the groom and taken to their new home.

1 What is a big dowry a sign of?
....
2 What did the dowry act as compensation for?
....
3 Which family normally gives the dowry?
....
4 Which family gives the dowry in Nigeria?
....
5 What do the guests at a Nigerian engagement party do, as well as dancing and having fun?
....
6 What two things does a Nigerian dowry consist of?
....

3 Complete the sentences with the words in the box. Then read again and check.

customary marks occasion on place rule symbolizes traditional

1 Dowry-giving .... different things, for example, a sign of wealth.
2 As a ...., in the past, brides did not work.
3 It's .... for a dowry to be given by the bride's family.
4 The engagement ceremony in Nigeria .... the beginning of the wedding celebrations.
5 The ceremony is an .... for people to have fun.
6 It takes .... on the evening or a couple of nights before the wedding itself.
7 It used to be .... for money to be thrown at the couple's feet.
8 .... the night of the wedding, the bride goes back to her own house.

10e Cultural differences

1 Writing skill **elision in informal writing**

Read the formal email (1) and the informal version (2). There are 16 differences. Find and underline as many as you can.

1

Dear Annabelle,

It was very good to see you the other day. I hope you had a safe journey back to Leipzig. I forgot to mention that I am traveling to Poland next month on business to visit a supplier. I am unfamiliar with business customs in Poland and wondered if there was anything that I ought to be particularly aware of. For example, should I take some gifts with me? Will they be offended that I do not speak any Polish? I certainly do not want to offend my hosts in any way.

I do not want to inconvenience you, but if you have a moment to write a few words of advice, I would be most grateful.

With kind regards,
Paul

2

Hi Annabelle,

Very good to see you the other day. Hope you got back to Leipzig safely. I forgot to mention that I'm traveling to Poland next month on business to visit a supplier. I have no idea about business customs in Poland and wondered if there was anything special I should know. For example, should I take some gifts with me? Will they be put out that I don't speak any Polish? I certainly don't want to seem rude to my hosts in any way.

I don't want to bother you, but if you've got a moment to write a few words of advice, I'd be really grateful.

Best,
Paul

Writing an informal email

2 Look at Annabelle's reply. Rewrite the underlined words and phrases so that they are in a more informal style.

[1] Dear Paul

[2] I enjoyed seeing you also and [3] thank you very much for [4] assisting me with my resume. [5] I regret to say I don't know very much about Polish business customs but [6] here is a little advice.

A small gift—a souvenir of your city perhaps—would be appreciated, I think. But [7] do not give them anything too [8] substantial as that would [9] cause embarrassment for them. [10] You will find that Polish business people [11] appear to be quite formal at a first meeting. [12] That is perfectly normal. Just spend time getting to know them and I [13] have no doubt that [14] they will relax.
[15] Regarding the language, "Milo mi" means [16] "It is nice to meet you" and "Dziekuje" means "Thank you."

[17] I hope it all goes well. Do [18] inform me about it [19] when you return.

[20] Yours sincerely,

Annabelle

1	....	11	....
2	....	12	....
3	....	13	....
4	....	14	....
5	....	15	....
6	....	16	....
7	....	17	....
8	....	18	....
9	....	19	....
10	....	20	....

Wordbuilding word pairs

1 Make matching pairs. Match the words in box A with their "partners" in box B.

A bride husband friends suit food singing plans formality fun

B arrangements dancing drink ceremony family games groom tie wife

2 Complete the sentences with matching pairs from Exercise 1.

1 We wanted a simple wedding, without the ________ of a normal wedding.

2 It was a small wedding. We just invited a few ________ .

3 The woman usually wears a white dress and the man wears a ________ .

Learning skills making full use of your teacher

3 Use your teacher as a resource. Read these tips to help improve your English.

1 Pay attention to the way your teacher pronounces words and phrases and try to imitate them.

2 Every teacher uses certain idiomatic phrases and expressions. Ask them what they mean.

3 Ask the teacher to correct your mistakes, particularly your pronunciation. Even teachers can feel shy about doing this.

4 Ask your teacher what they think your main fault in English is and how you can correct it.

5 Tell your teacher what kinds of books you like to read and ask them to recommend some in English.

6 Make sure that you have the vocabulary you need (e.g., to describe your job). Ask your teacher to supply these words.

4 Answer these questions. Then check with your teacher. Does your teacher agree with you?

1 Can you pronounce these words from Unit 10?
a disobey
b dairy
c future

2 Which one of these do you think you have most difficulty with?
a using the right tense
b lack of vocabulary
c pronouncing things correctly

3 What can you do well in English?
a study
b communicate at work
c get around in a foreign country

Check!

5 Complete these phrasal verbs and idiomatic phrases. You can find all the answers in Student Book Unit 10.

Quiz Time

1 Try not to give ________ to all your children's demands. (preposition)

2 We don't eat ________ much these days because restaurants are so expensive. (preposition)

3 Parents who are very relaxed and laid-________ don't push their children to be high achievers. (preposition)

4 Sarah and I have a lot ________ common. (preposition)

5 Bringing up children is complicated, but if you use your common ________ you won't go far wrong. (noun)

6 We didn't agree at first, but in the end we found some common ________ . (noun)

Unit 11 Knowledge and learning

11a Conserving languages

Reading enduring voices

1 Read a description of the work of Dr. K. David Harrison and the Enduring Voices team at National Geographic.

Dr. K. David Harrison believes that language diversity is just as important as biodiversity. He's part of a National Geographic project called "Enduring Voices," whose aim is to document languages which are little known and in danger of becoming extinct. It's estimated that over half the world's 7,000 languages will disappear by 2050 and so the race is on to trace and record these languages, and also to help keep them alive.

Diversity does not depend on the size of a territory or country. In Bolivia, which only has a population of twelve million, there are 37 different languages, belonging to eighteen language families. This is the same number as the whole of Europe.

Dr. Harrison seeks out these language "hotspots"—places where there is a great diversity of languages spoken and where some are in danger. Studies in the Oklahoma region of the US succeeded in discovering 26 languages, one of which, Yuchi, had as few as seven speakers. By highlighting this fact, researchers were able to help the community to keep this dying language alive.

2 Complete the sentences from the description using the correct form of these verbs.

document   record   seek out   trace

1 He is part of a National Geographic project called Enduring Voices, whose aim is to ________ languages which are little known.
2 The race is on to ________ and ________ these languages.
3 Dr. Harrison ________ these language hotspots.

Grammar *could, was able to, manage to,* and *succeed in*

3 Complete the sentences about learning a language using *could, was/were able to, manage to,* or *succeed in* and the verb in brackets. Sometimes more than one answer is possible.

1 The video I got was in Turkish, but I ________ (find) English subtitles on the main menu.
2 My sister is an amazing linguist: she ________ (speak) four languages fluently by the time she was twelve.
3 Esperanto was invented to be a world language, but supporters of it ________ (never / convince) enough people to use it.
4 When I first moved to New York, I ________ (not / understand) native speakers because they seemed to mumble when they spoke.
5 I had a friend who was brought up speaking three different languages, but I was never sure if he ________ (express) himself clearly in any of them!
6 I spent eight years learning Italian, but when I tried to use it a couple of years ago, I found that I ________ (remember) the grammar but not the vocabulary.

Vocabulary learning

4 Match the expressions (1–8) with the correct definition (a–h).

1 pick up	a become involved in
2 take in	b not know about
3 learn by trial and error	c learn as you go along
4 inspire	d understand simply
5 have a basic grasp of	e know about
6 engage with	f absorb
7 be ignorant	g motivate
8 be aware of	h learn by making mistakes

5 Complete the sentences using a verb or expression from Exercise 3.

1 Don't worry about explaining. I'm sure I'll ________ it ________.
2 She's a great teacher. She really knows how to ________ her students.

11b Memory loss

Reading memory loss

1 Read about two types of memory loss.

1 Prosopamnesia

Prosopamnesia is an inability to remember faces. It is something that many people have in a mild form, but in severe cases sufferers can forget the faces of even close friends or associates. People can be born with this syndrome or it can be acquired during their lives.

Philippa's story: "I'm terrible at remembering faces. I recall being at a conference at UC Berkeley in California and another academic came up and started chatting to me. I would have asked his name, but knowing my inability to remember faces I didn't in case he was someone I was supposed to know. Anyway, it turned out that we had a friend and colleague in common. 'Oh yes, I know William Child,' I said. 'We collaborated on a research project last year. He came to dinner at my house many times. How do you know him?' 'I am William Child,' the man replied."

2 Source amnesia

Also called "memory distrust syndrome," source amnesia occurs when a person is unable to recall the context in which they learned about something. Subconsciously, they then attribute the fact to some other, usually reliable, source. This can happen when the real source is not reliable and the person very much wants to believe that the fact is true.

Jon's story: "I work as a lawyer, and in my line of work I often come across people who have persuaded themselves of a version of events that may not be true. I had a witness who was going to give evidence in court that her neighbor had thrown a brick at her car. She clearly believed that this had happened, and was determined that her neighbor wasn't going to get away with it. But it turned out that it was not her own memory of events, but what another neighbor had told her."

Grammar future in the past

2 There are four examples of the "future in the past" forms in the text. Underline the examples. Which of the other future in the past forms could be used in each case?

was/were about to do	was/were going to	
was supposed to	would do	would have done

1 ....

2 ....

3 ....

4 ....

3 Complete the sentences using a future in the past form. Sometimes more than one form is possible.

1 "I'm so sorry. I .... (write) you a letter, but I lost your address."

2 "I promised her I .... (speak) to my boss about finding her a job, but I forgot."

3 "I .... (take) my driving test sooner, but I didn't feel ready."

4 "That's funny. I .... (just / ask) you exactly the same question."

11c Intelligent animals

Reading

1 Match the name of the animal with the correct picture.

Bonobo ape	border collie
crow	dolphin

1 ....

2 ....

3 ....

4 ....

2 Read a description of four intelligent animals. Write the number of the description (1–4) next to the intelligent behavior that this type of animal is known for.

1 Meg is a border collie, a smart breed of dog used by farmers because they understand instructions well and they like to be helpful. Their usual job is to round up and direct sheep. You can show Meg a picture of a toy and tell her its name (like a duck or a frisbee), then ask her to go and find it in a room full of toys. Once she has found it once and learned the name, all you have to do the next time is to ask her to fetch the the duck or the frisbee from the room and she will go and find it.

2 Betty is a New Caledonian crow. These animals are pretty inventive tool makers. In the wild, they use sticks, for example, to get insects out of trees. But what they found in the lab was that these birds were able to make tools from materials that they had never used before. Experimenters placed a piece of meat in a little basket and put it in a tube. Betty looked at the problem, then found a straight piece of wire, bent it into the shape of a hook using her beak and lifted the basket from the tube.

3 Maya is a dolphin. I think most people know that dolphins have incredible imitative abilities. They can see an action performed and then repeat it when ordered to. They also seem to understand spoken directions from humans very well. So you can get two of them to leap out of the water and turn a somersault at the same time. But in fact they do these kinds of synchronized tricks in the wild anyway, because they're naturally playful creatures, but no one really understands how they communicate with each other to get the timing so perfect.

4 Kanzi is a Bonobo ape who has been taught sign language so that he can communicate with humans. One anecdote about his intelligence is that on a walk in the woods, Kanzi indicated that he wanted marshmallows and a fire. He was given the marshmallows and some matches. He found some twigs, broke them into pieces, built a fire, lit it with the matches, and then, most amazingly, toasted the marshmallows on a stick over the fire. Bonobos are known for being expressive and good communicators, but even experts who study them were surprised by this behavior.

a They are good at copying what they see. ☐

b They are good at communicating. ☐

c They like to follow instructions. ☐

d They make implements to get different jobs done. ☐

3 Match the words from the descriptions with the adjectives below (1–4).

inventive	smart	expressive	playful

1 intelligent ....

2 creative ....

3 fun-loving ....

4 communicative ....

Word focus *learn*

4 Complete the sentences using expressions with *learn*.

1 You have to learn to w.................. before you can run.

2 It's never too l.................. to learn.

3 In life, you have to learn from your m.................. .

4 I learned a few t.................. of the trade.

5 Never again. I've learned my l.................. .

6 Just learn to l.................. with it!

7 I learned the hard w.................. .

8 I've learned the whole poem by h.................. .

11d Ask the teacher

Real life **getting clarification**

1 Complete these phrases with the correct verb.

1 What do you ________ by "difficult"?
2 Can you ________ up a little? I can't hear you.
3 Can you ________ what the test at the end of the course covers?
4 I'm sorry. I ________ not really with you.
5 Are you ________ that learning the historical dates isn't important?
6 Could you ________ me an example of an important historian of the last century?
7 There's a lot of information to ________ in.
8 I didn't ________ that last word. Can you repeat it?

2 Read a conversation between a student and a teacher. Answer the questions.

Student: Hi, have you got a minute? I just wanted to ask a bit more about what you covered in class.

Teacher: Sure, how can I help?

Student: Well, I don't really have the same background knowledge as some of the other students.

Teacher: Don't worry. I think a lot of people find it difficult at first. Things will become clearer.

Student: Well, can you explain what the course is going to be about, because I thought it was going to be about Roman history mainly.

Teacher: Well, it's a mixture of Greek, mainly Hellenistic, and Roman history.

Student: Sorry, I didn't catch that word. Helle-something?

Teacher: Hellenistic. Alexander the Great and so on.

Student: Oh, yeah... OK. And are you saying that no previous knowledge of ancient history is needed?

Teacher: Well, a little understanding of the geography of the Eastern Mediterranean is helpful, and if you've heard or read some Greek myths and legends, it helps too.

Student: Sorry, I'm not really with you. You mean stories like the Trojan War and so on?

Teacher: Exactly.

Student: OK, well could you give me an example of a book I could read now, outside class?

Teacher: Um, you could have a look at some texts by Herodotus. He was a historian of the 5th century BC and his histories read more like good adventure stories!

Student: Did you say Herodotus?

Teacher: That's right, H-E-R-O-D-O-T-U-S.

Student: OK, thanks. I'll do that.

1 What is the subject?
____
____

2 What is the student worried about?
____
____

3 What does the teacher recommend?
____
____

3 Grammar extra **verbs with indirect objects**

> **▶ VERBS WITH INDIRECT OBJECTS**
>
> Some verbs, e.g., *tell* and *show*, can be followed by an indirect personal object. Other verbs, e.g., *say* and *explain*, don't always need an indirect personal object. If you use an indirect personal object with these verbs, you must put *to* before the object.
>
> *He told **me** about the history course.*
> *I showed **him** a copy of the lecture notes.*
> *They explained **(to me)** that I could find the reading list online.*

Look at the sentences below and write the pronoun *me* where necessary.

1 Can you tell ________ how many hours of study we're expected to do each week?
2 Do you recommend ________ that I should read Stephen Hawking's book?
3 She said ________ that I could get most of the books from the library.
4 She also explained ________ that the library was open until 10 p.m.
5 Can you show ________ how that works?
6 He taught ________ that I didn't always need to write such long essays.

11e A letter to a college

Writing an email about a misunderstanding

1 Match the two parts of the sentences about a misunderstanding over an application for a course. What seems to be the problem according to the writer?

1 The website said the deadline for applications was August 20.
2 Despite the fact that my application arrived in time,
3 I am not someone who does things at the last minute.
4 While I appreciate that you have a lot of applicants,
5 Whereas most colleges seem to select applicants on the merits of their application,

a you choose people on a "first come, first served" basis.
b I cannot understand why you have chosen to ignore those people who applied after July.
c In fact, I sent in my application at the end of July.
d I am always careful to meet deadlines.
e I was told that I had missed the deadline.

2 Writing skill linking contrasting ideas

Rewrite these sentences from the reply to the applicant's letter using the words given.

1 We sympathize with your situation, but it is too late to do anything about it now. (while)

....

....

2 Despite the fact that you sent your form in before the deadline, we had already received too many applications. (although)

....

....

3 You say in your letter that we have no right to do this, but the college has the right to close the application process early. (in actual fact)

....

....

4 Most colleges would keep your application fee, but we are refunding it to you. (whereas)

....

....

3 Look at the notes and write a letter to a college. Include the following points.

a Reason for writing: you can't attend the accounting class this semester.
b Misunderstanding: you thought it was an evening class, but it's during the day.
c Effort on your part: your company would like to give you time off, but they can't.
d Apology: probably your mistake, but these things happen.
e Action required: want the college to refund the money paid for the class.

Dear Sir / Madam:

a ....

....

....

b ....

....

....

c ....

....

....

d ....

....

....

e ....

....

....

I look forward to ....

....

Sincerely, ...

Wordbuilding **idiomatic expressions**

1 Read the story. What do the idiomatic expressions in bold (1–6) mean? Match the idiomatic expressions with the definitions (a–f).

> I don't know when [1] **it first dawned on me** that it would be a good idea to grow my own vegetables. I know [2] **it struck me** some time ago that vegetables in the grocery store were getting very expensive. [3] **It occurred to me** that if more people grew their own, we wouldn't have to import so many. I [4] **didn't have a clue** about growing plants, but then I read a fantastic book written by woman called Joy Larkcom. The book really [5] **opened my eyes.** That was six years ago and it has become more than a hobby. [6] **It never crossed my mind** that I would become an expert, but now a lot of neighbors come and ask me for my advice.

a I had a strong impression ....
b helped me to see the truth ....
c was ignorant ....
d I realized ....
e I had the idea ....
f I didn't ever think ....

Learning skills **techniques for memorizing**

2 People remember things in different ways. Some remember better by hearing (auditory learners), some by seeing (visual learners), and some by doing or by action (kinesthetic learners). It is important to know how you remember things. What do you remember of the following items in Unit 11?

1 Maria Fadiman's work on conservation of plants. ....
2 How *could* is different from *managed to.* ....
3 The intelligence of Alex, the gray parrot. ....
4 Useful phrases for checking understanding. ....
5 Idiomatic expressions containing the word *learn.* ....

3 How did you remember the information? Was it through something:
a you heard? b you saw? c you did?

4 Look at these tips for memorizing. Check (✓) the one(s) you feel suit you best.

a **Auditory**: Record five words that you need to learn, putting each into a sentence. Then listen to them again last thing at night.
b **Visual**: Draw a picture of the words that you need to learn. Look at the pictures the following day and see if you can remember the words.
c **Kinesthetic**: Work with another student and simulate a situation that illustrates the meaning of the word. Or think of an action that would help you remember the word.

5 Try to memorize these words and expressions from Unit 11 using the tips in Exercise 4.

absorb grasp gut feeling learn your lesson a misunderstanding

Check!

6 Complete the crossword.

Across
1 Maria Fadiman's stories help students to .... with the subject (6)
5 a .... memory remembers only what it wants (9)
7 another word for advice (8)
8 the opposite of your "internal" memory (8)
10 "Sorry I didn't .... your name." (5)

Down
2 if you understand something in a simple way, you have "a basic ...." of it (5)
3 you can .... *in doing* something (7)
4 a person who studies plants (8)
6 the opposite of knowing is being .... (8)
8 one way of learning is by trial and .... (5)
9 "It's never too .... to learn."

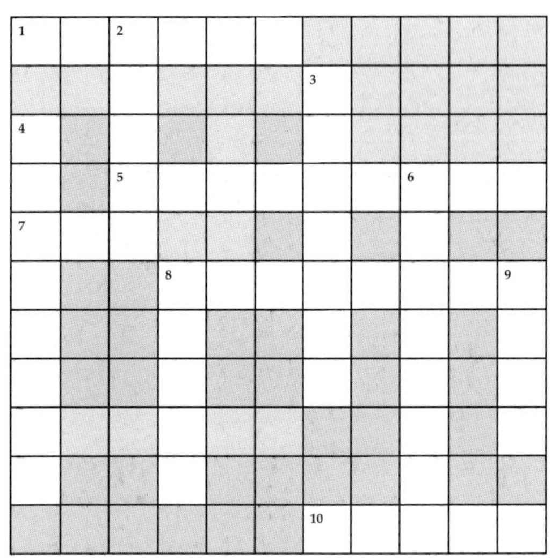

Unit 12 The economy

12a Economics

Vocabulary rich and poor

1 Find and circle the words in the word search that mean the following:

1 poor
2 have enough money
3 inexpensive (2 words)
4 expensive
5 income
6 comfortable
7 very rich

R	H	P	I	M	O	I	N
E	A	R	N	I	N	G	S
A	R	I	C	C	F	O	T
S	D	C	H	E	A	P	O
O	U	E	S	O	F	U	L
N	P	Y	B	A	F	L	E
A	W	E	L	L	O	F	F
B	I	L	E	F	R	A	T
L	O	A	D	E	D	E	S
E	S	T	O	N	R	I	A

Grammar focus adverbs *only, just, even, too, as well, also*

2 Complete the sentences with these adverbs. Sometimes more than one adverb is possible.

also as well even just only too

1 Let's .... consider people's attitude to money at its simplest level.
2 Of course, savers spend money ...., but .... when they can afford it.
3 People in these countries would have to work longer hours, pay more taxes, and .... accept lower wages.
4 You risk losing the money but you .... risk putting the borrower in a difficult situation.
5 We need both types of person, but .... if they lend and borrow responsibly.

3 Write the focus adverbs in the correct place in the sentences.

1 Some people believe that if you go through life saving money, you will never have any fun. ONLY
2 Some people keep spending money when they can't afford to. EVEN
3 You can guard against bad times by putting aside a small amount of money each week. JUST
4 If a few people save money, the banks won't have any to lend. ONLY
5 I'm not the only person who has debts. Other people have them. ALSO
6 Attitude to money is partly a cultural thing, but it has something to do with your upbringing. AS WELL
7 Some people are careful with money in hard times and in good times. TOO
8 Borrowers admit that they sometimes borrow money irresponsibly. EVEN

Vocabulary money

4 Complete these sentences with the correct noun. Use the verbs in brackets to help you.

1 To buy the car, I had to make .... of $90 a month for five years. (pay)
2 We need to cut back on our .... because the cost of living has become so high. (spend)
3 They say that gold is a good .... right now. (invest)
4 We took out a .... from the bank to finance the purchase of our apartment. (lend)
5 If you can't afford college tuition, then the government gives you a .... (give)
6 We wanted to increase our .... so that we could build an extension on our house. (borrow)
7 The public .... of the US are counted in trillions of dollars rather than billions. (debt)
8 Public sector workers are protesting because their .... have been frozen for the last two years. (earn)

12b Cheap labor

Reading the slave economy

The history of successful industries has always been a story of cheap labor. Clearly, if you can get people to work for very little, your business will be more profitable. Even in more recent times, you can track the movement of industry—textiles and tuna canning are two striking examples—to the places where the work can be done more cheaply.

But imagine the profits if your laborers work for nothing. In other words, if you use slaves as the European colonial powers of the 16th to the 19th centuries did. Those countries that had colonized the Americas became dependent on slave labor for their survival. Colonial officials believed that the land they had "discovered" in the Americas was useless without sufficient labor to exploit it. However, since there were not sufficient European or Native American workers, large numbers of African people were captured and transported to the Americas to work.

The trans-Saharan slave trade had long supplied slaves from central Africa to work on sugar plantations in the Mediterranean. Having proved themselves competent workers in Europe, enslaved Africans became the labor force of choice in colonial America.

1 Find words or expressions in the article with the following meanings.

1 follow (para 1) ____________

2 making a strong impression (para 1) ____________

3 enough (para 2) ____________

4 good at one's job (para 3) ____________

5 favored or preferred (para 3) ____________

Grammar causative *have* and *get*

2 Put the words in parentheses into the right form to complete these sentences.

1 It's evident that if you can ____________ (have / people / work) for very little money, your business is going to be more profitable.

2 Companies are always searching for a country where they can ____________ (get / their work / do) more cheaply.

3 Imagine how much more profitable it is if you ____________ (get / your laborers / work) for nothing.

4 The traders who sent slaves to the Mediterranean also ____________ (have / 10,000 slaves a year / send) to serve owners in America.

5 The slave owners ____________ (get / the slaves / work) first on the sugar plantations, then on tobacco plantations.

6 On the plantations, the owners ____________ (have / their slaves / work) as butlers, waiters, maids, etc.

7 In urban areas, their owners ____________ (get / them / learn) various trades.

8 In the 19th century, the British textile industry ____________ (have / cheap cotton / ship) over from America.

Vocabulary domestic jobs

3 Complete the sentences about repairs to a house. The first letter of each verb has been given.

1 We need to get someone to f____________ this carpet. The shape of the room is so irregular.

2 I've asked John to p____________ up some new shelves in the living room. He's a professional carpenter.

3 I think we can d____________ the room ourselves. We don't need to have it done by a professional painter.

4 The kitchen units came in pieces and I had to a____________ them by myself. It took me about seven hours.

5 Can you call a roofer? The roof's still leaking and we need to get it f____________ .

6 You know that guy who t____________ our bathroom walls—he did a terrible job. There are cracks everywhere.

7 Do you know anyone who can p____________ a ceiling? We have cracks in our living room and I'm worried the ceiling's going to come down.

8 Can you help me to h____________ this picture on the wall?

12c The world of barter

Word focus *hard*

1 Complete the text using an expression with *hard*. There are two extra expressions.

hard bargain hard work hard feelings hard up
hard-headed hard luck

If you are [1] ________ and short of cash, then barter, or trading, may be a good solution for you. You don't have to be a [2] ________ business person to make it work, because exchanges are done in a spirit of cooperation. In direct barter, the negotiation is friendly and there is no question of trying to drive a [3] ________. So there are never any [4] ________ between the barterers, with one person feeling they have "won" in the deal and the other feeling cheated.

2 **Grammar extra *hard* and *hardly***

> ▶ ***HARD* and *HARDLY***
>
> The adjective *hard* has two different adverb forms: *hard* and *hardly*.
> *I'm trying **hard** to see the advantage of it.* (I'm making a big effort.)
> *It **hardly** seems worth the effort.* (It's almost NOT worth the effort.)
>
> Note the position of the *hard* and *hardly* in relation to the verb.

Look at the grammar box. Then complete the sentences using *hard* and *hardly* and the verbs in the correct form.

1 runs / hard
  a He ________. He'll be in good shape if he manages to keep it up.
  b He ________. It's more of a walk.
2 works / hard
  a She ________ now. She goes in to the office once a week, I think.
  b She ________ now. She has a new boss who's very demanding.
3 know / hard
  I ________ him. We've met twice, I think.
4 thought / hard
  a I ________ about it. It wasn't an easy decision.
  b I ________ about work when I was away on vacation.
5 tried / hard
  a The team ________. It was as if they didn't care.
  b The team ________, but they weren't good enough to win.

3 Look at these DIY jobs and match each one with the professional who does it.

1 fixing a leaky faucet
2 rewiring a house
3 cutting the grass
4 demolishing a wall
5 hanging a new front door
6 painting the outside of a house

a a gardener
b a plumber
c a carpenter
d a general builder
e a painter
f an electrician

12d Organizing an event

Real life negotiating

1 Match the expressions (1–6) with phrases with the same meaning (a–f).

1	to be honest	a	in your shoes
2	the key thing	b	what's important
3	let's face it	c	when all's said and done
4	if I were you	d	to tell you the truth
5	at the end of the day	e	you have to understand
6	you have to appreciate	f	be realistic

2 Read a conversation between two people in a negotiation and answer the questions.

Client: So there'll be about 60 of us. We want some food but nothing too fancy. I suspect a lot of people will be going home and having supper later anyway.
Caterer: OK, so what did you have in mind? A few appetizers, some sandwiches?
Client: Well, I was hoping we could have something a little more exciting than sandwiches.
Caterer: Perhaps if we prepared some sushi, some smoked salmon…
Client: Yes, that would be much more like it. Is that going to be very pricey?
Caterer: About $15 per person.
Client: Mmm...that's expensive, but it is an important occasion. You know, it's a going away party for someone who's been working with us for 37 years, so we don't want it looking cheap.
Caterer: I think that's a good way to look at it. If I were in your shoes, I'd like to put on an event that people would remember. By the way, the $15 also includes the waitstaff for two hours.
Client: Oh, we don't need that. We can just help ourselves. Would that reduce the price a little, then?
Caterer: No, I'm sorry. You have to appreciate that we have to come and set it all up and take it away anyway, so we might as well serve it while we're there.
Client: I see. Well, the key thing for us is that it's a nice relaxing event, so we'll go with that, I guess.
Caterer: Great. Just let me know exact numbers when you have them.

1 What event are they discussing?

....

....

2 What does the client try to negotiate?

....

....

3 Grammar extra *would*

> ▶ ***WOULD***
>
> The function of *would* is to make what you say sound more polite or diplomatic, so it is often used in negotiations.
> *Yes, that **would** be much more like it.*
> ***Would** that reduce the price a bit, then?*

Rewrite these sentences using *would* to make the sentences more diplomatic.

1 I'm afraid that will be difficult for me.

....

2 Can you move a little on the price?

....

3 Are you willing to negotiate?

....

4 I need to have some kind of guarantee.

....

5 When do you need to know?

....

6 I don't want to put you to any trouble.

....

12e A proposal

1 Writing skill sub-headings and bullet points

Look at the first excerpt from a report. What is the report about?

....

> I have now spoken on the phone to two different caterers about the food to be served at the Annual General Meeting (AGM). One was Angel Foods, which is a local company, and the other is Carrick's, a large catering chain.
>
> **Summary**
> Two caterers have been contacted:
> - Angel Foods, a local firm
> - Carrick's, a large catering chain

2 Rewrite these excerpts from the rest of the report. Use bullet points and concise language.

> **1**
> There are several things that we ought to think about before we make a decision. How much food do we need to provide? How much is it going to cost us? Do people have any special dietary needs?
>
> **Three factors to consider**
> - ....
> - ....
> - ....

> **2**
> The caterer has suggested various types of food—some hot food which will cost about $15 per person (expensive, I think) and cold food which costs about $10 per person.
>
> **The caterer**
> - ....
> - ....

> **3**
> I suggest that we should go with Angel Foods, because they seemed to understand better what we want, and I think they will do it for a better price.
>
> **Recommendation**
> ....
> ....

Writing a report

3 Read the report. Then rewrite it in the framework given, making the language more concise and using sub-headings and bullet points.

> I met a caterer, Party Foods Ltd., yesterday and we discussed the food and arrangements for our office party on December 12, and this was what they proposed. They suggested that we have a range of different types of sandwiches and also hot and cold appetizers. Sandwiches on their own would cost $10 per person and a mixture of sandwiches and cold appetizers would be $12 per person. If the appetizers were hot this would be an extra $2 per person—so a total of $14 per person.
>
> Also, if we want, they can provide drinks. Alternatively, we can buy our own and they will charge a small amount for serving them—I think she said an extra $1 per person.
>
> I think we should go for the mixture of sandwiches and cold appetizers, and then provide our own drinks. I can organize that part of it.

> **Subject: Office party December 12**
>
> **Summary**
> ....
> ....
> ....
>
> **Food**
> - ....
> - ....
> - ....
>
> **Drinks**
> - ....
> - ....
>
> **Recommendation**
> ....
> ....

Wordbuilding *the* + adjective

1 Can you think of the right adjective for these groups of people in society?

1 People with a lot of money *the rich*
2 People without a job ______
3 People with very little money ______
4 People with nowhere to live ______
5 People over 70 ______
6 People who are well-known ______
7 People who can't see ______
8 People who can't hear ______
9 People who can't read or write ______
10 People who are ill ______

2 Which of the answers in Exercise 1 describe people in a positive situation (P), a negative situation (N), or neither positive or negative (X).

Learning skills using the Internet

3 The following ideas are ways you could use the Internet to help you learn. Check (✓) the ideas you could use.

1 Listen to or watch the news in English online. Make note of key words as you listen to each story. Check their meaning online or in a dictionary. Then listen again.
2 Search for articles relevant to your interests on news websites. Read the title and the first paragraph. Then think of two questions you would like answered by the article. Then read the article and find the answers.
3 If you are not sure how to pronounce a word, check in an online dictionary. Then practice saying it.
4 If you listen to English or American songs, search for the lyrics online. Follow them as you listen to the song. Look up any words you don't know.
5 Search for interesting quotations, sayings, and anecdotes on websites. Try to memorize them.

4 Use the Internet to find the following:

1 What does the word "spin" mean in the context of political news?
______
2 How do you pronounce "rhythm"?
______
3 What are the opening lyrics to "Big Yellow Taxi" by Joni Mitchell?
______
4 A good quotation on the subject of "success."
______

Check!

5 Complete the sentences about the economy using information from Unit 12. Then use the first letters of each word to make something that many of us dream of having!

1 Poverty is a ______ concept. You can be classified as poor if you earn less than 60% of the average person.
2 Norway is a country that has saved money for the future rather than ______ it all in its infrastructure.
3 The servant economy is growing in developed countries; even people who are not very well-off have a ______ come and clean the house once a week.
4 In the Stone Age, ______ gatherers had a kind of gift economy. This was because they had a lot and needed little.
5 "At the ______ of the day" is a commonly used phrase in negotiations.
6 The opposite of saving money is ______ it.

Word: ______

UNIT 3c, Exercise 11, page 38

Instructions

- Form a group of three or four people and ask the teacher which product you are going to present.
- Read the product description on page 154 or 155.
- Together prepare a brief presentation of the product: what it is, how it works, what it is appropriate for, and why it is special.
- Choose one person to give the presentation (the others will have to answer questions). Think about the questions you may be asked.
- Give and listen to the presentations, asking and answering questions as you go.
- Have a class vote for best product.

UNIT 4a, Exercise 10, page 47

Participation by art form

Art form	Creative participation %	Receptive participation %	Total participation %
Visual Arts & Crafts	22	38	49
Theater & Dance	7	40	42
Reading/ Creative Writing	16	84	84
Music	15	57	62

Participation in music

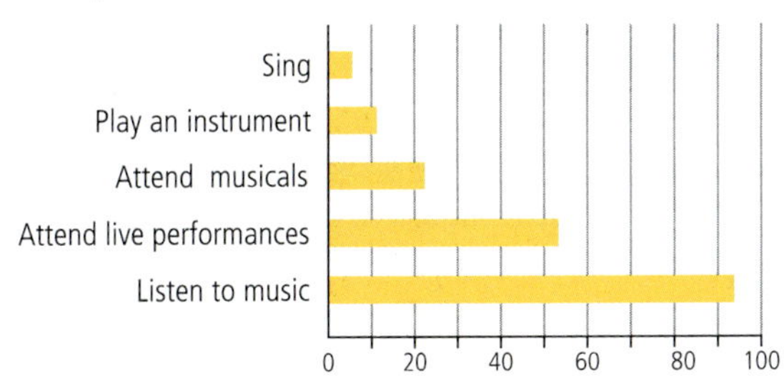

Reasons for non-participation

Reason	Non-participants %
difficult to find the time	54
not really interested	43
costs too much	41
not enough opportunities nearby	28

UNIT 8e, Exercise 4, page 101

- write to the university and ask them to speak to students about being considerate neighbors
- threaten to call the police if the students make noise after midnight
- have a friendly meeting with the students
- complain to town hall and ask them to put pressure on the university to find another solution

UNIT 5d, Exercise 5, page 64

Aston Homes for the Elderly

The bank gave the Aston Housing Association (AHA) a loan of $9 million in September 2009 to convert eight residential houses into groups of self-contained apartments for elderly people in the community who did not want to go into nursing homes.

Work started in December 2009, and so far five of the houses have already been converted, creating 40 self-contained apartments. The AHA has sold 30 of these, raising $4.5 million. It has also made repayments to the bank correctly and on time.

However, there have been complaints from local residents that AHA has sold some of the apartments to people who are not so elderly (one lady was in her late fifties), and that they have allowed people from outside the area to buy them. It seems that the price of the apartments is too high for many local people.

The AHA now intends to convert two more houses in the same area and is asking for an additional loan of $2.2 million.

UNIT 12d, Exercise 7, page 148

Student A

You want to buy this car. It is a seven-year-old VW Golf and the advertised price is $8,000. It is in good condition but has a lot of miles on it (100,000). Obviously you would like to get it for less, if you can. The problem is you have been looking for a long time and want to get a car quickly so that you can drive to work each day.

UNIT 3c, Exercise 11, page 38

Description 1

Portable Clay Cooler
Building on an ancient food-storage technique, the pot-in-pot system uses evaporation from a layer of wet sand between two pots to help keep produce fresh. Tomatoes can last weeks instead of days, meaning more income for farmers.

Developed by: Mohammed Bah Abba
Website: none available
Launch country: Nigeria

UNIT 9c, Exercise 10, page 110

* numbers in tens of thousands

UNIT 11c, Exercise 10, page 134

Quiz

Answer the questions then look at page 155 to see what type of learner you are. Do you agree?

1 WHEN I STUDY GRAMMAR, I LEARN BEST BY:
A reading clear rules. B writing down examples.
C putting it into practice in conversation.

2 IN CLASS, I PREFER:
A discussing. B looking at pictures, maps, diagrams, or videos.
C doing something practical.

3 I REMEMBER NEW VOCABULARY BEST WHEN IT IS ACCOMPANIED BY:
A a clear definition. B an image. C a demonstration.

4 IF I AM DISTRACTED IN CLASS, I USUALLY:
A hum or sing to myself. B doodle (draw) in my notebook.
C play with a pen or pencil.

5 WHEN LEARNING A NEW SKILL, I PREFER THAT:
A someone explain it to me. B someone demonstrate it.
C I just be allowed to get on with it myself.

6 WHEN I'M NOT SURE HOW TO SPELL A WORD, I:
A say the word aloud to myself. B try to visualize it in my mind.
C write down different versions.

7 I PREFER TO READ STORIES WITH LOTS OF:
A dialogue and conversation. B descriptive passages.
C action or adventure.

8 I PROBABLY LEARN THE MOST ENGLISH BY:
A listening to others. B watching movies.
C trying to use it.

UNIT 3c, Exercise 11, page 38

Description 2

Sugarcane Charcoal
Burning wood and dung, the main fuel sources for many in the developing world, has contributed to deforestation and breathing problems among inhabitants. These briquettes made from crushed sugarcane stalks not only make use of a local resource, they also burn more cleanly and allow residents to start a charcoal business for less than $50.

Developed by: MIT D-Lab
Website: http://d-lab.mit.edu/resources
Launch country: Haiti

UNIT 3c, Exercise 11, page 38

Description 3

Water Container

In poor rural areas, clean water is often miles away, leaving people vulnerable to diseases in unclean water. The strong Q Drum holds thirteen gallons in a rolling container that makes it easy to transport safe drinking water, a task that is usually done by women and children.

Developed by: P. J. and J. P. S. Hendrikse
Website: http://www.qdrum.co.za
Launch country: South Africa

UNIT 12d, Exercise 7, page 148

Student B

You want to sell this car. It is a seven-year-old VW Golf and the advertised price is $8,000. It is in good condition but has a lot of miles on it (100,000). You would like to get as close to the asking price as you can. However, it has been advertised for two months and you would like to sell it soon.

UNIT 11c, Exercise 10, page 134

Answers to quiz

Mostly As: you have an auditory learning style; you remember best when you hear things.

Mostly Bs: you have a visual learning style; you remember best when you see things.

Mostly Cs: you have a kinesthetic learning style; you remember best when you do things or when things are acted out.

UNIT 3c, Exercise 11, page 38

Description 4

Solar Wi-Fi Streetlight

The StarSight system consists of a series of pylons that use solar panels to power streetlamps, a Wi-Fi box for wireless Internet access, and if needed, closed-circuit TVs for security surveillance. The result is an integrated system of electricity and communication, plus better street lighting, which has been shown to help reduce crime.

Developed by: Kolam Partnership Ltd.
Website: http://www.starsightproject.com
Launch countries: Nigeria, South Africa, Turkey

UNIT 5b, Exercise 10, page 61

Questionnaire

1 HOW SATISFIED DO PEOPLE SEEM WITH THE AMOUNT OF MONEY THEY HAVE?

2 DO PEOPLE HAVE A GOOD BALANCE BETWEEN WORK AND FREE TIME?

3 HOW HAPPY ARE PEOPLE WITH THE EDUCATION THEY RECEIVE?

4 HOW CONFIDENT ARE PEOPLE IN YOUR COUNTRY'S HEALTH SYSTEM?

5 DO PEOPLE EAT HEALTHY FOOD?

6 HOW ENGAGED ARE PEOPLE POLITICALLY?

7 HOW OFTEN DO PEOPLE PARTICIPATE IN CULTURAL ACTIVITIES?

8 ARE PEOPLE TOLERANT OF OTHERS?

UNIT 8b, Exercise 8, page 97

1 false
2 true
3 half-true; it does increase life expectancy but no one can say how much
4 true
5 false; the zebrafish can heal its own heart, but not humans—yet!
6 true

UNIT 1

Present tenses review

Form

Simple present

Affirmative	Negative
I/you/we/they **live**	I/you/we/they **don't live** (don't = do not)
he/she/it **lives**	he/she/it **doesn't live** (doesn't = does not)

Interrogative	Short answer
do I/you/we/they **live**?	Yes, I/you/we/they **do**. No, I/you/we/they **don't**.
does he/she/it **live**?	Yes, he/she/it **does**. No, he/she/it **doesn't**.

Present continuous

Affirmative	Negative
I'm living ('m = am)	**I'm not** living ('m not = am not)
you**'re**/we**'re**/they**'re** **living** ('re = are)	you/we/they **aren't living** (aren't = are not)
he**'s**/she**'s**/it**'s** **living** ('s = is)	he/she/it **isn't living** (isn't = is not)

Interrogative	Short answer
am I **living**?	Yes, I **am**. No, **I'm not**.
are you/we/they **living**?	Yes, you/we/they **are**. No, you/we/they **aren't**.
is he/she/it **living**?	Yes, he/she/it **is**. No, he/she/it **isn't**.

Present perfect

Affirmative	Negative
I**'ve**/you**'ve**/we**'ve**/ they**'ve lived** ('ve = have)	I/you/we/they **haven't lived** (haven't = have not)
he**'s**/she**'s**/it**'s lived** ('s = has)	he/she/it **hasn't lived** (hasn't = has not)

Interrogative	Short answer
have I/you/we/they **lived**?	Yes, I/you/we/they **have**. No, I/you/we/they **haven't**.
has he/she/it **lived**?	Yes, he/she/it **has**. No, he/she/it **hasn't**.

Note the spelling rules for *-ed* endings:
*work → work**ed**; play → play**ed**; die → di**ed**; lie → li**ed**; try → tri**ed**; study → stud**ied**; stop → sto**pped***
Some verbs have irregular past participles, for example:
do → done; find → found; have → had; make → made

Present perfect continuous

Affirmative	Negative
I**'ve**/you**'ve**/we**'ve**/ they**'ve been living** ('ve = have)	I/you/we/they **haven't been living** (haven't = have not)
he**'s**/she**'s**/it**'s been living** ('s = has)	he/she/it **hasn't been living** (hasn't = has not)

Interrogative	Short answer
have I/you/we/they **been living**?	Yes, I/you/we/they **have**. No, I/you/we/they **haven't**.
has he/she/it **been living**?	Yes, he/she/it **has**. No, he/she/it **hasn't**.

Note the spelling rules for *-ing* endings:
work → working; play → playing; live → living; have → having; stop → stopping; run → running; die → dying; lie → lying

Use

Simple present

We use the simple present to talk about:

- facts or things which are generally true. *Orangutans **eat** fruit and leaves. The Earth **doesn't move** around the Moon. Where **do** polar bears **live**?*
- daily routines and habits. *I **work** in that factory every day. I always **take** a shower in the morning.*
- a permanent state or situation. *She **doesn't play** the piano. **Do** you **live** in Bahia?*

We often use adverbs of frequency (*always, usually, often, sometimes, rarely, never*) and expressions of frequency (*once a week, on Fridays, on the weekend, in the summer, every Saturday*) with the simple present to talk about how often we do something.
*We **always** play football on Saturday morning.*
*She **never** talks to strangers.*

Present continuous

We use the present continuous to talk about a situation in progress or things which are happening now or around now. With the present continuous, we often use these time expressions: *at the moment, (right) now, this week, this summer.*
*The boys **are playing** tennis in the park.*
*Paul **isn't living** in San Miguel this summer.*
***Are** you **doing** your report, Vikram?*

Present perfect

We use the present perfect to talk about a recent action or situation which started in the past. The situation may also continue into the present or have a result in the present.
*Michael can't come with us because he **hasn't renewed** his passport.*
***Have** you **visited** your grandparents lately?*

Present perfect continuous

We use the present perfect continuous to talk about an action or situation that was in progress in the recent past. The situation may also continue into the present or have a result in the present. We use the present perfect continuous, not the present perfect, to emphasize the duration of an action.

*I've **been working** here for months.* (And I still am.)
*They've **been behaving** like this since they arrived.*
*What **have you been doing** since I last saw you?*
*She **hasn't been working** hard enough lately!*

We often use the present perfect and present perfect continuous with *since* and *for* to talk about how long a situation has continued. We use *since* with the point of time when the activity started, for example *since Monday, since I was a boy*. We use *for* to talk about a period of time up to now, for example *for an hour, for a long time*.

*We've been friends **since** we were twelve years old.*
*We've been playing at the club **since** 2010.*
*I've lived in this house **for** six months.*

Practice

1 Choose the correct option.

Can you believe these other amazing and unlikely friendships between animals?

- A baby hippo [1] *has been living* with a giant tortoise since a devastating tsunami in 2004. They [2] ______ and [3] ______ together.
- One intrepid explorer says that his Eskimo dogs [4] ______ an extraordinary relationship with some polar bears. They [5] ______ together each year since 2008, when the dogs first traveled through the Arctic lands of Canada.
- Ellie, a dog, and Hattie, an elephant, [6] ______ the best of friends since they met in 2009.
- At a reserve in South Africa, a leopard cub and a dog often [7] ______ together, and at the moment, they [8] ______ in the same kennel.

People are amazed by these friendships. "It's true to say that there has been an evolution in the animal kingdom recently," says one animal expert.

1 a has been living b has lived c is living
2 a are eating b have eaten c eat
3 a are sleeping b have slept c sleep
4 a have been b have been getting c have got
5 a are playing b have played c have been playing
6 a become b are becoming c have become
7 a play b are playing c have played
8 a sleep b are sleeping c have slept

The passive voice

Form

We form the passive voice with the correct tense? of the verb *to be* + past participle.

Tense	Active	Passive
Simple present	makes/make	**is/are** made
Present continuous	is/are making	**is/are being** made
Present perfect	has/have made	**has/have been** made

Use

We use the passive voice when we want to focus on an action or the object of the action, rather than the person doing the action. The object of the active sentence becomes the subject of the passive one.

Active: Parents (subject) are questioning the new values (object).
Passive: The new values (subject) are being questioned by parents (object).

In a passive sentence, we can say who did the action (the agent) using *by*. We use *by* + agent when it is important to know who did the action. It isn't always necessary to use *by* + agent. We don't usually use the agent when it is obvious who has done the action, when we don't know, or when it isn't important.

*The best products are selected **by the product manager**.*
Guests are asked ~~by the hotel~~ to sign the visitors' book.

We also use the passive when we don't want to identify the agent.

I'm sorry, but the window has been broken ~~by my son~~.

Practice

2 Rewrite the sentences in the passive voice. Use *by* + agent where appropriate.

1 They are changing people's lives every day.
People's lives are being changed every day.
2 We make new plans all the time.
______
3 The government is making some new laws.
______
4 They have changed the whole system since I was a student.
______
5 Young people are forgetting the old way of life.
______
6 We haven't seen good manners for a long time.
______
7 We are still respecting a lot of the old customs.
______
8 Are they respecting the way that people used to live?
______

UNIT 2

Simple past and present perfect

Form

Simple past

We add *-ed* to regular verbs to form the simple past.

Affirmative	Negative
I/you/he/she/it/we/they **worked**	I/you/he/she/it/we/they **didn't work** (didn't = did not)

Interrogative	Short answer
did I/you/he/she/it/we/they **work**?	Yes, I/you/he/she/it/we/they **did**. No, I/you/he/she/it/we/they **didn't**.

Note the spelling rules for other regular verbs:

- for verbs ending in *-e*, we add *-d*: *realize* → ***realized***
- for verbs ending in *-y*, we change the *-y* to *i* and add *-ed*: *carry* → *carr**ied***
- for verbs ending in vowel + consonant (not *-w*, *-x*, or *-y*), we double the consonant: *plan* → ***planned***

Some verbs have an irregular affirmative form in the simple past:
be → *was/were; do* → *did; go* → *went; see* → *saw; write* → *wrote*

Present perfect

We form the present perfect with the simple present of the verb *to have* + past participle.

See page 156: Present perfect

Use

Simple past

We use the simple past to talk about finished actions in the past when there is a clear link to a specific time in the past. We often use a time phrase (*yesterday, last week, five years ago*) with the simple past.
*He **finished** the movie script two hours ago.*
*They **didn't go** to the movies last night.*
***Did** you **meet** Alex earlier?*

We use the simple past to talk about someone's life when they are dead.
*He **fought** as a soldier in the Civil War.*

Present perfect

We use the present perfect to talk about a recent action or situation which started at some time in the past. The situation may also continue into the present or have a result in the present. We use the present perfect when the experience is more important than the time, and the time is not stated.
I've seen a lot of different movies in the last five years.
He hasn't seen the new Lord of the Rings *movie yet.*

We also use the present perfect to talk about life experiences (when the people are still living).
I've never been to Peru. Have you ever gone?

When we talk about a period of time that is not finished, we use the present perfect, even if the action itself is finished.
Have you talked to him today? (It is still today.)

When the period of time is finished, we use the simple past.
Did you talk to him earlier? (It is now later.)

Practice

1 Choose the correct option.

1 I *saw* / *have seen* a very interesting movie yesterday.
2 *Did you ever read* / *Have you ever read* poetry?
3 I *didn't like* / *haven't liked* the end of the movie.
4 They *enjoyed* / *have enjoyed* watching the play last night.
5 Elena *didn't study* / *hasn't studied* literature for a long time.
6 The students *wrote* / *have written* some very original short stories in last year's class.
7 Lately his parents *told* / *have told* him a lot of funny anecdotes from when he was a child.
8 When *did you find out* / *have you found out* about the stories of Borges?

Past tenses review

Form

See page 158: Simple past

Past continuous

Interrogative	Short answer
was I/he/she/it **working** there?	Yes, I/he/she/it **was**. No, I/he/she/it **wasn't**.
were you/we/they **working** there?	Yes, you/we/they **were**. No, you/we/they **weren't**.

Past perfect

Affirmative	Negative
I**'d**/you**'d**/he**'d**/she**'d**/it'**d**/we**'d**/they**'d worked** ('d = had)	I/you/he/she/it/we/they **hadn't worked** (hadn't = had not)

Interrogative	Short answer
had I/you/he/she/it/we/they **worked**?	Yes, I/you/he/she/it/we/they **had**. No, I/you/he/she/it/we/they **hadn't**.

Past perfect continuous

Affirmative	Negative
I**'d**/you**'d**/he**'d**/she**'d**/it'**d**/we**'d**/they**'d been working** ('d = had)	I/you/he/she/it/we/they **hadn't been working** (hadn't = had not)

Interrogative	Short answer
had I/you/he/she/it/we/ they **been working**?	Yes, I/you/he/she/it/they **had been working.** No, I/you/he/she/it/they **hadn't been working.** (hadn't = had not)

Use

Simple past

We use the simple past to talk about the sequence of the main events of a story.
*Giles **got up** at six o'clock and **left** the location early.*

Past continuous

We use the past continuous to describe a background event which was in progress around the time of the main event. We often use the past continuous with the simple past.
*The sun **was coming up** as Paul arrived at the park.*

Past perfect

We use the past perfect to talk about what happened earlier, before the main event.
*When Julieta saw the animals, she remembered what the trainer **had said** the day before.*

Past perfect continuous

We use the past perfect continuous to describe an action that was in progress before or up to the main event in the past.
*When Salma arrived, the other actors **had** already **been rehearsing** for two hours.*

We don't usually use stative verbs in either the past continuous or the past perfect continuous.
*I **knew** the route well.* (Not *I ~~was knowing~~ the route well.*)
*I **had known** him for ten years.* (Not *I ~~had been knowing~~ him for ten years.*)

Practice

2 Complete the text with the correct past tense form of the verbs.

Elena [1] .... (walk) in the park near her home. It [2] .... (be) a beautiful evening. The sun [3] .... (shine) all day and now it [4] .... (set) behind some tall trees by the river. Suddenly she [5] .... (hear) a scream. She thought that it [6] .... (come) from the direction of the river so she [7] .... (run) there as fast as she could. When she [8] .... (reach) the river, she [9] .... (see) a young boy in the water. He [10] .... (slip) on the muddy bank and [11] .... (fall) head first into the water. Now he [12] .... (struggle) and unable to swim. Elena quickly [13] .... (take) off her shoes and [14] .... (jump) in. She [15] .... (catch) the boy by the arm and [16] .... (drag) him out.

UNIT 3

Future forms review

Form

will

Affirmative	Negative
I/you/he/she/it/we/they**'ll** go ('ll = will)	I/you/he/she/it/we/they **won't** go (won't = will not)

Interrogative	Short answer
will I/you/he/she/it/we/ they go?	Yes, I/you/he/she/it/we/they **will**. No, I/you/he/she/it/we/they **won't.**

going to

Affirmative	Negative
I**'m going to** visit	I**'m not going to** visit
you**'re**/we**'re**/they**'re going to** visit	you/we/they **aren't going to** visit
he**'s**/she**'s** /it**'s going to** visit	he/she/it **isn't going to** visit

Interrogative	Short answer
am I **going to** visit?	Yes, I **am.**/No, I**'m not.**
are you/we/they **going to** visit?	Yes, you/we/they **are.** No, you/we/they **aren't.**
is he/she/it **going to** visit?	Yes, he/she/it **is.** No, he/she/it **isn't.**

about to

Affirmative	Negative
I**'m about to** start	I**'m not about to start**
you**'re**/we**'re**/they**'re about to** start	you/we/they **aren't about to** start
he**'s**/she**'s**/it**'s about to** start	he/she/it **isn't about to** start

Interrogative	Short answer
am I **about to** start?	Yes, I **am.**/No, I**'m not.**
are you/we/they **about to** start?	Yes, you/we/they **are.** No, you/we/they **aren't.**
is he/she/it **about to** start?	Yes, he/she/it **is.** No, he/she/it **isn't.**

See page 156: Simple present, Present continuous

Use

will

We use *will* to talk about:

- a prediction. *I expect he'**ll** be here in a minute.*
- a decision we have made at the time of speaking. *"I can't start my car." "Don't worry. I'**ll give** you a ride."*
- a future event in an *if* or *when* clause. ***If** the population increases, there **won't be** enough food.*

going to

We use *be* + *going to* + base form

- to talk about a plan or intention for the future. This has been decided before the moment of speaking. *When I'm in Chile, **I'm going to travel** to Arica.*
- to make a prediction about the future based on present information. *My team is playing very badly. They**'re going to lose** this game.*

about to

We use *be* + *about to* to talk about an event in the immediate future.
*I can't talk to you now—**I'm about to go** into a meeting.*

We often use *just* in front of *about to*.
*Tell me the details later—**I'm just about to go** into town.*

Present continuous

We use the present continuous to talk about:

- an intention or previously made decision or arrangement. *They **aren't coming** to the theater.*
- a formal arrangement. *They**'re coming** at noon.*

We often use the present continuous with a specific (or understood) time in the future.
*I'm traveling to New York **on Thursday evening**.*

Simple present

We use the simple present to talk about:

- a scheduled event. *The concert **starts** at eight o'clock. What time **does** the train **leave**?*
- a simple statement of fact. *Water **boils** at 212°F.*

Practice

1 Complete the conversation with the correct future tense of the verbs.

A: The first talk [1] ………………… (start) at five.
B: [2] ………………… you ………………… (go) to it?
A: No, I think I [3] ………………… (pass). It's not really a subject that interests me.
B: Really? I think it [4] ………………… (be) really interesting.
A: Well, I [5] ………………… (meet) a colleague in half an hour anyway to discuss the presentation we [6] ………………… (give) later.
B: Oh. When does that [7] ………………… (start)?
A: It [8] ………………… (be) at 2:00 p.m.
B: Oh good. I [9] ………………… (try) to come to that.
A: Great! Anyway, you'd better go. Your talk [10] ………………… (be) to start.

Future continuous and future perfect

Form

Future continuous

We form the future continuous with *will be* + *-ing*.

Affirmative	Negative
I/you/he/she/it/we/they **will be doing**	I/you/he/she/it/we/they **won't be doing**

Interrogative	Short answer
will I/you/he/she/it/we/they **be doing**?	Yes, I/you/he/she/it/we/they **will**. No, I/you/he/she/it/we/they **won't**.

Future perfect

We form the future perfect with *will have* + past participle.

Affirmative	Negative
I/you/he/she/it/we/they **will have done**	I/you/he/she/it/we/they **won't have done**

Interrogative	Short answer
will I/you/he/she/it/we/they **have done**?	Yes, I/you/he/she/it/we/they **will**. No, I/you/he/she/it/we/they **won't**.

Use

Future continuous

We use the future continuous to talk about an action which you know or think will be in progress at or during a certain period of time in the future.
*In five years' time, everyone **will be using** HD phones.*
*This time tomorrow I **won't be sitting** in this office.*
*What **will** scientists **be researching** ten years from now?*

Future perfect

We use the future perfect to talk about an action which is going to be completed at or before a certain point of time in the future.
*In 50 years' time, people **will have stopped** using cash.*
*He **won't have finished** the work by the weekend.*
***Will** you **have sent** that email by five o'clock?*

Practice

2 Choose the correct option.

1 Next year people *will be using* / *will have used* wind power for their electricity.
2 By next January the company *will be designing* / *will have designed* a smaller computer chip.
3 Scientists *will be making* / *will have made* some important breakthroughs by 2020.
4 It is predicted that *we will be living* / *will have lived* on Mars in the next 50 years.
5 I expect that I *will be working* / *will have worked* in a laboratory next month.
6 I'm sure he *will be studying* / *will have studied* biology all his life.

UNIT 4

Expressions of quantity

Form

***(not) many, (a) few, a (small/large) number of, several* + plural count noun**

*There were **not many people** at the concert.*
*Eda has only been to **a few** classical **concerts**.*

***(not) much, (a) little (of) a (large/small) amount of* + noncount noun**

*There isn't **much live music** at the festival.*

***a lot of, lots of, plenty of, loads of, (a) lack of, (almost) no, (not/hardly) any, some, enough* + plural count or noncount noun**

*You can buy **plenty of food and drink** at the show.*
*There were **hardly any cars** in town today.*

Use

We use quantifiers with count or noncount nouns to talk about quantity (how much or how many of something).

Large quantities

To express large quantities, we use:

- *a large number of, a huge number of* with plural count nouns
- *a large amount of, a huge amount of* with noncount nouns
- *some, a lot of, lots of, loads of, plenty of* with plural count or noncount nouns

***An enormous number of** people are involved.*
***Some** visitors return three or four times a year.*
*There were **a lot of/loads of** great bands at the festival.*
Note that *loads of* is less formal than *a lot of/lots of*.

Small quantities

To express small quantities, we use:

- *(not) many, (a) few, a (small) number of, several* with plural count nouns.
- *(not) much, (a) little (of), a small amount of* with noncount nouns.
- *some, a lack of, (almost) no, (not/hardly) any* with plural count or noncount nouns.

*In most towns, there are **a few** interesting places to visit.*
***Hardly any** artists become rich in their lifetime.*

We use *little/a little* and *few/a few* to talk about small quantities in affirmative statements. *A little* and *a few* have a positive meaning (= some, but not many). *Little* and *few* have a negative meaning (= only a small number of).
***A few** people watched his latest play.* (= at least some, if not many)
***Few** people watched his latest play.* (= almost none)
*They arrived very late so they only saw **a little** of the show.* (= some, but not much)
*He ate **little** of his dinner in the restaurant because he didn't like seafood.* (= almost none)

We don't usually use *much* in affirmative statements. We normally use *a lot of/lots of.*
They don't have much knowledge of the local area.
We have a lot of brochures about the area.

Several usually means three or more things or people.
*There were **several** people in the audience.*

enough

We use *enough* to say we have the correct or sufficient quantity. We use *not enough* to say we have less than we want or need.
*There are **enough** members of the orchestra now.*
*There **aren't enough** artists signed up for the festival yet.*

We can use *a large amount, enough, plenty, several, not much, not many* without nouns when the meaning is clear.
*Do you have many theaters in your town? Yes, we have **several**. / No, there are**n't many**.*

Practice

1 Choose the correct option.

1 There aren't *much / many / a little* movies playing this week.
2 There is *a few / several / lots of* gas in the car.
3 Is there *many / much / a few* interest in art?
4 *Few / Not much / A little* people were there.
5 *Much / Many / Some* art books are on the shelf.
6 There is only *a little / lots of / plenty of* talent among these new actors.
7 The exhibition had *a little / not much / almost no* good paintings.
8 Are there *a bit of / enough / not much* bands playing at the festival?

Determiners

Form

***each, every, either, the whole* + singular noun**

***Each visitor** to the gallery receives a plan of the exhibition.*
***Every exhibit** in the museum is catalogued.*
*People can buy **either** a one-day or a season ticket.*

***all, both* + plural noun**

***All** the shortlisted artists gained a lot of publicity.*
***Both** artists exhibited three pictures.*

***any, no* + singular or plural noun**

*Have you seen **any** good movies this month?*
*They received **no** complaints.*

all, any, no + noncount noun
__All__ literature has value.
Can we use __any__ material we like?
__No__ culture is superior to another.

Use

every, each, all

We use *every, each,* and *all* to talk generally about people or things.
__Every__ musician played well.
__Each__ artist had some interesting work on display.
__All__ the paintings were very good.
We use *each* and *every* to refer to the individuals or individual parts of a group. We use *all* to refer to the whole group.

We use *every* (+ singular noun) and *all, all the, all of the* (+ plural noun/noncount noun) when the plural noun refers to **three** or more people or things.
__Every__ person had the opportunity to be an artist for a day. (There were three or more people.)
__All of the__ participants wrote a poem about nature. (There were three or more participants.)
We use *each* (+ singular noun) to talk about **two** or more people or things.
__Each__ member of the group made some form of contribution. (There were two or more people.)

both, either

We use *both* and *either* to talk about **two** things or people. We use *both/both of the* (+ plural noun) to say the same thing about two people or things. We use *either* (+ singular noun) to say there are two possible options.
__Both (of the)__ sculptors made three works of art.
They could choose to use __either__ stone or clay.

We use *neither* to express the opposite of *both*.
__Neither__ contestant made it to the final.

(not) any, no

We use *(not) any* or *no* to talk about a negative idea.
They __didn't__ allow __any__ graffiti on the walls at all.
There are __no__ original ideas left in art.

We can use *(not) any* without a noun when the meaning is clear.
Did you get the tickets? No, there __aren't any left__.

Practice

2 Complete the sentences with a suitable determiner. More than one answer is possible.

1 There were ten pianists in the competition, and they were all very good.
2 .... member of the band is talented.
3 Gilberto and Jorge work as a pair, but .... men are artists in their own right.
4 They were both good players, so .... of them could have won.
5 .... performer was better than the others.
6 .... student was asked to bring a sketch.

UNIT 5

Verb + infinitive or *-ing*

Form

Verb + infinitive	
verb + infinitive	*They __wanted to create__ a luxury resort.*
verb + *someone* + infinitive	*He __asked his father to lend__ him the money for the deposit.*
verb + *someone* + base form	*She __helped her friend establish__ a new theme park.*

Verb + *-ing*	
verb + *-ing*	*I __enjoy going__ to shopping malls.*

Use

verb + infinitive
After certain verbs we use infinitive. This is often to talk about hopes, intentions and decisions.
He offered __to draw__ the plans for the redevelopment.
They didn't want __to work__ on the project any more.
Common verbs which are followed by infinitive include: *agree, appear, arrange, choose, decide, expect, hope, intend, manage, need, offer, plan, prepare, pretend, promise, refuse, seem, want, wish, would like.*

verb + _someone_ + infinitive
Some verbs are followed by an object and infinitive.
He reminded __his employees to arrive__ early.
They'd like __the contractors to submit__ their proposal.
Common verbs which are followed by *someone* + infinitive include: *allow, ask, expect, force, help, invite, like, need, remind, teach, tell, want, would like.*

verb + _someone_ + base form
Some verbs are followed by an object and the base form.
She __helped her daughter expand__ her business.
Common verbs which use this form are: *feel, hear, help, notice, see, watch.*

verb + _-ing_
We use verb + *-ing* after certain verbs.
The architect __suggested adding__ some green space.
Common verbs which are followed by *-ing* are: *avoid, can't help, like, love, enjoy, prefer don't like, hate, can't stand, (not) mind, keep, miss, practice, risk, suggest.*

Practice

1 Choose the correct option.

1 I always enjoy *going* / *to go* to work.
2 Dubai *growing* / *grows* richer every day.
3 Ana asked them *sending* / *to send* help.
4 We decided *to invest* / *investing* in property.
5 The ministers suggested *to start* / *starting* an investment bank.
6 The government refused *giving* / *to give* them planning permission.

Verb + *-ing* or infinitive

Form

verb + *-ing* and verb + infinitive (two different meanings)

*He **remembered listening** to the program.*
*They **remembered to record** the program.*

verb + *-ing* and verb + infinitive (no change in meaning)

*He **continued traveling** around Asia.*
*He **continued to travel** around Asia.*

Use

Some verbs can be followed by either *-ing* or infinitive but the meaning changes.
*Jan **stopped talking** to journalists.* = action has ended (Jan used to talk to journalists but then he stopped.)
*Jan **stopped to talk** to a local resident.* = the reason for stopping (Jan stopped so that he could talk to a local resident.)
Common verbs which can be followed by *-ing* or infinitive with a change in meaning are: *forget, go on, mean, regret, remember, stop, try*.

Some verbs can be followed by either *-ing* or infinitive with very little or no change in meaning.
*Lizze **likes reading** business economics books.*
*Lizzie **likes to read** business economics books.*
Common verbs which can be followed by *-ing* or infinitive with little or no change in meaning are: *begin, continue, hate, love, prefer, start*.

Practice

2 Complete the sentences with the correct form of these verbs.

ask bring borrow ~~buy~~ change inform

1 I forgot *to buy* some milk.
2 I don't remember .... any money from Mike but he says I did.
3 We regret .... you that your bank account has been closed.
4 I meant .... them if the water was safe to drink or not.
5 Did you remember .... the plans with you?
6 If we want the company to be profitable, it means .... our prices.

UNIT 6

not

Form

Negative infinitive

We form the negative infinitive by putting *not* in front of the infinitive. Note that *not* goes before *to*.
*We decided **not to go** abroad on vacation this year.*

want, would like

To make a sentence negative with *want* or *would like*, we make the main verb negative.
*She **didn't want** to visit India.*
*They **wouldn't like** to work there.*

must not and *don't have to*

The negative form of *must* is *must not* and the negative form of *have* to is *don't/doesn't have* to. (Note that in British English, the contracted form *mustn't* is commonly used in place of *must not*.)
*You **must not** travel without your passport.*
*You **don't have to** go.*

hope and *think*

The negative forms of *hope* and *think* are different. When we form a negative sentence with *hope*, we make the verb that follows negative. When we form a negative sentence with *think*, we use *don't/doesn't think*.
*I **hope** he **isn't** late.*
*He **doesn't think** she should travel alone.*

let's

To form the negative of *let's*, we use *let's not*.
***Let's not** go on vacation this year.*

Use

Negative infinitive

We often use the negative infinitive to give advice or orders about what **not** to do.
*It would be better for you **not to meet** him tomorrow.*

want, would like

We use *don't/doesn't want* and *wouldn't like* to talk about a wish not to do something in the future.
*I **don't want** to go.* (Not *I ~~want not~~ to go.*)
*I **wouldn't like** to read that book again.*

must not and *don't have to*

We use ***must not*** to say that it is important not to do something.
*You **must not** forget to apply for your visa.* (= It's important that you not forget.)

We use *don't/doesn't have to* to show that something is not important or essential.
*He **doesn't have to** get a new passport before he goes.*

hope and *think*

*I **hope** my vacation **won't be** a disappointment.* (not *I ~~don't hope~~…*)
*I **don't think** her hotel **will be** cheap.* (not *I think her hotel ~~won't be~~ cheap.*)

let's

We use *let's not* + base form when we want to make a negative suggestion: ***Let's not** go out.*

Practice

1 Complete the sentences using *not* and the correct form of the verb. Use contractions where possible.

1 He told me *not to spend* (spend) too much.
2 Bo .... (want) to go to the museum.
3 Let's .... (tell) Ping about it—it will upset him.
4 Orel asked me .... (book) the flights.
5 We .... (think) the airplane will take off on time.
6 We decided .... (stop) off in Managua on the way.

Negative and tag questions

Form

Open questions (no confirmation of opinion demanded)

We form open questions using an auxiliary verb (like *do, have*) and inverting the subject and verb.
***Do you enjoy** traveling by train?*
***Has he played** tennis before?*

Negative questions

We form negative questions using the negative form of the verb. We usually use the contracted form.
***Don't you enjoy** traveling by train?*
***Hasn't he played** tennis before?*

Tag questions

To form tag questions, we use the auxiliary of the verb in the main sentence. When the main verb in the sentence is affirmative, the tag question is negative:
*They **were** at the party, **weren't they**?*
When the main verb in the sentence is negative, the tag question is affirmative:
*He **didn't** stay late, **did he**?*

When you write tag questions, put a comma between the main sentence and the tag.

Note that when the subject is a pronoun, we repeat it in the tag question. When the subject is a noun, we use an appropriate pronoun in the tag question.
***It**'s very interesting, isn't **it**?*
***Mike** travels to South Africa every year, doesn't **he**?*

Tense	Positive-negative	Negative-positive
to be (*am, is, are, was, were*)	***It's** a long way, **isn't it**?* ***I was** bad, **wasn't I**?*	***It isn't** a long way, **is it**?* ***I wasn't bad, was I**?*
Simple present (*do/does*)	***She works** there, **doesn't she**?*	***She doesn't work** there, **does she**?*
Present continuous (*am, is, are*)	***They're arriving** soon, **aren't they**?*	***They aren't arriving** soon, **are they**?*
Simple past (*did*)	***She went** there, **didn't she**?*	***She didn't go** there, **did she**?*
Past continuous (*was, were*)	***They were eating, weren't they**?*	***They weren't eating, were they**?*
Present perfect and present perfect continuous (*has, have*)	***You've been** here before, **haven't you**?* ***They've been studying** late, **haven't they**?*	***You haven't been** here before, **have you**?* ***They haven't been studying** late, **have they**?*
Past perfect (*had*)	***They'd gone, hadn't they**?*	***They hadn't gone, had they**?*
will	***You'll do** it, **won't you**?*	***You won't do** it, **will you**?*
Modals (*must, should, can, would*)	***I can** go, **can't I**?* ***He should** know, **shouldn't he**?*	***I can't** go, **can I**?* ***He shouldn't** know, **should he**?*

Use

Open questions

We use open questions when we don't know what the answer will be or when we don't expect a particular answer.
Are you going on vacation this year? (Possible answers: *Yes, I am. No, I'm not. Well, maybe. I don't think so.*)
Did he tell you where he was going? (Possible answers: *Yes, he did. No, he didn't. I can't remember.*)

Negative questions

We use negative questions to check information that is probably true. We answer with *yes* or *no*.
***Don't** you always visit your parents on Sunday? Yes, I do.*
***Wouldn't** you prefer to stay in a hotel? No, I wouldn't.*

We also use negative questions.

- to show surprise. *Don't you enjoy eating out?*
- to make a suggestion. *Don't you need to go now?*
- to request something, especially when we expect a negative answer. *Can't I have a different room?*

Tag questions

We use tag questions to ask for information, or to check and confirm information.

We're meeting at two o'clock, ***aren't we****?*

Practice

2 Complete the negative and tag questions.

1 *Don't* you want to stay here? It's nice.
2 India is a very diverse country, *isn't it* ?
3 Ana didn't go out, ______ ?
4 ______ you booked the flights yet? I thought I asked you to last week.
5 The group won't be taking a train to Cuzco, ______ ?
6 They wouldn't be much use, ______ ?
7 ______ he pay for his hotel before he arrived?
8 ______ she like to go somewhere else for a change?

UNIT 7

Mixed conditional sentences

Form

	If-clause	Main clause
First conditional	*If* + simple present	*will* + base form
	If *it* ***rains****, the drought* ***will end****.*	
Second conditional	*If* + simple past	*would/could/might* + base form
	If *we* ***recycled****, we* ***could reduce*** *our trash.*	
Third conditional	*If* + past perfect	*would/could/might have* + past participle
	If *they* ***had saved*** *more water, there* ***wouldn't have been*** *a drought.*	
Mixed second and third conditional	*If* + simple past	*would have* + past participle
	If *the policy* ***worked,*** *the government* ***wouldn't have needed*** *extra food.*	
Mixed third and second conditionals	*If* + past perfect	*would/could/might* + base form
	If *the water* ***hadn't been stored****, there* ***wouldn't be*** *a harvest this year.*	

Remember, we can use *if* in two positions:

- *If*-clause first: *If we use less water, we should be able to provide enough for the whole population.*
- Main clause first: *We should be able to provide enough water for the whole population if we use less water.*

When the *if*-clause is at the beginning of the sentence, we use a comma to separate it from the main clause.

Use

First conditional

We use the first conditional to talk about a possible future action or situation. We can also use it to talk about things that are generally true.

If they ***pollute*** *the water, we* ***won't be able*** *to drink it.* (It's possible that they will pollute the water in the future. Then we won't be able to drink the water.)

Second conditional

We use the second conditional to talk about hypothetical situations in the present or future.

If they ***changed*** *their environmental views, perhaps they* ***would get*** *the contract.* (This is a possible situation in the future.)

Note that when we use the simple past with *if*, it refers to the present or future. It does not refer to the past.

We can also use *could* and *might* instead of *would* in the main clause.

If they ***changed*** *their environmental views, they* ***might/could get*** *the contract.*

Fossil fuels ***might not*** *run out if people conserved more.*

Third conditional

We use the third conditional to talk about imagined past situations or events that did not happen and their hypothetical consequences.

If they ***had built*** *the dam, those villages* ***wouldn't have flooded.*** (But they didn't build the dam and the villages were flooded.)

We can use *could/might (not) have* to speculate on a possible consequence of the imagined past situation.

If they had built the dam, those villages ***might not*** *have flooded.* (They did not build the dam; it's possible that the villages wouldn't have been flooded but we are not certain.)

Mixed conditionals

We use mixed conditionals to talk about unreal situations when the *if* clause and the main clause don't refer to the same time.

We use mixed second and third conditionals to talk about an imagined situation in the present or future with the hypothetical past result or consequence.

If the pro-forest organization ***didn't exist****, more of the Amazon forests* ***would have disappeared.*** (But the organization does exist, and so more of the Amazon forests didn't disappear.)

We use mixed third and second conditionals to talk about an imagined situation or action in the past, with the imagined consequence in the present or future.
*If the activists **hadn't intervened**, the Amazon **would be** much smaller now.* (But the activists did intervene, so the Amazon is bigger than it would have been without their help.)

Practice

1 Complete the sentences. Use mixed conditionals.

1 Rafa didn't say anything at the summit meeting because he didn't know anything.
If Rafa ___*had known*___ (know) anything, he ___*would have said*___ (say) something.
2 They didn't dam the river because people protested about it.
If people ______ (not protest) about it, the river ______ (be) dammed today.
3 The job required environmental knowledge. Katrin doesn't know about the environment, so she didn't apply.
Katrin ______ (apply) for the job if she ______ (know) about the environment.
4 They need people with experience in conservation, but I don't have any.
If I ______ (have), I ______ (join).
5 I worked hard on the mining project, so I felt I needed a rest that weekend.
If I ______ (not work) so hard on the project, I ______ (be) tired that weekend.
6 You were writing reports last week. You're feeling very tired today.
If you ______ (not write) so many reports, you ______ (not feel) so tired today.

wish, would rather, and *if only*

Form

wish / if only **+ noun/pronoun + simple past**
*I wish / If only I **knew** more about the plan.*

wish / if only **+ noun/pronoun + past perfect**
*I wish / If only he **hadn't signed** the contract.*

wish / if only **+ noun/pronoun +** ***would*** **+ base form**
*I wish / If only they **would approve** the plan.*

would rather **+ base form**
*They **would rather save** the rain forest than mine for oil.*

would rather **+ object + simple past**
*The company **would rather you proposed** a more energy efficient solution.*

Note that when we use the verb *to be*, we use *was* in everyday speech; we use *were* in formal speech and writing, for example:
- Informal spoken: *I wish I was on vacation.*
- Formal spoken/written: *I wish I were on vacation.*

Use

We use *wish* and *if only* to talk about regrets and to describe an imaginary situation which is the opposite of the real situation.
- To express a wish about a present situation, we use *wish / if only* + simple past.
I wish I knew the answer. (But I don't.)
- To express a wish about a past situation, we use *wish / if only* + past perfect.
I wish I'd bought a smaller car. (But I didn't.)
- To express a wish for someone to do something differently in the present or future, we use *wish / if only* + noun/pronoun + *would* + base form.
I wish you would be more environmentally friendly. (You won't be more environmentally friendly, but I want you to be.)
Notice that you can't use the same subject in both clauses with *would*. You can't say: *I wish I would be more environmentally friendly.*

We use *would rather* + base form to talk about preferences.
*I **would rather use** my car less.*

When we use *would rather*, we can also include *than* + an alternative.
*I'd rather use my car less **than** spend more on gas.*

We use *would rather* + object + simple past to state what we would prefer someone else to do.
***I'd rather you used** energy-saving lightbulbs.*

Practice

2 Complete the sentence using the correct conditional form of the verbs.

1 If only there ___*were*___ (be) a way to stop people from using fossil fuels, but there isn't.
2 I wish they ______ (stop) using pesticides on crops, but they won't.
3 If only the river ______ (not flood) their village, things would be OK now.
4 I wish they ______ (understand) how to protect their environment, but they don't.
5 If only people ______ (consider) the consequences before cutting down the forest, but they didn't.
6 I wish there ______ (not be) a nuclear power station here, but there is.
7 I wish they ______ (leave) the downtown area alone, but they didn't.

UNIT 8

Reporting verbs

Form

Reporting verbs use different patterns.

verb + base form
*She **promised to investigate** the story.*
Reporting verbs with this pattern include: *agree, offer, promise, refuse, threaten.*

verb + someone + base form
*He **asked the photographer to send** the files.*
Reporting verbs with this pattern include: *advise, ask, convince, encourage, invite, persuade, remind, tell, urge, warn.*

verb + *-ing*
*He **admitted faking** the document.*
Reporting verbs with this pattern include: *advise, admit, deny, mention, propose, recommend, suggest.*

verb + preposition + *-ing*
*He **complained about working** long hours.*
Reporting verbs with this pattern include: *apologize (for), complain (about), insist (on), object (to).*

verb + someone + preposition + *-ing*
*The editor **blamed him for not checking** his facts.*
Reporting verbs with this pattern include: *accuse* (+ *of*), *blame* (+ *for*), *compliment* (+ *on*), *congratulate* (+ *on*), *criticize* (+ *for*), *forgive* (+ *for*), *thank* (+ *for*), *warn* (+ *about*).

Other common verb patterns are:
verb + someone + *that*
*He **warned us that** the journey would be difficult.*
Reporting verbs with this pattern include: *advise, persuade, tell, warn.*

verb + *that*
*We **agreed that** she was the best candidate.*
Reporting verbs with this pattern include: *admit, agree, explain, deny, know, realize, say, think, warn.*

Use

Say, tell, think, and *ask* are the most common reporting verbs, but we often use others to report what people said. When we decide what reporting verb to use, we think about the function or the purpose of the speaker's words.
"Remember to download your photos." = **remind** *(He reminded me to download my photos.)*
"I'll sign up later." = **promise** (*She promised to sign up later.*)

Practice

1 Report the statements using these verbs. You may need to use a preposition after the verb.

admit apologize complain invite offer tell thank ~~urge~~

1 I really think you should go to the meeting.
Ki *urged me to go to the meeting.*
2 It was me that informed the press.
Rebecca ....
3 I'm really grateful that you read my article.
Fatima ....
4 I really dislike having to write business reports.
Leo ....
5 I'm sorry, but I made a mistake.
Clara ....
6 Please come to my house tomorrow.
Ji-hu ....
7 I'll give you a ride to the press conference.
Jaime ....
8 Don't send that email.
Aisha ....

Passive reporting verbs

Form

Passive reporting verbs are formed with *It* + *be* + past participle of reporting verb + *that* + clause.

When we report ideas in the present, we use the verb *be* in the simple present.
*It **is** believed that…*

For a present report of a present event, we use the simple present in the *that*-clause.
*It is said that people **are** less happy nowadays.*

For a present report of a past event, we use the simple past in the *that*-clause.
*It is believed that they **lived** unknown to the outside world for over 200 years.*

For a present report of a future event, we use *will* + base form in the *that*-clause.
*It is understood that reporters **will leave** them alone.*

When we report ideas in the past, we use the verb *be* in the simple past.
*It **was** believed that…*
*It **was** reported that…*

For a report and event at the same time in the past, we use the simple past in the *that*-clause.
*It was claimed that the break-in **happened** that morning.*

For a report in the past of an event that happened before the report, we use the past perfect in the *that*-clause.
It was believed that the break-in ***had happened*** *earlier.*

For a past report of a future event, we use *would* + base form in the *that*-clause.
It was understood that the survivors ***would go*** *straight to the hospital when they returned.*

Use

We use passive reporting structures to talk about events when the speaker is unknown or unimportant, or when someone wishes to remain anonymous. We can report ideas in the present or in the past.
It ***is*** *said that people consume on average 50 times more sugar than they did ten years ago.*
It ***is*** *believed that tickets will be available soon.*
It ***was*** *reported that there had been violence.*
It ***was*** *thought that there wouldn't be enough money.*

For passive reporting, we use verbs such as *believed, claimed, considered, estimated, expected, known, reported, said, suggested , thought,* and *understood.*

Practice

2 Write sentences using the prompts.

1. Present report about a present event: report / story / not be / true
   It is reported that the story is not true.
2. Present report about a past event: understand / those people / live / there / for twenty years
   ....
3. Present report about a future event: suggest / people / travel / to Mars / next year
   ....
4. Past report about a past event: think / women / be / less intelligent
   ....
5. Past report about a distant past event: said / men / not see / the Arctic ice / then
   ....
6. Past report of a future event: not believe / newspapers / become / so powerful
   ....

UNIT 9

Articles: *the* or no article?

Form

Definite article *the*:
Armstrong walked on ***the*** *Moon.*

No article:
He was a hero to ***millions****.*

Use

We use *the* + singular count noun, plural count noun or noncount noun:

- to refer back to the same thing or person. *I applied for a job. It was* ***the*** *perfect job for me.*
- when there is only one. *He was the youngest person to cross* ***the*** *Atlantic Ocean by boat.*
- before a superlative adjective: *That was* ***the*** *most terrifying experience I've ever had!*
- to talk about a specific thing or things, person or people.
  Did you see ***the*** *space shuttle landing earlier?*
  I have a lot of admiration for ***the*** *relief workers there.*
- to talk about professional groups. *He worked in* ***the*** *navy for many years.*
- with certain countries, place names, geographical regions, oceans and seas, deserts, mountain ranges and rivers, for example: *the USA, the UK, the Republic of China, the Philippines, the United Arab Emirates, the Great Wall, the White House, the Middle East, the Antarctic, the Pacific, the Indian Ocean, the Atacama Desert, the Andes, the Himalayas, the Amazon.*

We use no article + plural count and noncount nouns:

- to talk in general about things or people. *Do you use computers in your job? I don't like potatoes.*
- before certain familiar places (*work, home, college, school*). *What time do you go to work?*
- before most cities, countries, continents, lakes, mountains, languages, and names of people. *Have you ever been to* ***Beijing****? She lives in* ***Bolivia****. He worked in* ***India*** *for many years.* Other examples are: *New York, Lima, Argentina, China, Asia, South America, Lake Titicaca, Mount Everest, Mandarin, Spanish, Japanese, Christopher Columbus.*
- before certain time expressions. *I'll meet you* ***next week****. He was born in* ***1953****.*

Notice that there are exceptions, for example:
time expressions: *in* ***the*** *sixties, on* ***the*** *weekend, in* ***the*** *summer, in* ***the*** *18th century*

Practice

1 Complete the text with *the* or no article (–).

I was listening to [1] *the* news at ten o'clock [2] .... last night, when it was reported that [3] .... President of [4] .... United States was on [5] .... vacation for [6] .... two weeks. They said that he was visiting [7] .... town where he was born. Apparently he doesn't like going to [8] .... places where there are lots of people, preferring [9] .... peace and quiet. [10] .... reasons why someone in his position does this are obvious!

Relative clauses

Form

Relative pronouns introduce defining relative clauses. To give information about:

- people, we use *who* or *that*. *He's the man* ***who*** *got the job.*
- things, we use *which* or *that*. *That's the network* ***which*** *is used for public access.*
- places or times, we use *where or when*. *This is the place* ***where*** *the information is stored. It was a time* ***when*** *space was unknown.*
- possession, we use *whose*. *She's the person* ***whose*** *job was advertised.*

Reduced relative clauses

We can sometimes shorten relative clauses by omitting the relative pronoun and using a present or past participle.
If the verb in the relative clause is in the active, we use the present participle.
People ***who visit*** *the area have admired its lakes.*
People ***visiting*** *the area have admired its lakes.*

If the verb in the relative clause is in the passive, we use the past participle:
It is a subject ***which is studied*** *by many people.*
It is a subject ***studied*** *by many people.*

We can't use a reduced relative clause when the relative pronoun is the object of the relative clause.
The expedition, which I am leading, is in June.
Not: ~~*The expedition leading is in June.*~~

Use

We use a relative clause to give more information about a noun in the main clause of the sentence.
We use a **defining** relative clause when the extra information in the relative clause is essential for identification. The meaning in the main clause is unclear without it.
This is the forest ***where the new species was discovered.***

We use a **non-defining** relative clause when the extra information is not essential. The meaning of the main clause is still clear. The non-defining relative clause is separated from the main clause by commas.
Stefano Calabrio, ***who is eighty-five,*** *still works as a mountain guide.*
The ship Arctic Krestrel, ***which was built in Glasgow,*** *is registered in Russia.*

The relative pronoun in a relative clause can be:

- the subject of the clause. *Explorers are people who make discoveries.*
- the object of the clause (with a noun or pronoun following it). *He's the explorer who I met in Laos.*

We can omit the relative pronoun when it is the **object** of a **defining** relative clause.
That's the explorer (who) I met in Laos.
We cannot omit the relative pronoun when it is the subject of a defining relative clause or in a non-defining relative clause.

We often use reduced relative clauses in announcements and reports.
Passengers ~~who are~~ traveling to Mumbai, please proceed to gate 25.
Due to the bomb scare, all bags ~~which were~~ left unattended were removed and destroyed.

Practice

2 Write sentences using relative clauses. Use reduced relative clauses where possible.

1 He is an explorer. He likes traveling to remote places.
He's an explorer who likes traveling to remote places.

2 This is the lake. The fish was discovered here.
....

3 Equipment is often left on Mount Everest. It is regularly removed.
....

4 That is the biologist. Her papers were lost in the storm.
....

5 Lake Titicaca is very large. It is on the border of Bolivia and Peru.
....

6 GreenSpace created the prototype. The prototype was copied by a rival company.
....

UNIT 10

Simple present, present continuous, and *will* for repeated actions

Form

Simple present

Adverbs of frequency come before the main verb with the simple present, but after the verb *be*.
We ***always have*** *a family celebration at Thanksgiving.*
*He****'s usually*** *on time for his extra class.*

Present continuous with *always*

Always comes between the verb *be* and the *-ing* form of the verb.
They're ***always*** *criticizing their children.*

will

Children ***will*** *naturally choose to play rather than study.*

Use

We use the simple present for repeated actions (often with adverbs of frequency) or to talk about a simple fact or general truth.

*He **listens** to the radio news every morning.*
*Water **freezes** at 32° Fahrenheit.*

We use the present continuous with *always* to talk about a habit which we find annoying or which we wish to criticize.

*I try to avoid Zhang at work. He **is always talking** about his children's achievements.*
*She**'s always complaining** about work.*

We use *will* to talk about typical behavior.

*Westerners **will** often avoid unfamiliar food.*

Practice

1 Write sentences using the prompts. Use the simple present (SP), present continuous (PC) with *always*, and *will* (W).

1 (SP) Mary / read / detective novels
Mary always reads detective novels.

2 (W) Cats don't like swimming. They / do / anything to avoid getting wet
....

3 (SP) James / ride/ his bike everywhere
....

4 (PC) Ria / talk / with / her mouth full
....

5 (SP) Kumar / stay / at work until 7:00 or 8:00 at night
....

6 (W) Cats / sleep / all day / rather than go out
....

7 (PC) My mom / complain / about my messes
....

8 (SP) Li Wei / get / to work early most days
....

used to, usually, be used to, and *get used to*

Form

Affirmative	Negative	Interrogative
used to + base form I/you/he/she/it/we/they **used to** live	I/you/he/she/it/we/they **didn't use to** live	**did** I/you/he/she/it/we/they **use to** live?
usually + simple present I/you/we/they **usually play**	I/you/we/they **don't usually play**	***do*** I/you/we/they ***usually*** play?
he/she/it **usually plays**	he/she/it **doesn't usually play**	**does** he/she/it ***usually*** play?
be used to + noun or *-ing* **I'm used to** playing	**I'm not used to** playing	**am** I **used to** playing?
you**'re**/we**'re**/they**'re used to** playing	you/we/they **aren't used to** playing	**are** you/we/they **used to** playing?
he**'s**/she**'s**/it**'s used to** playing	he/she/it **isn't used to** playing	**is** he/she/it **used to** playing?
be getting used to + noun or *-ing* **I'm getting used to** playing	I***'m not getting used to*** playing	**am** I **getting used to** playing?
you**'re**/we**'re**/they**'re getting used to** playing	you/we/they **aren't getting used to** playing	**are** you/we/they **getting used to** playing?
he**'s**/she**'s**/it**'s getting used to** playing	he/she/it **isn't getting used to** playing	**is** he/she/it **getting used to** playing?

Use

We use *used to* (+ base form) to talk about past habits, situations, and states.

*I **used to go** out to eat a lot when I lived in Paris.*
*She **didn't use to enjoy** opera when she was younger.*

We use *usually* + simple present to talk about present habits.

*We **usually have** dinner with my parents on Sundays.*
***Do** you **usually go** shopping on Friday nights?*

We use *be used to* to talk about familiar (and unfamiliar) habits and situations.

***Is** he **used to using** his new laptop yet?*
*He **isn't used to** his new laptop yet.*

We use *get used to* to talk about habits that are becoming familiar.

*Sara **is getting used to working** in the store now.*
*Sara **is getting used to** the store now.*

Practice

2 Choose the correct option.

1 Since his illness, he .... very healthy food.
a usually eats
b used to eat
c is getting used to eat

2 Paul has worked for a multinational company for years, so he .... now.
a usually travels
b used to travel
c is used to traveling

3 They both .... golf when they were boys.
a usually play
b used to play
c are used to playing

4 Li ______ at her new college.
a usually studies
b used to study
c is getting used to studying

5 Didn't Jana ______ to her co-director every day?
a usually speaks
b usually speak
c is getting used to speaking

6 Jorge ______ different food since he went to Thailand last week.
a used to
b is used to trying
c didn't use to try

7 Petra's worked here for years, so she ______.
a used to get up early
b is used to getting up early
c is getting used to getting up early

8 My brother ______ very late on Saturday nights.
a usually stays out
b is used to staying out
c is getting used to staying out

UNIT 11

could, was able to, manage to, and *succeed in*

Form

Affirmative	Negative	Interrogative
could + infinitive base form I/you/he/she/it/we/they **could do**	I/you/he/she/it/we/they **couldn't do**	**could** I/you/he/she/it/we/they **do**?
was/were able + infinitive I/he/she/it **was able to do** you/we/they **were able to do**	I/he/she/it **wasn't able to do** you/we/they **weren't able to do**	**was** I/he/she/it **able to do**? **were** you/we/they **able to do**?
manage + infinitive I/you/he/she/it/we/they **managed to finish**	I/you/he/she/it/we/they **didn't manage to finish**	**did** I/you/he/she/it/we/they **manage to finish**?
succeed in + *-ing* I/you/he/she/it/we/they **succeeded in making**	I/you/he/she/it/we/they **didn't succeed in making**	**did** I/you/he/she/it/we/they **succeed in making**?

Use

To talk about a general ability in the past, use *could.*
*He **could swim** when he was three years old.*
*He **couldn't find** the herbal medicine he was looking for.*

We use *was / were able to, manage to* + base form and *succeed in* + *-ing* to talk about the ability (or lack of ability) to successfully complete a particular task or activity, but not to talk about general ability.
*She **was able to find** the quickest route immediately.*
*They **weren't able to finish** the journey.*
*He finally **managed to publish** his book.*
*Did she **manage to get** that scholarship in the end?*
*We **succeeded in raising** enough money for our trip.*
*Unfortunately, she **didn't succeed in getting** the job.*
We use *manage to* + base form only with people or living things.
The plant managed to grow without light.
Not: *~~The car didn't manage to accelerate.~~*
We often use expressions such as *finally* and *in the end* with *manage to* and *succeed in* to emphasize that the activity was an effort.
*I **finally** managed to pass my exams.*
***In the end**, I succeeded in becoming a doctor.*

Practice

1 Look at the sentences (a and b) and choose the best option.

(1a) Did you manage to find out about the Mexican cure for blisters?
1b Could you find out about the Mexican cure for blisters?
2a In the past, people didn't succeed in accessing as much information about plants as they can today.
2b In the past, people weren't able to access as much information about plants as they can today.
3a A recent survey found that most people in the US weren't able to identify common plants.
3b A recent survey found that most people in the US didn't manage to identify common plants.
4a The medicine didn't always succeed in treating the illness.
4b The medicine didn't manage to treat the illness.
5a Sally didn't manage to publish her latest article. She submitted it too late.
5b Sally couldn't publish her latest article. She submitted it too late.

Future in the past

Form

***going to*: See page 159**

***about to* + base form: See page 159**

Affirmative	Negative	Interrogative
would + base form I said (that) I/you/he/she/it/we/they **would do**	I said (that) I/you/he/she/it/we/they **wouldn't do**	they asked if I/you/he/she/it/we/they **would do**
would have + past participle I/you/he/she/it/we/they **would have made**	I/you/he/she/it/we/they **wouldn't have made**	**would** I/you/he/she/it/we/they **have made?**
be supposed to + base form I/he/she/it **was supposed to finish** you/we/they **were supposed to finish**	I/he/she/it **wasn't supposed to finish** you/we/they **weren't supposed to finish**	**was** I/he/she/it **supposed to finish?** **were** you/we/they **supposed to finish?**

Use

We use *was / were going to* to talk about:

- an intention which may or may not have been fulfilled. *I **was going to call** you, but I got too busy.*
- a plan or arrangement which changed. *We **were going to meet** at 2:00 but came late.*

We use *be about to* to say that we were very close to doing something, but were prevented at the last moment.
*I **was about to leave** the house when the telephone rang.*

We use *would* to report what somebody said they would do.
*Jane said that she **would work** that evening.*
*He promised he **would send** me the report.*

We use *would have* to refer to a future action in the past which didn't happen.
*I **would have bought** it, but I didn't have enough money.*

We use *supposed to* to talk about actions which people should have done, but didn't.
*They **were supposed to get** here at eight o'clock! Where are they?*

Practice

2 Complete the second sentence so it has the same meaning as the first. Use the words in bold.

1 He planned to tell you, but he didn't see you.
going He *was going to tell* you, but he didn't see you.

2 "I'll work harder next week."
would John said that he .... harder next week.

3 She intended to tell you, but she forgot.
would She .... you, but she forgot.

4 Maria was going to bring enough food for everyone! Where is it?
supposed Maria .... enough food for everyone! Where is it?

5 They intended to start studying tomorrow, but they went out instead.
going They .... studying tomorrow, but they went out instead.

6 He wanted to say something, but decided not to.
about He .... something, but decided not to.

7 Why didn't you ask? She wanted to tell you.
would She .... you if you had asked.

8 "I'll remember."
would Lin said that she ....

UNIT 12

Focusing adverbs: *only, just, even, too, also, as well*

Form

only, just, even

Only, just, and *even* always come directly before the word they are emphasizing.
***Only/Just** Dave knows how hard they worked.*
*It is **only/just** two days since I saw him.*
*A lot of people don't **even** have any savings.*

too, also, as well

- sentence + *too*:
  *We can invest in that company **too**.*
- sentence + *as well*:
  *We bought a new iPad **as well**.*
- *Also* + sentence:
  ***Also**, she runs a successful accounting business.*
- *also* + main verb:
  *Most people **also** want to plan for their future.*
- be + *also*:
  *He's good at tennis. He's **also** a good badminton player.*
- auxiliary verb + *also* + main verb:
  *They are **also** going to the game.*

Use

We use focusing adverbs to emphasize a particular piece of information. Sentences which include focusing adverbs can exist without them.

Only and *just* focus on one particular thing to the exclusion of all others.

Only/Just *she and I know her secret.*

It's ***only/just*** *banks that accept travelers checks.*

We use *even* to show that we think something is unusual or surprising.

The question was so easy that ***even*** *Bill knew the answer.*

Even *football doesn't interest him any more.*

We use *also, as well,* and *too* to emphasize an additional piece of information in a sentence. *Also* comes before most verbs, but after the verb *to be*, or at the beginning of a sentence. *As well* and *too* come after the verb (and the object if there is one).

He likes sports, but ***also*** *enjoys playing chess.*

He likes sports, but enjoys playing chess, ***as well/too****.*

Practice

1 Choose the correct option.

1 I *only* / *too* heard about his financial situation yesterday.
2 Did you want to go to the bank *even* / *too*?
3 He *even* / *too* asked the accountant about it!
4 He usually works late on Thursdays *even* / *as well*.
5 They *only* / *as well* have a few thousand dollars left.
6 The money has *just* / *as well* been deposited in your account.
7 The boys *also* / *too* wanted some of the money.
8 The recession is a big problem for us *too* / *only*.

Causative *have* and *get*

Form

have/get + something + past participle

I ***had/got my car repaired*** *last week.*

have + someone + base form

I ***had a gardener help*** *me with the garden.*

get + someone + infinitive

I ***got a gardener to help*** *me with the garden.*

Use

We use *have/get something done* to explain that we asked someone to do something for us but we don't say who. We often pay for the work.

She ***has her house cleaned*** *by a cleaning company.*

We ***get our car serviced*** *every six months at the local auto shop.*

We use *have someone do / get someone to do* to explain that you have asked someone to do something for you. With these expressions, we say who does the job. Notice that with *get* we use infinitive. With *have* we use the base form.

I ***have a gardener mow*** *the lawn.*

I ***get a window cleaner to clean*** *the windows.*

Practice

2 Write sentences using the prompts. Use causative forms.

1 I / get / hair cut / yesterday
I got my hair cut yesterday.

2 I / have / accountant / go over / my accounts / on Saturday
....

3 We / get / mortgage rate / fix / last week
....

4 She / get / neighbor / pay for / new fence / this afternoon
....

5 He / get / friend / open / an account / last summer
....

6 She / have / new credit card / send out / this morning
....

Unit 1

1

It's known that animals often cooperate in their own social groups, helping each other to hunt or raise their young. Some highly intelligent animals, like elephants, go even further than this, and help other animals who are not in their own family group. But cooperation between animals of different species is unusual, so that's why the story of Suriya, the orangutan, has attracted a lot of interest.

Suriya lives with his keepers at the Institute of Greatly Endangered and Rare Species in Myrtle Beach, South Carolina, which is a kind of sanctuary for rare animals. Recently this orangutan has made an unlikely friend in a local hound dog. Now most dogs avoid apes because they are scared of them basically, but these two have formed a strong bond.

Each day the dog comes into the compound and searches out Suriya. When he finds him, they carry on like long-lost friends, wrestling and hugging and playing together. They've been doing this every day since they first met, and their friendship has attracted the curiosity of millions of viewers on the National Geographic Channel. The founder of the institute, Dr. Antle explains: "It's clear they are having the time of their life. What is more striking is that Suriya has also understood that the hound dog is very hungry, so he regularly shares his monkey biscuits with him. Orangutans are very generous creatures. If you give one a piece of candy, often they will break it in half and hand one piece back to you."

So how does he explain the fact that their relationship has a lot of the characteristics of what we call friendship? Antle says that the two animals are fulfilling a basic social need in each other that perhaps we don't normally associate with animals. "It's a relationship with attributes of fun and interaction that they are not getting from anyone else."

2

G = Greta; T = Tan

G: Tan, hello! Imagine bumping into you here! How are you?
T: Greta! Wow, what a surprise! Hi!
G: It's been a long time. What have you been up to?
T: I know. It's been way too long. Umm, I've been working abroad for the last eighteen months.
G: Anywhere exciting?
T: Yes, in India, actually. I had a contract with the consulate to do teacher training.
G: Well, it obviously suits you: you're looking very tanned and relaxed.
T: Oh, thanks, it's been a lot of fun. And you? You're looking well too. How are things?
G: Oh, you know, busy as ever. I've been completely swamped with work the last few months, trying to get my online shoe store off the ground.
T: Is it going OK?
G: Well, you know. It has its ups and downs. But we're getting there.
T: And what about Amanda? Do you see much of her?
G: Yeah, we still get together now and then. She was asking about you the other day, actually.
T: Oh. Well, I probably won't have time to look her up this time. I'm only back for a week. But do tell her I said hi.
G: I will.
T: And the next time I'm back, maybe we can all meet and catch up.
G: Yeah, that'd be great. How long will you be gone for?
T: I've just got to do another two months over there. Then I'll be back in the US for a while, I hope.
G: OK. Well, give me a call when you're back. You've got my number, don't you?
T: Yes, if it's still the same one.
G: Yeah, it is. I'll look forward to that. Is Shan going out there with you?
T: She has been with me, but uh, she's not coming this time.
G: Oh. Well, say hello to her from me. Look, I don't mean to be rude, but I need to get back to work—but it was really nice seeing you. Hope the trip goes well.
T: Thanks. Yeah, I've got to run too. Anyway, great to see you too, Greta. Take care… and see you soon. Good luck with the business.

3

1 Imagine bumping into you here.
2 I had a contract with the consulate.
3 Is it going OK?
4 Do you see much of her?
5 We still get together now and then.
6 I'm only back for a week.

Unit 2

4

P = Presenter; M = Mark Mowlam

P: Take a best-selling book, a great storyline and a great cast, add an experienced director and a large budget and what do you get? A box office success, you would think. Think again. There's no guarantee that a book that has enjoyed great success will make a good movie. Some movie adaptations have worked, others have flopped. So what's the secret? That was the question I put earlier to film critic Mark Mowlam, who's followed the progress of many book-to-film adaptations in his time and has recently reported on the making of Tolkien's *The Hobbit*.

M: Well, the goal is really to make a good movie that remains true to the spirit of the book. There are many examples of adaptations which have failed because they tried to remain too faithful to the plot and the characters of the book. Probably because at the time, the producers worried that they'd alienate loyal readers if they departed too much from the original text. But in fact, that's a mistake: what works well on the page doesn't necessarily work well on the screen; you have to give the screenwriter freedom to create a script that flows, even if that means changing the original. So what we find is a lot of good films—*Sense and Sensibility*, *The Shining*, for example—that are completely unlike the original book. And readers are generally OK about this because they think of books and movies as two separate works of art. But there are movies that have managed to stay true to the book and still be good. What they've done—a little like in cooking, I suppose—is to put in all the book's good ingredients and then boil them down to a concentrated mixture that's packed with the flavor of the original work. Probably the best example of this is *The Lord of the Rings* trilogy by Peter Jackson. The central theme of the book—which is a struggle between the forces of good and evil—perhaps wasn't so difficult to portray, but J.R.R. Tolkien created a very original other world and reproducing that was a much more difficult task, because each reader has his or her own very distinct idea of what this world was like. I think Jackson did a fantastic job, using the spectacular scenery of New Zealand for the film's location. The other thing about the *The Lord of the Rings* is that it's a very substantial work—three books, each containing over twenty long chapters—so Jackson had to leave some elements of the story out. To compensate for this, he took the most important scenes and then put all the emotional force behind them. The result is that it has become one of the most successful movies of all time, a blockbuster that has grossed almost $3 billion.

5

1 I haven't been to India.
2 It isn't far.
3 You aren't allowed.
4 It doesn't matter.
5 I hadn't noticed.
6 They weren't late.
7 She hasn't called.
8 We didn't care.

6

Conversation 1

A: The bus broke down on the highway, so we were all left stranded until help could arrive.
B: What did you do?
A: Luckily another bus came within about 15 minutes and we all transferred to that one.
B: That must have been a relief.

Conversation 2

A: My pants got caught on the door handle and as I walked away, they tore.
B: Oh, that's awful.
A: Yes, I had to walk right across the restaurant back to our table with my hands over the hole.
B: How embarrassing!

Conversation 3

A: I bent the key trying to force it into the lock and when I tried to straighten it, it snapped.
B: How did you get in?
A: I went to the neighbors', but they weren't at home, so I just had to wait 'til someone came home.
B: Yeah, something like that happened to me once.

Conversation 4

A: The elevator got stuck between floors twenty-five stories up, and two of the occupants were completely panic-stricken.
B: What a nightmare!
A: It was. Then the lights went off and one of them started screaming.
B: Yeah, I think I would have done the same thing.

Conversation 5

A: The tires on my bicycle were badly worn and when I hit a bump in the road, one of them burst.
B: Poor you!
A: Well, I fell off and cut my hand. Thank goodness there were no cars behind me.
B: That was lucky.

Conversation 6

A: My computer froze while I was working.
B: Really? How strange!
A: Yeah, I thought I'd lost about four hours' work, but I when I rebooted the computer, I searched for some of the key words in my document and found a temporary file which had most of the document in it.
B: That was good thinking.

7

That must have been a relief.

So what did you do?

8

1 What a nightmare!
2 Oh, that's awful.
3 How embarrassing!
4 Really? That's odd.
5 That was good thinking.
6 Something like that happened to me.

Unit 3

9

Hello everyone… one moment, I'll just adjust my microphone… OK, that's better. I can see a lot of hopeful-looking faces out there. I'm speaking to a government committee tomorrow and I hope they look as bright-eyed as you do… Let me just say that I'm afraid that those of you who have come looking for immediate answers to overpopulation are going to be disappointed, but I hope I can at least give you some cause for optimism. I'm not going to speak for too long because I'd like to hear what you have to say too, but let me tell you first how I see the situation…

In 1798, an English economist, Thomas Malthus, claimed that the population always grows faster than the food supply until war, disease, or famine arrive to reduce the number of people. A century and a half later in 1968, Paul Ehrlich wrote in his book *The Population Bomb* that medical science was keeping too many people alive and that we had failed to control the birth rate. He predicted that as a result hundreds of millions of people would soon starve to death.

But his bomb was a dud. Yes, medical science has extended life expectancy and the population carries on growing: around 7 billion today and it will probably peak at around 9 billion by 2050. But mass starvation? It hasn't happened. Why? Because science stepped in with better seeds and better pesticides to boost food production, and it's about to step in again with nanotechnology, which will help us to engineer safer and cheaper foods.

So what about overpopulation? Let me give you a fact: if in 2045 there are 9 billion people in the world, the population density will still be only half that of France today. And no one complains about overcrowding there: France is the world's favorite vacation destination! Some of the new megacities of Asia might not be such pleasant places to live… But the problem is not just the number of people. The problem is how people consume resources.

By 2030, more than a billion people in the developing world will belong to the "global middle class." That's a good thing, but it will be a bad thing for the planet if those people start eating meat and driving big cars every day. Some ultracautious people say we should bring in wartime emergency measures to conserve resources. I don't think that's the answer, but then I'm a scientist at heart even if I'm semi-retired now. For me the answer lies in innovations like biofuels and other alternative energy sources.

I'll talk about these specific solutions in the second part of my talk, but let's just go back to Malthus for a moment. People, he argued, are basically lazy. They won't do anything unless they are forced to by necessity. But what he didn't take into account is that faced with disaster, people are not lazy. Mankind and science will rise to the challenge—that is my sincere belief.

10

B = Ben; S = Sophie

B: Can you give me a hand? I'm having trouble printing this map.
S: Hang on, I'm just finishing a letter. I'll be with you in a second… OK. What do you want to do exactly?
B: I'm just giving directions to some friends who are staying in our house next week. I'm trying to paste this map into a Word document.
S: Are you going to email it to them? Because if so, you could just email them the link to the map.
B: No, I'm going to print it out and give it to them when they get here, because we're going away… The trouble is, it won't allow me to copy it.
S: Let me take a look. Oh, I see… It's a Google map; you can't select and copy them, I'm afraid.
B: Oh… what should I do then?
S: Well, there are two possibilities. You can either take a screen shot or…
B: What does that involve?
S: Here I'll show you. Just press alt print screen like this, then open a new Word document and paste it in. That should do the trick.
B: Oh, I see, but it came out very small. That's going to be too hard for them to read. What else do you suggest?
S: Have you tried looking for a different map? If you do a search, you might find one that you can copy.
B: OK. I'll give that a try. Thanks.
S: Feel free to ask me again if that doesn't work.

11

What do you suggest?

What does that involve?

It won't allow me to copy it.

First select the picture,…

What are you trying to achieve?

What solution do you propose?

Did you attach the document?

Unit 4

12

"Nature has done everything for Sydney, man nothing; man has done everything for Melbourne, nature nothing," a visitor to Australia once noted. Herein lies the essential difference between Australia's two largest cities. Melbourne is Australia's second city, but it has plenty of first-class qualities, from a buzzing art scene to an enormous range of restaurants. It may have a few gray days, and a muddy river instead of a beautiful harbor, but don't let that worry you. The lack of natural attractions has meant that Melbourne has had to create its own man-made pleasures, and in doing so it has become Australia's cultural capital. Theater, music, street sculpture, fashion—in fact, there are hardly any forms of artistic expression which you can't find here. All thrive, alongside a cosmopolitan mix of cafés, restaurants, and bars.

What's great about Melbourne for the visitor is how accessible all these arts are. In addition to traditional museums and galleries like the National Gallery of Victoria and concert halls like Hamer Hall, there is an enormous number of smaller art spaces and venues which cater to every kind of taste. Art is not something for a small minority. In fact, for most inhabitants of Melbourne a weekly visit to the movie theater or an art exhibition is a routine event. Several festivals take place during the winter months, including the International Film Festival in July and the Fringe Festival in September, which has loads of interesting (even if not always good!) comedy, dance, and theater acts.

If the locals appreciate their art, they absolutely love their sport. Lots of people around the world will know the Australian Formula One Grand Prix and the Australian Open Tennis, which attracts over half a million spectators to Melbourne in a carnival atmosphere, but few people will be familiar with the sports Melburnians themselves follow. Australian Rules football and cricket enjoy a huge amount of support and, if you have enough time, a visit to see either is well worth it just for the atmosphere. If you're looking to participate rather than just watch, why not try some surfing or swimming? Biking, jogging, or a visit to one of Melbourne's many gyms are other possibilities. All this information is on our website…

13

a huge amount of support

a huge number of galleries

a lack of natural attractions

a lot of information

lots of people

14

I = Interviewer; W = Walid

I: OK, Walid, I'm going to fire some statements at you about what various people say art should be, and I want to know which of these you agree with. OK?

W: Uh, OK, but I'm already a little suspicious, because I don't really think that "should" has a lot to do with it. People have a very fixed idea about what art "should" be—a certain kind of portrait or landscape, very often—but, anyway, anyway, I'll play the game, so… let's hear what they say…

I: Good, here's the first one then: *Art should be pleasing for the viewer.*

W: Mmm, no, not necessarily—the artist's intention might be to make you feel uncomfortable, not to give you a warm feeling.

I: OK. What about this, then? *Art should involve effort on the part of the artist.*

W: Well, that's more interesting, but still the answer is "not necessarily." Monet did some of his paintings in five minutes.

I: Did he? I didn't know that. That's amazing! Well, that ties in with the next one, perhaps. *Art should involve technical skill.*

W: Um, I can think of quite a lot of examples of successful art that wasn't technically difficult, but was just based on a clever idea.

I: OK, *Art should have a social message or make a political point.*

W: No, certainly not. Is the Mona Lisa political? I don't think so. Look, an artist's role is simply to present an idea in a visual form. The viewer's role is to give that effort their time and attention and then say either "Yes, I really like that," or "That moves me," or "No, I'm afraid that doesn't do anything for me."

15

J = Jae; T = Tomas

J: Hey, Tomas, how was *The Lion King*?

T: I loved it, even though I'm not generally a fan of musicals.

J: No, me neither. I never feel particularly inspired by the music in them, which should really be the whole point of them, with a few exceptions maybe—like *West Side Story* or *Grease*, which have terrific music. So what was so good about it?

T: Well, visually it's absolutely stunning, the opening scene in particular. All the animals—giraffes, wildebeest, zebra, antelope—congregate on the stage to set the scene, which is the plains of the Serengeti where the story takes place. And they're in these fabulous costumes. They're difficult to describe, but the effect is that they actually seem to move like real animals. Everyone in the audience was spellbound.

J: But is the story the same as in the Disney movie? I remember there were a couple of pretty annoying characters in the movie, like that bird who's supposed to be there for comic effect—well at least I think it is—but after a while, really begins to annoy you.

T: You mean Zazu. Yeah, I know what you mean about that kind of Disney character. They can get on your nerves, but this production's different. It actually seems much more adult than the movie. It's very well done. I found the story really moving.

J: What about the music?

T: It's essentially the same score as the film—I think Elton John wrote most of it, but it's all based on African rhythms and vocals.

J: Doesn't really sound like my kind of thing.

T: Oh, well, I'm really into Elton John. I think he catches the mood of this really well. Have you heard *Circle of Life*?

J: Uh, no, I don't think so.

T: Well, I'm not going to sing it. Anyway, I really recommend it. It's not cheap to go, but if you get a chance you should. I can't stand the high prices they charge for musicals these days, but actually I didn't mind for this one. It was worth it.

Unit 5

16

I = Interviewer; J = Journalist

I: I know you like exotic places. Have you tried visiting India?

J: I was just there actually, in Kerala, in the southwest. I was meaning to go on to tour other parts of India, but Kerala was so fascinating I stayed longer.

I: Were you on vacation?

J: No. Well, it was meant to be a vacation, but it actually turned into more than that.

I: Oh dear…

J: Oh, no! I don't regret changing my plans! I became so interested in the place that I started to write an article about it for the newspaper I work for.

I: Really? Is it a travel article?

J: Not really. It's more sociological, I guess. I'm trying to show what a remarkable place Kerala is in the developing world. You see, it's a small state with a big population, and the average income is only about $300 a year. Usually that would mean people having a fairly poor quality of life, but that's not the case. In fact, Kerala stands out as a kind of model of social development. The population is highly literate and well-educated and they seem very well-off, compared to other parts of India. They're healthy and live almost as long as Americans or Europeans. It seems that infant mortality is also very low. Also, women, who've, uh, traditionally been the head of the household, continue to be very active (and equal) participants in society.

I: Huh, that's really interesting. I remember going there with my wife in the 1990s. But we were just tourists and my memories of it are as a very tranquil and beautiful place, with gorgeous beaches and lagoons.

J: Well, of course that's the part of it that tourists like to spend time visiting. But tranquil is not necessarily the adjective I would use. Trivandrum, the main city where we stopped to visit an Indian journalist I know—a highly cultured man, by the way—is absolutely hectic. The people there are very politically engaged: they never stop debating. There are often strikes on the buses or parades of demonstrators. Some medical students started protesting when we were there and went on protesting for four days.

I: So why do you think it's such a successful society?

J: Well, there are essentially two reasons, I think. The first is that the Keralites are naturally tolerant people: you find Hindus, Muslims, and Christians all living peacefully beside each other, and foreigners are treated no differently than anyone else. And second, the government has invested a lot in health and education and goes on investing a lot. The land is incredibly fertile and well managed. Small farmers cultivate every inch of it so none is wasted, which I regret to say is not always the case in some developing countries.

I: Sounds fascinating. Please remember to send me a copy of the article when it's published.

J: Of course I will.

17

1	state weight	5	main plane
2	low though	6	stopped opt
3	head said	7	none fun
4	course force	8	waste faced

18

P = Patricio; A = Ana; I = Isabel

P: OK, Ana, I believe you've prepared a brief summary of the Howard Park project. [**Ana:** Yup]. Could you just take us through the main points?

A: Yes, sure. Well, the Howard Park project began two years ago. We agreed to lend the local government $750,000 to redevelop a green space in the Howard's Hill area of the city. The aim was to give the local residents a nicer park, first of all, but also some new recreation facilities: a mini-golf course, two tennis courts, a small café, and a new children's play area. The play area was in terrible condition—full of trash—so it was actually pretty dangerous. So here we are two years later, and what progress have they made? Well, they've done a good job of cleaning the area up: they've planted trees and laid new grass, so it looks much, much better. They've also built the café and the children's play area. However, they've also done some things that weren't part of the original plan. For example, they've built a fountain near the café, and six months ago they also bought a sculpture, at a cost of $80,000, to place near the fountain. Now they've run out of money and are asking for a new loan of $250,000 to complete the tennis courts and mini-golf course. What do you think?

I: If you ask me, that's completely wrong. They've been spending money on things they had no right to. I don't think we should give them another cent.

P: Well, hang on a minute. Let's not be too hasty. I agree that they should have told us about these other changes, but we need to consider whether they are in the spirit of the original aims of the project.

A: That really depends on the opinion of the local residents. The way I see it, it's probably a good thing if residents like it and it means they'll use the park more.

I: Well, I just find it arrogant of them.

P: OK, so what should we do? Personally, I don't think we should lend them any more until we know what local people think of the work they've already done.

A: Yes, I'd go along with that. We need to ask them to conduct a survey of local opinion and then show us the results.

P: Exactly. Are we all in agreement, then?

I: Yes, I guess so. Yes, that seems fair to me.

Unit 6

19

P = Presenter; K = Katie Samuel

P: Now, have you ever thought of doing a little building work during your vacation? Or helping to look after animals on a wildlife preserve? You probably thought that kind of vacation was for eighteen-year-olds in their gap year, didn't you? But it seems more and more working adults are opting for volunteer vacations. With us today is Katie Samuel, author of *Good Travel*, a guide to alternative vacations. Katie, I can see that this might attract a few people, but wouldn't most people who only get a few weeks off a year prefer a more relaxing option?

K: Well, that depends very much on how your volunteer vacation is organized. The good companies in this field are certainly conscious of the fact that this should be a rewarding travel experience, not just a work trip.

P: But isn't the whole point to go and lend a hand to people in need of help? It's not really a vacation as we know it, is it?

K: Well, no, perhaps it isn't, but it is more like what real travel should be about: a cultural experience where each side gives something and takes something. A good example is a program next to Kenya's Tsavo National Park, where volunteers help local people to find ways of making a living that don't involve poaching or killing local wildlife. So they help them to plant crops, build fences, develop ideas for tourist businesses, and so on. In return, the locals take them for bush walks, which are like mini-safaris, teach them about local wildlife, talk about the history of their community.

P: But the volunteers pay for the trip, don't they?

K: Yes, of course, they have to pay for their flight, their living expenses, and something to cover the organization's costs.

P: And do you need to be qualified to volunteer? I imagine organizations don't want people turning up to teach or build or whatever who have no idea of what they're doing, do they?

K: Again, it depends. There are a few projects which are only open to people with professional experience, uh, like people with a medical background, but for the most part, volunteers can be trained to do the work. The Cultural Restoration Tourism Project (CRTP), which helps to restore cultural heritage sites around the world, gives volunteers the chance to work with local architects and artists. They have a project restoring a 300-year-old monastery in Nepal where you can get training in doing wall paintings from a world-famous painter.

P: So, you could actually come back with a skill you didn't have when you left?

K: Absolutely. It might not be a skill you'll ever use again: helping to bottle-feed milk to orphaned lion cubs—that's a project in Zambia—is unlikely to be of direct use to you back at the office, but we all benefit from new and different experiences, wouldn't you agree?

P: Yeah, I'm sure that's true. So could you tell us a bit more about…

20

Do you like visiting new places? Yes, now and then.

Don't you like visiting new places? No, not at all.

You like visiting new places, don't you? Yes, I love it.

You don't like visiting new places, do you? No, you're right. I don't.

21

1 You like the idea of volunteer vacations, don't you?
2 Don't you think it's an interesting idea?
3 You've been on a volunteer vacation, haven't you?
4 Didn't it seem strange to pay money in order to work?
5 You won't be going again this year, will you?

22

M = Manuel; P = Paul

M: Hi Paul, this is Manuel, your host. You emailed me about staying next Thursday for a couple of nights.

P: Oh hi, hi Manuel. Thanks for getting back to me. Is that still OK?

M: No, that's all fine. I just thought I'd give you a call to explain how to get here, because it's a little complicated. How are you getting to Hamilton, first of all?

P: I'm coming in by train sometime in the afternoon.

M: OK. I wanted to pick you up, but my car's in the garage that day.

P: Hey, that's nice of you, but I can find my own way.

M: OK. Well, I'm at work 'til about five thirty, so feel free to come over any time after six.

P: That sounds perfect. And how do I get to you from downtown?

M: Well, you could just catch a taxi, but it's about eleven miles from downtown, so it won't be cheap. Alternatively, you can hop on a bus to Stoney Creek. Look out for the Stoney Creek Arena on your right and get off there. It's only a twenty-minute ride. From there, Cherry Heights is another fifteen minutes on foot, straight up King St. Once you reach the crossroads at Gray Road, the easiest thing is to give me a call and I'll come out and meet you.

P: So: bus to Stoney Creek, walk up King St. to Cherry Heights and call from there?

M: Yup. Call when you get to the crossroads at Gray Road.

P: OK, got it. That sounds great. If I get held up in any way I'll let you know, but otherwise expect a call around six thirty.

M: Great. See you next Thursday then. Bye.

P: Bye.

23

I wanted to pick you up, but my car's in the garage that day.

You could just catch a taxi, but it's about eleven miles from downtown.

Unit 7

24

Speaker 1: Liam from the United Kingdom

I live in Manchester, which is probably one of the wettest places in the UK. If I had been brought up somewhere like Saharan Africa, where I had to walk miles each day just to fetch water, I'd obviously be a lot more conscious of water conservation. But I'm afraid I don't set a very good example. I probably waste a lot—leaving the tap running when I brush my teeth and so on. Clearly we're not going to run out of water in the UK, but I know water conservation is important. If we all used less water, the water companies wouldn't have to use so much energy treating water to make it clean. And of course that would be more environmentally-friendly.

Speaker 2: Gemal from the United Arab Emirates

I'm not saying the idea of desalination plants is wrong. If desalination methods didn't exist, this country would not have been able to develop in the way it has. Nowadays we use water in our homes more or less as we want to. But I don't think we can continue like this. You see, the waste from the desalination process is a kind of brine with a dangerously high salt content which will eventually destroy life in the sea. I am interested in discovering farming techniques that use salt water. There are grasses and other types of plant that can grow with sea water. If we were to use more of these, it would give our natural fresh water springs a chance to recharge.

Speaker 3: Daniel from the United States

Americans (and I'm as guilty as the rest) use water like there is no tomorrow. I think it's well-known that the Colorado River doesn't reach the sea anymore. If you had visited the area around the old delta in Mexico 100 years ago—rich wetlands, full of wildlife—you'd be shocked to see it now. It's all dried up, a kind of salt flat. The reason is agriculture. The river has been dammed and diverted in various places along its route to irrigate fields and provide enough water for people living in the desert areas of Nevada and California. Unless we change the way we think about water and stop wasting so much, the river will keep on getting smaller.

Speaker 4: Carmen from Mexico

My water needs are the same as most people's, I think: I have a small vegetable garden; I have to wash myself and my clothes. I don't have to save water, but I want to, you know. I collect rainwater for the garden, I fill a basin to wash in rather than running the tap, I wash my dishes every other day. But now governments are discussing big projects for transporting water from one part of the world to another using huge pipes and tankers. I think if more people thought and acted like me, things would not have come to this point, you know.

25

E = Elena; A = Anne; J = Jim; R = Rick

A: Elena, what do you think about all these people who say that there's no proof that climate change is man-made?

E: My position is that I don't know if climate change is man-made and I'm not sure anyone can say for sure. Let me give you an example, an analogy. Imagine you were losing your hair and I told you that some people had found that if they ate a banana every day it prevented hair loss. Even though you had no proof it worked, you would probably try eating a banana every day, wouldn't you? Well, it's the same with global warming. We don't know that we're causing it, but some people say we might be, with all the fossil fuels we burn. And I, for one, am happy to be a little more careful in how I pollute in case they're right.

A: Mmm, well, I don't accept that. I used to believe in climate change, but the last few winters here in the US have been much colder than normal. To be honest with you, I'd believe it more if I wasn't getting up in the morning and scraping ice off the inside of my windows rather than the outside.

E: Yeah, but that's not the point, Anne, is it? You know, regional temperatures may be lower, but average global temperatures keep on rising.

J: Well, look, there's no doubt that the weather's changing, but I don't believe it's a man-made problem. It's just part of a natural weather cycle. Yeah, I know you'll say "Oh, that's just your excuse to drive a big car and fly to exotic places for your vacations," but actually that's not the reason. I don't believe it simply because no scientist has successfully proved it yet.

R: We're approaching this debate all wrong by saying "it's a big environmental problem that we need to address." Because it's not just an environmental problem. It's an economic problem, a social problem, even an ethical problem. We all need to do what we can to prevent climate change.

26

I don't know and I'm not sure anyone knows for sure.

27

1 We don't know that we're causing it, but some people say we might be.
2 …scraping ice off the inside of my windows rather than the outside.
3 Regional temperatures may be lower, but average global temperatures keep on rising.
4 Because it's not just an environmental problem. It's an economic problem, a social problem, even an ethical problem.

Unit 8

28

And finally… it was thought that the Large Blue butterfly was extinct in Britain, but it seems to have made a remarkable comeback. The Large Blue, which disappeared 30 years ago, is only found in certain fields. What these fields have in common is that their grass is very short because rabbits, sheep and cows graze there. Originally it was believed that greedy butterfly hunters had killed off the Large Blue, but it is now agreed that changes in farming techniques were responsible for its decline. As a result of recent efforts to protect its natural habitat, it is estimated that around 20,000 of these beautiful creatures will be seen in the British countryside this summer.

And finally, researchers believe they may have found a cure—or at least some relief—for the common cold. In tests, it was reported that people who started taking zinc at the first signs of a common cold got well sooner. There have been many previous studies into the effectiveness of zinc but they were inconclusive. The new study, involving over 1,000 people of various ages, found that, on average, people who took zinc supplements recovered from their colds one day earlier than those who took nothing. The effectiveness of zinc in preventing a cold in the first place was less certain, although it was said that those who took it regularly suffered less serious symptoms than those who didn't.

And finally, believe it or not, eating chocolate might be good for you after all. In the past it was thought that eating candy would result in tooth decay and weight gain. But now it is claimed that a new chocolate bar, invented by the world's largest chocolate maker, can actually slow the aging process of your skin. The special chocolate contains antioxidants, which help hydrate the skin and fight wrinkles. The market for healthy foods has grown by over five percent a year in recent years and it seems now that even the sellers of traditionally unhealthy snacks are trying to get in on the act. However, doctors have warned against rushing out to buy extra chocolate—good skin and chocolate are not generally natural partners, they say.

And finally, Costa Rica today has the honor of being named the world's happiest nation. According to the latest Happy Planet Index, it is said that Costa Rica has the best balance of human well-being—that is to say, good health, a long life, low levels of poverty—and a low ecological footprint, in other words the amount of natural resources it uses. In fact, Latin American countries took nine of the top ten places, while richer, so-called developed countries, like the US at number 74, were much further down in the list.

29

J = Jess (female); P = Phil

J: Hey, Phil. Did all that noise in the street wake you up last night?

P: No, it didn't, but then I'm a deep sleeper. What happened?

J: Well, I didn't see it myself but I heard that it was an argument between two drivers and supposedly it got pretty nasty.

P: Really? Who told you about it?

J: Tara at number 42. It seems that both drivers got out of their cars and started shouting at each other. She says they almost started fighting.

P: Well, I'd take what Tara says with a grain of salt, if I were you. She tends to blow things out of proportion.

J: No, I believe her actually—people do get very frustrated not being able to pass each other in this street. Anyway, the police were called…

P: The police? It wasn't that serious, was it?

J: Well, no. The cars didn't crash or anything. But Tara says that they got out of their cars and started arguing. She figures that if the police hadn't arrived, there would have been a fight.

P: Did the cars make contact?

J: No, they were just coming in opposite directions and they met where the street gets narrow and neither one would back up to let the other pass. So they just stayed there, in the middle of the road, with neither one giving way.

P: How childish.

J: Yeah, right? Someone said they'd seen one of the drivers before. Apparently he's a local politician.

P: It wasn't Tara getting her facts mixed up again, was it?

J: No, it was Chris. I think I'd take his word for it; he's not the type to spread gossip.

P: So what did the police do about it?

J: Well, according to Chris, they took them both away for questioning.

30

apparently	generally
supposedly	happened

Unit 9

31

Q: Can you tell us something about the Emerging Explorers program?

A: It's an awards program set up by the National Geographic Society to encourage young adventurers, scientists, photographers, and storytellers to continue their work and to realize their potential. Each year, between eight and fifteen explorers whose work is really outstanding are selected and given money to help them continue their research and exploration.

Q: So Emerging Explorers are generally young people?

A: Not necessarily. Emerging Explorers are generally people who are at an early stage of their careers. What they have in common is that they are all people who are pushing the boundaries of their field, whether that's exploring undiscovered deep-water caves or watching the stars through a telescope.

Q: And how does National Geographic encourage them?

A: Well, first of all National Geographic awards each one of them $10,000, which is intended to go towards further research and exploration. Of course their profiles are also raised by the articles and news that appear in *National Geographic*. In other words, the magazine is a place where other interested people can read about their work.

Q: And what kind of fields do the winners come from?

A: We have so many different types of explorer, chosen from fields as diverse as anthropology, space exploration, mountaineering, and music.

Q: You mentioned storytellers earlier. What did you mean by that, exactly?

A: Well, there are all these people doing important work out there in the various fields that I've described. And that's great, but it's also very important that everyone hears about this work. That's the skill of the storytellers: communicating with pictures and words important facts about the planet and life on the planet in a way that grabs everyone's attention. A really good example is Alexandra Cousteau, whose father Philippe Cousteau was well-known for his documentaries about marine life. She works as a conservationist, trying to persuade people to protect scarce resources like water. Alexandra, inspired by her father's success as a storyteller, is researching ways in which the environmental community can use new media—social networks, video games—to communicate its message.

32

S = Sarah; P = Panit

S: So, you're 24 years old, you graduated a year ago, and you're looking for work with a charity. What attracted you to Shelterbox?

P: Well, I'm familiar with your work because I have a friend who volunteered for you last year packing boxes, and I think it's a fantastic concept. But, umm, mainly I'm really interested in working abroad in foreign countries.

S: Mm, I see. And what makes you think you'd be suited for that? I see you studied economics at Stanford. Don't you think that's a pretty different world?

P: Yes, it's true that I specialized in economics but, actually, I'm good at coping with difficult environments. I spent three months helping to build a school in Chennai in India last summer. And the year before that, I trekked across the Mojave Desert. So I think I'd be well-suited for the work.

S: OK, well, they're certainly not easy places to adapt to, although in fact you'd also be spending a good part of the time here in the office doing paperwork.

P: Yeah, that's also fine. I was expecting that. I have quite a lot of experience sitting at a desk for my studies. What sort of paperwork is it?

S: Well, each trip involves a lot of preparation and a certain amount of follow-up, too. Keeping spreadsheets, writing reports. Are you OK doing that sort of thing?

P: Yeah, I'm pretty good with computers. I'm comfortable with all the usual programs—Excel, Word, some financial software…

S: OK. There's just one thing that's worrying me though. You're clearly a bright person and you have a good degree. How do I know that you won't just do this job for a few months and then go and get a better-paid job with a bank or a consulting company?

P: That's a good question. It's actually what a lot of my friends from college have done, but I'll tell you why that's not for me. First, I'm really serious about wanting to help people in need. Second, I think I need to become more knowledgeable about the world, before I use my economics degree to do something else. If you put your faith in me, I will be absolutely committed to doing the best job that I can for two or three years at least.

33

although, comfortable
environments, foreign
knowledgeable, months
specialized, suited
world

34

clothes, February, folk, island
lengths, receipt, surface, thorough

Unit 10

35

Different people's diets rarely surprise me these days. We didn't use to think so much about what we ate. But today, well, we live in an age when people are just very conscious of their diets. A day hardly ever passes without a story in the news about a particular food that's good for your health or bad for you if you eat too much of it.

So I was very interested to read a story the other day about the diet of the Nochmani tribe of the Nicobar Islands in the Indian Ocean. People used to think that these tiny islands—which are about 600 miles from the coast of India—that they were uninhabited by humans. But in 2004, aid workers in helicopters spotted some tribespeople on a mountainside. Scientists were particularly surprised that there were inhabitants there, because people usually need mammals—you know, cows, goats and so on—and their produce—meat, milk, et cetera—in order to live. But the Nicobar Islands have almost no mammals. So what were the Nochmani surviving on? Fish, perhaps? No. Amazingly, their diet consisted largely of insects, in particular beetles, of which there were over 1,700 varieties on the islands, but also other insects including spiders.

This presented a problem for the aid workers, who'd brought with them standard survival meals, including chicken, beef, and pork. The Nochmani, who weren't used to eating meat at all, were disgusted by these offerings. All they'd take from the aid workers were sweets and cakes. It wasn't just a matter of taste, either. If you're used to a certain type of food—even insects—other types may be completely indigestible.

Insects are, in fact, very nutritious: high in protein and fat and low in carbohydrates, making them an ideal food source for humans. But what was even more amazing was that just as we usually help our animals to live by providing food for them, so the Nochmani cultivate certain fungi and mosses to attract and feed the insects they eat. Perhaps we can learn from this tribe. If more of us could get used to eating unconventional foods such as insects, it might help the world's food problems.

36

M = Marie; E = Esther

M: I know of henna painting as a custom from Indian weddings, but you came across it in Turkey, didn't you?

E: Yes, in eastern Turkey when I was traveling there. It takes place a few nights before the wedding.

M: Was it a little like a bachelorette party?

E: Well, in the sense that it marks the last evening that a bride spends with female family and friends, I suppose it is a little like that. What happens, typically, is that women from both families get together with the bride, to celebrate with music, song, and dance. But it's not just a party. It's an occasion for sadness too, because it symbolizes the end of life as a single person and the start of another stage.

37

M = Marie; E = Esther

M: So what happens exactly?

E: Well, the ceremony begins with preparation of the henna. It's traditional for this to be done by the daughter of a couple who have had a successful marriage themselves. Then, after the bride's head has been covered in a red veil, her hands and feet are decorated with henna. After that, a gold coin is put into the remaining henna. While this is happening, the guests sing, umm, separation songs—these are rather sad, as you can imagine. The party continues well into the night. Then, on the morning of the wedding, a child presents the hennaed coin to the groom as a symbol of future prosperity and good fortune.

38

M: I know of henna painting as a custom from Indian weddings, but you came across it in Turkey, didn't you?

E: Yes, in eastern Turkey when I was traveling there. It takes place a few nights before the wedding.

M: Was it a little like a bachelorette party?

E: Well, in the sense that it marks the last evening that a bride spends with female family and friends, I suppose it is a little like that. What happens, typically, is that women from both families get together with the bride, to celebrate with music, song and dance. But it's not just a party. It's an occasion for sadness too, because it symbolizes the end of life as a single person and the start of another stage.

M: So what happens exactly?

E: Well, the ceremony begins with preparation of the henna. It's traditional for this to be done by the daughter of a couple who've had a successful marriage themselves. Then, after the bride's head has been covered in a red veil, her hands and feet are decorated with henna. After that, a gold coin is put into the remaining henna. While this is happening, the guests sing, umm, separation songs—these are rather sad, as you can imagine. The party continues well into the night. Then, on the morning of the wedding, a child presents the hennaed coin to the groom as a symbol of future prosperity and good fortune.

39

custom, dress, friends
music, suppose, weddings

40

across, eastern, lose, place
rings, single, spends, surprise

Unit 11

41

Have any of these things happened to you? You were about to give a speech or make a comment at a meeting, and then your mind went blank. You were supposed to send a friend a card for his birthday, but then you forgot. You recognized someone in the street and would have spoken to her, but you didn't because you couldn't remember her name. You promised you would mail a letter for someone and two days later you found it still in your pocket. You were going to write down a great idea you had, but when you found a pen and paper, the idea had gone. I could go on, but I won't because I'm sure everyone recognizes these common failures of memory.

42

We all would like to remember more but would it actually make us any happier?

I want to tell you the story of a 41-year-old woman from California known in medical literature as AJ, who remembers almost every day of her life since the age of 11. She remembers that at 12:34 p.m. on Sunday, August 3, 1986, a young man she was attracted to called her on the telephone. She remembers that on March 28, 1992, she had lunch with her father at the Beverly Hills Hotel. It's a bit like certain smells that evoke strong memories: AJ's memory is stimulated in the most intense way by dates.

You'd think that being able to retrieve facts and knowledge in this way would make us more confident and wiser. But in fact for AJ, an incredible memory is as much a burden as it is a benefit. That's because most memories are selective: they provide us mostly important things, and mostly good things too. AJ remembers every detail, good or bad, important or not.

So when we curse our poor memories for forgetting to send a birthday card, actually we should be grateful also for all the things that our memories hide away because they don't need to be remembered or thought about. Umm, technology, of course helps us with this. We don't need to remember the precise content of a report or the exact time of a meeting, because it's stored on our computer or in our smart phone.

But interestingly, the growth of this technology—what psychologists call our external memory—is having an effect on what and how much we remember. Even our memories of happy events—like parties or vacations—get stored in photograph albums on our computers. So our internal memories are probably worse than those of people 100 years ago. Medical science is trying to address the problem of poor memory and this is what I want to talk about next.

43

Have any of these things happened to you? You were about to give a speech or make a comment at a meeting, and then your mind went blank. You were supposed to send a friend a card for his birthday, but then you forgot. You recognized someone in the street and would have spoken to her, but you didn't because you couldn't remember her name. You promised you would mail a letter for someone and two days later you found it still in your pocket. You were going to write down a great idea you had, but when you found a pen and paper, the idea had gone. I could go on, but I won't because I'm sure everyone recognizes these common failures of memory.

We all would like to remember more but would it actually make us any happier?

I want to tell you the story of a 41-year-old woman from California known in medical literature as AJ, who remembers almost every day of her life since the age of 11. She remembers that at 12:34 p.m. on Sunday, August 3, 1986, a young man she was attracted to called her on the telephone. She remembers that on March 28, 1992, she had lunch with her father at the Beverly Hills Hotel. It's a bit like certain smells that evoke strong memories: AJ's memory is stimulated in the most intense way by dates.

You'd think that being able to retrieve facts and knowledge in this way would make us more confident and wiser. But in fact for AJ, an incredible memory is as much a burden as it is a benefit. That's because most memories are selective: they provide us mostly important things, and mostly good things too. AJ remembers every detail, good or bad, important or not.

So when we curse our poor memories for forgetting to send a birthday card, actually we should be grateful also for all the things that our memories hide away because they don't need to be remembered or thought about. Umm, technology, of course, helps us with this. We don't need to remember the precise content of a report or the exact time of a meeting, because it's stored on our computer or in our smart phone.

But interestingly, the growth of this technology—what psychologists call our external memory—is having an effect on what and how much we remember. Even our memories of happy events—like parties or vacations—get stored in photograph albums on our computers. So our internal memories are probably worse than those of people 100 years ago. Medical science is trying to address the problem of poor memory and this is what I want to talk about next.

44

Have any of these things happened to you? You were about to give a speech or make a comment at a meeting, and then your mind went blank. You were supposed to send a friend a card for his birthday, but then you forgot. You recognized someone in the street and would have spoken to her, but you didn't because you couldn't remember her name. You promised you would mail a letter for someone and two days later you found it still in your pocket. You were going to write down a great idea you had, but when you found a pen and paper, the idea had gone. I could go on, but I won't because I'm sure everyone recognizes these common failures of memory.

45

1 I was going to ask Sanjip to come, but I asked Kumar instead.
2 She was supposed to be in Cairo this week, but she's sick.
3 He promised he would send me the original, but he sent me a copy.
4 We would have been there by ten o'clock, but the train didn't get in until eleven fifteen.
5 He was about to announce that he would retire, but now he thinks he'll stay another year.
6 The city planners were going to build a new shopping mall downtown, but residents opposed it.

46

A = Ahmad; L = Liz

A: Hi there, I'm interested in taking a class at your college—umm, the history of art course.

L: Is that the two-year advanced course?

A: Excuse me, what do you mean by advanced?

L: The advanced art history course is a two-year college-level course with exams at the end of each year.

A: Oh no, no, no! I don't want to take any exams. It's just for interest.

L: OK. In that case, we have a one-year art appreciation course.

A: Sorry. Can you speak up a little? I can't hear you very well.

L: Yes, we have a one-year art appreciation course.

A: Umm, can you explain what the course involves?

L: Yeah, it's a two-hour class once a week and, basically, it teaches you how to look at art so that you get the most from the experience.

A: No, sorry, I'm not really with you. Are you saying that it doesn't really deal with the history of art?

L: No, there's some history of art in it, of course, but it's mainly learning about composition, techniques, references and so on.

A: Hmm… Could you give me an example of the kind of thing students do in the class?

L: Sure. Typically, students look at works of art and then comment on them. Then they're told more about the artist, what he or she was trying to achieve, and then they look at their work again, with fresh eyes, so to speak.

A: Mmm, OK. It sounds pretty interesting. What was the course called again?

L: Art appreciation.

A: And when is it?

L: Every Tuesday from 7 p.m. til 9 p.m., starting on… one minute… yeah, starting on September 29th. The cost is $298 for the year, unless you're a registered student.

A: Hang on a second. That's too much to take in all at once. I'm trying to write it down. I didn't catch the start date. Did you say November 29th?

L: No, September 29th.

A: OK. Well, thanks. I'll think about it, but it sounds good.

L: OK, bye.

47

Are you saying the course is full?

Can you speak up a little?

Could you give me an example?

Did you say Tuesday?

What do you mean?

Unit 12

48

I = Interviewer; D = David Stiles

I: Thirty years ago, the idea of getting a worker to hand-wash your car would have been unthinkable—except to the very rich. Either you washed it yourself at home on a Sunday morning, or you took it the carwash. Nowadays, you can have it washed inside and out by a team of willing and capable workers for as little as $6. So, what's changed? I have here with me David Stiles, author of *The Servant Economy*. David, are we just getting too lazy to do our own domestic chores. or is this part of some new economic phenomenon?

D: Well, first of all hi and thanks for having me on your show. In answer to your question, yes, it's said that in the US today there are more workers doing domestic jobs than there were in the 19th century—perhaps as many as two million: gardeners, nannies, maids. And this is a direct consequence of globalization and the freeing up of the labor market. You see, many of these workers are migrants—in the case of the US, mostly Latin Americans. Umm, and I think that in capitalist economies, anyway, the richer classes will always provide employment for the poorer classes. As the Victorian satirist Hilaire Belloc famously said, "It is the duty of the wealthy man to give employment to the artisan."

I: Yes, but that's the point, isn't it? A 19th-century-style servant economy actually emphasizes the inequalities between rich and poor in a society.

D: Well, yes, it can, but it also creates employment. You don't have to be especially rich to have a house cleaner come once a week. Quite a lot of working people do that. A lot of so-called ordinary people get their windows cleaned every few months. But there are some—uh, rich—people who get it into their heads that they're too busy or important to do any domestic chores. So they'll hire a personal shopper, and have someone walk their dog every day. If they're having a party at home, they'll get an outside catering company to prepare the food. I know some people who even have their Christmas tree installed in their living room and then decorated for them. That really *is* a statement of wealth.

I: Hmm… It seems more a statement of confused priorities to me. Walking the dog and decorating the Christmas tree are supposed to be a pleasure, aren't they?

D: Well, of course they are. But look at it another way: these are all things that create employment. As long as the staff are treated well—you know, as employees, not as servants—and are fairly paid and their skills are valued, just as you would show respect to your hairdresser when you get your hair cut, then I don't see a problem.

49

carwash	shelves
shopper	chores
richer	watch
decision	garage
pleasure	change
college	fridge

50

agent	arrange
champagne	cheese
choice	fashion
general	January
sugar	television
usual	

51

LA = Leasing agent; W = Woman

LA: So, you've had a look at the offices. What do you think?

W: Well, yeah, I really like the building. To be honest, it's absolutely perfect for our needs.

LA: That's wonderful! So you'd like to take it?

W: Well, yes, ideally I would but, umm, a key thing for us is how long we'd be tied into the lease.

LA: Well, it's a fifteen-year lease. I think that was in the details I sent you.

W: Yes, it was, but I was hoping we could negotiate that down. Because if you look at it from our point of view, we're a young business and we don't really know how things are going to go for the next few years. Who does? And let's face it, fifteen years is a big commitment. So if your client could give a little on that…

LA: Hmm… I think what you have to appreciate is that our client's main concern is securing a rental for a reasonable length of time. You know, at the end of the day, it gives them some security. To tell you the truth, that's why the rent is so low. The fifteen-year period is a kind of compensation for that. So I'm not at all sure we're going to get anywhere there.

W: Oh, that's somewhat of a sticking point then, isn't it? Is there no way around that?

LA: Uh, not that I can think of offhand. What did you have in mind?

W: Well, maybe if we signed a fifteen-year lease but with an exit clause after, say, six years, then we could pay some kind of penalty to get out of the contract.

LA: Umm, well, the normal penalty would be that you paid the remaining nine years' rent, so I don't really think that would work.

W: Oh, I see. Well, that's a shame because I really like it and we need a place pretty urgently.

LA: Look, we have other people interested in the premises, so someone will take it. If I were in your shoes, and found the terms of the lease difficult, I think I'd just leave it. When all's said and done, it has to feel right to you.

W: But that's just the problem, it does feel right to us. Give me a moment. I'm just going to call my business partner and see what he thinks.

LA: OK, no problem.

52

1 To be honest…
2 A key thing for us is…
3 Let's face it…
4 At the end of the day,…
5 To tell you the truth…

Inside Photo: 3 tl (Shivji Joshi), 3 tc (Dario Mitidieri/Hulton Archive/Getty Images), 3 tr (sellingpix/Shutterstock.com), 3 tl (EMANUELE PICCHIRALLO/National Geographic Creative), 3 tc (GEORGE STEINMETZ/National Geographic Creative), 3 tr (SUDRES Jean-Daniel / hemis. fr/Alamy), 3 cl (DAVID DOUBILET/National Geographic Creative), 3 c (CHINA OUT Reuters/Stringer/Reuters), 3 cr (Robert Harding Travel/ Photolibrary Group/Getty Images), 3 bl (NIGEL SWINN/National Geographic Creative), 3 bc (GEORGE STEINMETZ/National Geographic Creative), 3 br (JODI COBB/National Geographic Creative), 8 tr (IS09908XU/Image Source / Alamy), 8 tc (Patrick Aventurier/Getty Images/ News/Getty Images), 8 tl (Barry Bland/Barcroft Media/Getty Images), 8 bl (TIM LAMAN/National Geographic Creative), 8 bc (MICHAEL NICHOLS/National Geographic Creative), 8 br (David Ewing/INSADCO Photography/Alamy), 8 cr (Andrew Peacock/Aurora Open/Aurora Photos / Alamy), 9 t (© Regien Paassen/Shutterstock.com), 10 t (Stevi Calandra/National Geographic Channel/National Geographic Creative), 12-13 (RANDY OLSON/National Geographic Creative), 15 t (PAUL THOMPSON/National Geographic Creative), 16 br (Corbis), RF/ Alamy), 17 b (© iStockphoto.com/hadynyah), 18 (Edwin Levick/ Hulton Archive/Getty Images), 20 cl (JOEL SARTORE/National Geographic Creative), 21 t (Dario Mitidieri/Hulton Archive/Getty Images), 22 b (Adam Woolfitt/Corbis), 24 b (STEVE WINTER/National Geographic Creative), 27 br (JOEL SARTORE/National Geographic Creative), 28 br (Oote Boe 2 / Alamy), 29 b (© Ralph Loesche/Shutterstock.com), 30 (John Springer Collection/Corbis), 32 tl (BEVERLY JOUBERT/National Geographic Creative), 33 t (© sellingpix/Shutterstock.com), 34 t (RANDY OLSON National Geographic Creative), 35 br (© Michael Rosskothen/Shutterstock.com), 36 b (OLIVER UBERTI /National Geographic Creative), 38 bl (RENEE COMET/National Geographic Creative), 38 bc (RENEE COMET/National Geographic Creative), 38 bc (Renee Comet/ National Geographic Creative), 38 br (RENEE COMET/National Geographic Creative), 39 b (KENNETH GARRETT/National Geographic Creative), 44 bl (AMY WHITE & AL PETTEWAY/National Geographic Creative), 45 t (EMANUELE PICCHIRALLO/National Geographic Creative), 46 t (ANNIE GRIFFITHS/National Geographic Creative), 48 b (Alexandre Orion), 51 b (DAVID ALAN HARVEY/National Geographic Creative), 52 t (STEPHEN MORRISON/epa/Corbis), 53 tr (Justin Kase zfivez / Alamy), 54 (Patrick Aventurier/Getty Images), News/Getty Images), 56 cl (STEPHEN SHARNOFF/National Geographic Creative), 57 t (GEORGE STEINMETZ/National Geographic Creative), 58 b (Smar Jodha/ National Geographic Creative), 60 tl (Frans Lanting/Frans Lanting Studio / Alamy), 60 tr (MICHAEL MELFORD/National Geographic Creative), 63 b (CHIEN-CHI CHANG/MAGNUM PHOTOS/National Geographic Creative), 64 b (© thebezz/Shutterstock.com), 66 (IS09908XU/Image Source / Alamy), 69 t (SUDRES Jean-Daniel / hemis.fr/Alamy), 70 br (CHRIS JOHNS/National Geographic Creative), 72 bkgd (©Pichugin Dmitry/Shutterstock.com), 73 tr (Ivo Roospold/Alamy), 75 tr (Ian Trower/Age Fotostock/Photolibrary Group/Getty Images), 75 tr (RICHARD NOWITZ/National Geographic Creative), 75 cr (Sextantio Press), 75 br (Juergen Henkelmann Photography / Alamy), 76 b (KEENPRESS/ National Geographic Creative), 78 (David Ewing/INSADCO Photography/Alamy), 80 c (FARRELL GREHAN/National Geographic Creative), 81 t (DAVID DOUBILET/National Geographic Creative), 82 b (Liysa/Perspectives/Getty Images), 83 cr (GERD LUDWIG/National Geographic Creative), 84 t (PANORAMIC IMAGES/National Geographic Creative), 87 bkgd (©Nazzu/Shutterstock.com), 88 b (©Tinna/Shutterstock. com), 90 (TIM LAMAN/National Geographic Creative), 92 cl (XPACIFICA/National Geographic Creative), 93 t (CHINA OUT Reuters),/Stringer/ Reuters), 94 cl (STEVE MCCURRY/National Geographic Creative), 94 bl (Steve McCurry/National Geographic Creative), 96 bl (IS098Q1KE/ Image Source / Alamy), 96 inset (©Holger Wulschlaeger/Shutterstock.com), 96 bl (©withGod/Shutterstock.com), 96 bl (©Cheryl E. Davis/ Shutterstock.com), 97 br (Corbis), Cusp/Alamy), 99 br (Cate Gillon/Getty Images News/Getty Images), 102 (Andrew Peacock/Aurora Open/ Aurora Photos / Alamy), 104 tl (Wong Maye-E/Associated Press/Press Association Images), 106 b (courtesy of nasaimages.org/NASA), 109 t (Robert Harding Travel/Photolibrary Group/Getty Images), 109 t (Wes C. Skiles/National Geographic Creative), 109 bl (Kira Salak), 109 bc (Stephon Alexander/Diana Rogers), 109 br (Wes C. Skiles/National Geographic Creative),111 t (KENNETH GARRETT/National Geographic Creative), 111 b (Kenneth Garrett/National Geographic Creative), 112 tl (Shelterbox), 112 tl (Bjoern Bertheau/Synthesis International),113 tr (©wavebreakmedia/Shutterstock.com), 114 (Ben Ramos / Alamy), 117 t (NIGEL SWINN/National Geographic Creative), 118 br (Asiaselects/ Alamy), 120 t (©jeep2499/Shutterstock.com), 123 t (STEFANO MASSAI/National Geographic Creative), 124 br (JAMES L. STANFIELD/ National Geographic Creative), 125 (©zhu difeng/Shutterstock.com), 126 (Barry Bland/Barcroft Media/Getty Images), 128 cl (KRISTA ROSSOW/National Geographic Creative), 129 t (GEORGE STEINMETZ/National Geographic Creative), 130 cr (Renee Fadiman), 132 l (Maggie Steber/National Geographic Creative), 135 b (Vincent J. Musi/National Geographic Creative), 136 br (©Lisa F. Young/Shutterstock.com), 138 (MICHAEL NICHOLS/National Geographic Creative), 140 cl (©Michael Klenetsky/Shutterstock.com), 141 t (JODI COBB/National Geographic Creative), 142 br (LUKA TAMBACA/National Geographic Creative), 144 t (MARIA STENZEL/National Geographic Creative), 145 br (JOEL SARTORE/National Geographic Creative), 147 b (XPACIFICA/National Geographic Creative), 148 br (Sterba Martin/CTK / Alamy), 150 t (MATTIAS KLUM/National Geographic Creative), 150 bkgd (Sam Abell/National Geographic Creative), 152 tl (Justin Guariglia/National Geographic Creative), 153 c (Motoring Picture Library / Alamy), 154 tl (RENEE COMET/National Geographic Creative), 154 cr (RENEE COMET/National Geographic Creative), 155 tl (Renee Comet/National Geographic Creative), 155 tr (Renee Comet/National Geographic Creative), 155 c (Motoring Picture Library / Alamy).

Illustration: Bob Lea P 42, Celia Hart P 100, David Russell P 40, National Geographic Maps/National Geographic Creative P 8.

Credits

Inside Photo: 6 bc (©Stephen Bures/Shutterstock.com), 7 cr (Robert Fried/Alamy), 9 cr (©Matej Hudovernik/Shutterstock.com), 10 t (©BMJ /Shutterstock.com), 14 cl (©iStockphoto.com/Fitzer), 17 cr (Stefano Cavoretto/Alamy), 18 c (Renee Comet/National Geographic Creative), 22 bl (©Viktor Kovalenko/shutterstock.com), 23 cl (©1000 Words/Shutterstock.com), 23 c (©Natalia Bratslavsky/Shutterstock.com), 25 br (© faberfoto -it/Shutterstock.com), 28 br (James Nielsena/AFP/Getty Images), 29 tl (Terry Donnelly/Alamy), 29 cr (©iStockphoto.com/AKauroraPhotos), 30 tl (©iStockphoto.com/chinaface), 32 l (©iStockphoto.com/fotoVoyager), 34 r (©iStockphoto.com/PanosKarapanagiotis), 35 r (©iStockphoto.com /MShep2), 37 l (©Radu Razvan/Shutterstock.com), 40 c (Greatstock Photographic Library/Alamy), 41 tl (©iStockphoto.com/Brad Martin), 41 tr (©iStockphoto.com/leezsnow), 41 cl (©Robert J. Beyers II/Shutterstock.com), 41 cr (©iStockphoto.com/MichaelUtech), 41 cl (©iStockphoto.com /alantobey), 41 cr (©chippix/Shutterstock.com), 41 bl (©iStockphoto.com/Spinkle), 41 br (©iStockphoto.com/nesjerry), 42 cl (©iStockphoto.com /woraput), 42 cr (©iStockphoto.com/lilly3), 43 c (Andrew Woodley/Alamy), 48 r (Paul Nicklen/National Geographic Creative), 49 r (©iStockphoto .com/pierredesvarre), 52 c (Alliance Images/Alamy), 53 t (courtesy of Hayat Sindi), 54 c (KeystoneUSA-ZUMA/Rex Features), 56 c (©iStockphoto.com /Rich Legg), 57 cl (Robert Harding Travel/Photolibrary Group/Getty Images), 57 cr (Wes C. Skiles/National Geographic Creative), 58 l (©iStockphoto .com/rossario), 59 l (Wholly Owned/National Geographic Creative), 61 bl (Kersten Geier/Gallo Images/Corbis), 66 tl (©Andraž Cerar/Shutterstock .com), 66 tr (©Steve Byland/Shutterstock.com), 66 cl (©L. S. Luecke/Shutterstock.com), 66 cr (©Robbie Taylor/Shutterstock.com), 73 r (©Stefano Viola/Shutterstock.com), 75 r (Xpacifica/National Geographic Creative).

Illustration: Kevin Hopgood Illustration PP 19, 60.